Granada Television

The first generation

GRANADA TELEVISION

The first generation

edited by
JOHN FINCH

in association with
MICHAEL COX *and* MARJORIE GILES

Manchester University Press
Manchester and New York

distributed exclusively in the USA by Palgrave

Published by Manchester University Press
Oxford Road, Manchester M13 9NR, UK
and Room 400, 175 Fifth Avenue, New York, NY 10010, USA
www.manchesteruniversitypress.co.uk

Distributed exclusively in the USA
by Palgrave, 175 Fifth Avenue, New York, NY 10010, USA

Distributed exclusively in Canada
by UBC Press, University of British Columbia, 2029 West Mall,
Vancouver, BC, Canada V6T 1Z2

British Library Cataloguing-in-Publication Data
A catalogue record for this book is available from the British Library

Library of Congress Cataloging-in-Publication Data applied for

ISBN   0 7190 6514 3   hardback
0 7190 6515 1   paperback

First published 2003

11 10 09 08 07 06 05 04 03   10 9 8 7 6 5 4 3 2 1

Designed in Scala with Scala Sans
and Clarendon display
by Max Nettleton FCSD
Typeset by Koinonia, Manchester
Printed in Great Britain
by Biddles Ltd, Guildford and King's Lynn

Contents

List of illustrations

Dates included where known

Editors' foreword

Somewhere in the following pages Colin Clark, an early recruit to Granada, writes, 'I met this same spirit some years later when I helped to start up Channel 13, the educational station in New York, but it is incredibly rare. Most people working in television spend their time jockeying for promotion and power. Ratings become the only criterion of success and any idea of excellence is thrown out of the window.' Christopher Morahan, doyen of television directors, writes, 'I doubt if we shall see its like again.' Sir Denis Forman describes it as 'a kind of happy magic.' What they refer to is a climate of creative activity which attracted so many people to work at Granada in what are now sometimes referred to as the Golden Years.

It is a little late to describe television as being at the crossroads. Most of it is well down the chosen road. In the hope that some may feel it worthwhile to retrace and take another look at the signpost we have gathered together these observations of a part of the journey before the signpost came in sight. Some of it will undoubtedly be imbued with nostalgia. It was a probability we were aware of when we invited people to write what they most wanted to write in their own words. One or two may have described some aspects of the journey more critically than others, but the overwhelming majority record an experience which was positive and, in a diverse and growing industry, possibly unique.

We hope that there might be lessons for today in this experience from yesterday.

When we asked our colleagues to record their memories, nearly a hundred of them responded and we are grateful to them all. Some of their memoirs are reproduced in full but, in order to keep the book to a manageable length, some have been edited and others put in the Apocrypha or to one side. The whole body of material makes up a very special archive which we hope will remain available to historians and students of the medium.

John Finch
Marjorie Giles
Michael Cox

The editors wish to express their very special thanks
to Sandra Cox who found us a publisher
and to Cynthia Finch who put up with
a great deal of hassle over a number of years

Preface: Granada 1957–92

DAVID PLOWRIGHT CBE

Granada Television was the most precocious of the independent television companies formed in the 1950s. It was also the most innovative, self-opinionated, insufferably arrogant for some of its competitors, and defiant of authority if it tried to obstruct the transmission of programmes Granada considered to be in the public interest. It was swashbuckling and successful and it was irresistible for the first generation of commercial television programme makers keen to challenge the monopoly of the BBC.

Many Granada graduates have since had a major influence on the development in the UK, of television, theatres, films, journalism and politics. One of them ran the BBC; another the Royal Opera House and two more are helping to run the country from the front bench of the Labour Party. Most of them are contributors to this impression of the early days of commercial broadcasting in Britain inside a company that was a phenomenon of the time.

Paradoxically, it was the exercise of regulatory control that Granada so often considered humbug that created the opportunity for the company to adopt an almost Reithian view of the purposes of broadcasting. From the beginning of the commercial services, Parliament had decided that ITV was to follow the tradition of the BBC in adopting values of public service such as universal availability and appeal; recognition of the needs of the disadvantaged in society; the importance of information and education as well as entertainment; the protection of culture by the imposition of quota restrictions on imported programme material; devolved responsibility to the regions of the UK; beyond the influence of advertisers in matters of programme content; freedom from state control.

Granada's founder, the charismatic, waspish and sophisticated Sidney Bernstein, would have judged the claim of the BBC's first Director General Lord Reith that 'few (listeners) know what they want and very few want what they need,' to be unduly authoritarian. However, there was no discernible public outcry for *Marathon*, a four hours a day opportunity to see and hear every candidate in every constituency of the North of England during the 1959 General Election or in the decision to offer gavel-to-gavel coverage of the political parties' annual conferences.

These were the no-go areas of television coverage and significant omissions in the service of the BBC that Sidney Bernstein openly admired. He had started his programme service with a tribute to the BBC and declared with due immodesty that Granada would beat them at their own game. The task was made easier by a piece of imaginative legislation that allowed commercial television to compete with the BBC for audiences and prestige but not for money; and the ITV companies to compete with each other but in a well organised way which ensured that they all played at separate grounds and never met face to face. Each would serve its own nominated territory, be the sole supplier of ITV programmes there and enjoy the exclusive right to such television advertising revenue as was available in its area. ITV thus provided the rare instance of a commercial enterprise making one thing – programmes – and selling another – advertising air time – in a market environment where the acceptance of non-competitive practices was a prior condition of permission to trade – a quaint piece of governance when contrasted with the one off blind bids of the 1990 licensing process. Parliament had legislated in the interests of programme range and diversity and appointed a guardian body, the ITA, later the IBA, to monitor programme performance and empowered it to remove licensees who did not come up to scratch.

Such a monopoly could clearly not have an indefinite life. For one thing its sheer cosiness was irritating to those who did not have a place within it. But there is no escaping the fact that it worked well for a remarkably long time. From the early fifties to the late eighties Britain had a television service which grew to four national channels, which, though not perfect, was a great deal better than most others in the world. Granada grew to become an internationally recognised broadcaster, acclaimed for many of its programmes, most notably *Brideshead Revisited, The Jewel in the Crown* and *World in Action,* and in 1985 was described by one international commentator as the best commercial television company in the world.

A number of attempts to write Granada's history have been made, but none was considered by those who sat in judgement to capture the uniqueness of the institution, adequately recognise its principles or explain why it happened the way it did. Certainly the name of Denis Forman must be coupled with that of Sidney Bernstein as architects of the environment which encouraged so many creative people to excel.

This is not an attempt at a history but an assembly of recollections in tranquility by those who enjoyed the adventure or found it a nightmare.

Introduction: the development of commercial TV in Britain

JULIA HALLAM

Dr Julia Hallam, School of Politics and Communications, University of Liverpool

In the preface to this volume of engaging personal accounts, David Plowright contributes an eloquent overview of the development of Granada Television from its beginnings to the end of his chairmanship in 1992. The purpose of this introduction is to flesh out the background behind these events, providing in the process a necessarily brief guide to the development of commercial television in Britain. It includes a summary of the debates that surrounded the passing of the Television Act in 1954, the establishment of the Independent Television Authority and Granada's role in this process.

Sidney Bernstein, co-founder of Granada Television, was an ardent admirer of the BBC although critical of what he called the BBC's 'stuffiness' and cultural snobbery. The BBC led the television revolution that swept through Britain in the 1950s; as the reach and spread of its transmitters was extended, the goal of providing a nation-wide service came ever closer. Because of its influence on the development of commercial television and Granada in particular, this account begins with the televising of an event that marked the BBC's success in creating a national network and a nation-wide audience even as it was losing ground to the campaign for a commercial alternative. It situates television amid the changes that rocked British society in the 1950s, primarily the increased spending power of ordinary people and the steady growth of a consumer-orientated society. Many establishment figures saw these changes as a grave threat to traditional values and the British way of life; they blamed an influx of American culture, with commercial television in particular singled out as a potentially malignant force. Once the campaign for commercial television had been won, however, the Conservative government of the day wasted no time in passing the Television Act and setting up the infrastructure that would regulate the new companies. Granada was awarded a licence to broadcast in the north, one of the four largest franchise areas, and quickly established itself as the most socially conscious of the commercial companies making distinctive programmes that included innovative drama and ground-breaking coverage of current affairs.

Television in Britain came of age with the Coronation.

(Harry Hopkins 1964:295)

The explosion of television viewing in Britain occasioned by the coronation of Queen Elizabeth II was a symbolic marker of the beginning of the end of the old society in Britain, a social order based on inherited wealth and the cultural traditions and values of a small minority of the population. The coronation marked the beginning of a period of change and transformation in which television played a major role, not only by becoming a leading sector of post-war economic regeneration but by mediating change in many areas of British life. The development of commercial television as a regional networked service played a key role in this process. By showing the nation to itself in ways that radio, cinema and the press could never hope to do, live television ('radio with pictures') brought current events and entertainment into the home as they happened. Commercial television was, as the first Director General of the Independent Television Authority Sir Robert Fraser put it, 'people's television' because for the first time people in Britain could choose what they wanted to watch and were released from the paternalistic dictates that characterised the BBC's attitude to viewers and listeners.

The coronation of the young queen is regarded by many as the earliest national 'event' in British television's short but eventful history. For the first time, the BBC was given permission to televise a state occasion live from Westminster Abbey and, for the first time, television could reach an audience justifiably 'national' in terms of geographical reach and the numbers of people watching. A tremendous feat of BBC engineering made it possible to transmit images of the royal occasion to more than two and a half million television sets in pubs, clubs, village halls and private houses up and down the land as well as receivers in France, Germany and Holland. Almost half the UK population – around twenty million viewers – crowded around the small screens to watch a flickering black and white image of the young queen being crowned. This shared experience of witnessing an event as it happens even though you're not there, of being an 'absent presence' in the crowd, is television's most unique attribute. For many watching that day it was the first time they'd experienced live television and it fuelled desire for a set of their own; over a million TV licenses were issued between 1953 and 1954.

The take-up rate of TV licences continued apace throughout the 1950s, with licence figures revealing that numbers of households owning a television set increased from 343,882 in 1950 to 10,469,753 by the end of the decade. Taking its place as the country's number one leisure occupation, television ousted cinema and radio as principal sources of entertainment and information. This massive growth in popularity was not solely due to the increased availability of BBC programmes or the televising of the coronation. It was the brasher, more down-to-earth style of commercial television that secured a place for the TV set in living rooms nationwide, and its tremendously popular status as a source of news and entertainment. When ITV began transmitting programmes in 1955 it reached only 3 per cent (180,000) of all television homes; five years later 82.8 per cent (10,040,000) of the 12,120,000 television sets in operation could receive it.[1] By 1958, almost half the population were regularly watching television on Sunday nights, with 45 per cent of working-class viewers tuning in for an average of four hours every night of the week (Hopkins 1964:404). Many of these viewers deserted the BBC's evening schedule of home grown comedy shows, drama series and serious programming for the more light-hearted, escapist fare of American style quiz shows, westerns and imported comedies such as *I Love Lucy* (Desilu Prod, ITV tx 1955–61) offered by the new network.[2] The success of ITV confirmed the worst fears of many critics and commentators; commercial television was yet another example of how 'Americanisation' was corroding the soul of British society epitomised by a quest for material comfort provided by 'things' and a desire for mindless distraction.

In *The New Look*, his account of the social revolution that shook Britain in the twenty years following the end of the Second World War, Harry Hopkins notes the disquieting effect that the arrival of commercial television had on certain sectors of the Establishment. In the days leading up to the first commercial broadcast there was a feeling that something critical was about to happen that would change Britain for ever, but only the vaguest idea of how severe it might be or how it might have come about. Among the paternalistic upper middle classes, particularly those associated with education, the universities and the church, television was viewed with considerable suspicion (if it was viewed at all!). The extremist opinion was that the dawn of commercial television would mark the beginning of the end of civilisation as then known or, more appropriately, the end of the old society. Television, they complained, killed conversation, turned intelligent children into monosyllabic morons and induced 'narcotic dysfunction'. By 1958 television's grip on the adult population upset and disturbed a range of powerful vested interests across the commercial, intellectual and professional sectors. For the next five years, television became a scapegoat for all the ills of society. It was cited in divorce courts, mentioned in suicide notes, alluded to as a reason for robbery, blamed for juvenile delinquency, seen as the cause of typists' bad spelling and the source of children's nightmares. 'Doctors diagnosed "TV Neck", "TV Crouch", "TV Dyspepsia" and "TV Stutter"'; dentists issued a solemn warning against bucked teeth produced in children by 'viewing' from the floor, chin cupped in hands' (Hopkins 1964:403).

Such ill effects were seen by critics as yet further evidence that the shallow, superficial values and attitudes they associated with American culture were undermining not only the psychological and physical health of children and other vulnerable individuals (particularly the working classes) but the spiritual and cultural health of the entire nation. Commercial television, along with pop music, comics, Hollywood movies and a passion for fashion among the young was deemed responsible for eroding British traditions and the British way of life. Visible signs of this destruction manifested themselves in the heartlands of British theatre and the literary establishment. From the late 1940s, on the orthodox as well as the musical stage, American productions such as *Death of a Salesman* and *Oklahoma!* dominated London's West End; an American novel, *The Philanderer* successfully challenged the outdated Obscene Publications Act in the courts and in popular music, American artists frequently topped the record charts. These changes in taste, away from the staid satire typified by the drawing-room comedies of Noel Coward towards more psychologically realised characters in everyday surroundings, were indicative of a seismic cultural shift led, at least in part, by the increased purchasing power of growing numbers of young people. Teenagers, newly enfranchised as consumers, came of age in the 1950s reflecting enhanced opportunities for employment in the rapidly expanding economy. Prime Minister Harold Macmillan's famous credo 'you never had it so good' might not have rung true for everyone in the UK, but for many people during the 1950s life improved beyond measure. With full employment came the possibility of higher standards of living; a building boom created opportunities for families to leave the overcrowded inner cities and move to green field sites on the periphery. Although some equated greater affluence and geographic mobility with the break-up of traditional working-class communities and the end of a collective way of life, many were only too happy to leave the congested inner cities and the grimy Dickensian terraces for a healthier life in a bright modern home in the suburbs. Owning a car and the latest labour saving domestic appliances such as vacuum cleaners, washing machines and refrigerators were indicative of a family's financial and social status in the new neighbourhoods. Householders demonstrated that they were 'keeping up with the Joneses' by flaunting TV aerials on their chimney stacks and fashionable TV sets in their living rooms. Innovative 'rent to buy' hire purchase and credit schemes helped to make these new goods widely available.

Caught up in the consumer boom of the 1950s and the changing lifestyles of people eager to modernise not only their homes but also their social aspirations, British television grew up and came of age. For the first time the BBC, which had been the only provider of television programmes, was forced to defend its monopoly as the campaign for commercial television gathered momentum. Surprisingly perhaps, it was not the demand from growing numbers of TV owners for more or different programmes that stimulated the campaign; commercial television came about because a few well-organised entrepreneurs recognised the potential of the new medium for making a great deal of money. A group of businessmen with interests in the manufacturing of television sets, advertising revenue and programme production led a well-orchestrated campaign that resulted in the passing of the Television Act in 1954. To succeed, they had to overcome opposition from those who considered themselves guardians of the nation's cultural heritage and spiritual values, primarily the BBC and its core supporters, the universities and the church.

'Quality' versus 'vulgarity': monopoly versus competition

Citizens expected to be capable of choosing their political governors should be capable of choosing their television programmes. (Altman et al. 1962:3)

By the end of the Second World War, the BBC was highly regarded in Britain and internationally for the quality of its radio services, a quality that many within the BBC and among its supporters thought could only be maintained if the BBC continued to operate as a monopoly. Television was a young, undeveloped medium, regarded by the BBC as a subsidiary activity to the expansion of its radio networks; the BBC imbued its programmes with the same paternalistic ethos that pervaded its radio broadcasts. Closed down for the duration of the war, the BBC resumed its development of television services in 1946 amid an atmosphere of some concern about the close cooperation between the broadcasters and government. In the post-war period, the BBC saw itself as 'the voice of the nation' and staunchly defended its right to remain so: expansion of the television service was part of a wider programme of change in radio broadcasting that included the introduction of the Third programme. There were renewed calls for an end to the BBC's monopoly and the arguments for an alternative, commercially run service grew louder and more persistent.

Debates about the introduction of a commercial element into the British broadcasting system accompanied the development of television from the outset. The first government body to consider the future of television, the Selsdon Committee (1934), concluded that the cost of developing the new medium could be offset by 'a modicum of screen advertisements'. The following year this proposal was rejected by the Ullswater Committee, who recommended that the BBC should have sole responsibility for television services (Sendall 1982:4). In 1936, the BBC established the first television service in the world as a small experimental unit that could reach anyone living within a 25-mile radius of the London transmitter at Alexandra Palace. Programmes were broadcast for an hour in the afternoon and an hour in the evening six days a week, excluding Sundays. The price of the set ensured that in these early years television was a luxury enjoyed by a wealthy minority; by the time war broke out in 1939 around 20,000 people had a licence to receive 'radio with pictures'.

While television services were closed for the duration of the war two government committees (one officially appointed by Parliament, the other an interest group) debated the future of television. The official group recommended that after the war television should be run as a BBC monopoly funded by the licence fee. The other group debated a range of commercial alternatives but no clear consensus emerged amongst them. The post-war Labour government accepted the recommendations of the official committee, extending the BBC's Charter and its monopoly until 1952, but not without stormy opposition in the House of Commons from both Liberal and Conservative MPs. For the next five years the campaign for commercial television, led from 1950 by the former head of BBC television Norman Collins, steadily gained momentum. In Collins' view, the development of television was far too restricted and subordinated to the interests of radio. He formed and registered one of the first commercial television companies, the Associated Broadcasting Development Co. Ltd which led ultimately to the appointment of its successor, Associated Television Ltd, as one of the first independent programme contractors (Altman *et al.* 1961:26). In Parliament, Collins's efforts to introduce reform were supported by an informal backbench broadcasting 'group' who brought pressure to bear on the government and were the hard core of successive Conservative Broadcasting Policy Committees. Subsequently, the activities of this group were acknowledged as a remarkable example of political lobbying, not least because the commercial interests of those involved were well known to their peers in the House.

The moving force in the campaign, The Popular Television Association (PTA), is now regarded as an archetypal lobby group because it spawned the practice of supplying draft letters for lobbying purposes. Established in 1953 'to help in the task of setting television free', the PTA organised an extensive letter-to-the-editor campaign that called for the immediate introduction of competitive TV. Identical letters appeared in numerous local newspapers, some of them with different signatories but from the same address. One, signed Leonard, London, claimed to be from a Labour party member objecting to being compelled to oppose a piece of Conservative legislation that he considered highly desirable.[3] Unsurprisingly, amongst the PTA's most prominent supporters were advertising agents and those who stood to gain commercially from the outcome. Electronic equipment manufacturers such as Pye Radio and Rediffusion donated funds for the campaign, companies that later held stock in programme companies (Paulu 1961:34).

Fierce opposition to the very idea of commercial television was vociferously expressed by the BBC's former Director General, John Reith, a man who fervently believed that broadcasting was a force for social improvement and had created an organisation whose ethos was firmly rooted in pre-war paternalistic notions of public service. By 1949 he was arguing that the ethos and value of public service broadcasting would be unable to survive without 'the brute force of monopoly'. The same year Reith announced his continuing support for the BBC, the Labour government appointed Beveridge to chair a Committee on Broadcasting; its remit was to anticipate the renewal of the BBC's Charter in 1952 and recommend how broadcasting should continue to be organised and funded. Paradoxically, Gallup polls of the time indicated that most Conservative voters opposed the introduction of commercial television even though their party supported it, while many Labour voters favoured it in spite of their party's strong objections. The biggest fear was that sponsoring of programme production by advertisers would distort television's public service mandate to tell the truth and remain impartial; and that in the quest for ratings, only the most popular forms of entertainment would survive. The conflict was waged around distinctions between monopoly and competition, terms that were seen as synonymous with maintaining 'standards' in opposition to 'vulgarity', of protecting British (high) culture from American (low) culture and its associated values. Taking a cue from Reith, the BBC summarised its defence of monopoly by stating that competition would mean a lessening of responsibility, a lowering of standards, an elimination of the rights of minorities, a failure to serve educational and cultural purposes and a likelihood of making 'listeners' more passive citizens. In other words, broadcasting's public service remit would no longer be upheld and it would be impossible to maintain a service committed to informing, educating and entertaining the audience.

The majority of the Beveridge Committee concurred, concluding that if television were to have any kind of social purpose, it had to be protected from forms of competition that would create a debasing rivalry. The Labour government of 1950–51 accepted their conclusions, but was slow to enact the legislation that would renew the BBC's Charter. Events overtook them; Labour lost the next election, leaving the field open for the Conservatives who favoured Selwyn-Lloyd's minority report. In a highly influential paper, he argued that competition would be healthy for British television so long as the BBC continued to set the standards and an independent commission regulated the new channel. The incoming Conservative government favoured Selwyn-Lloyd's report and expressed their intention to break the BBC's monopoly. In May 1952 they issued a White Paper that renewed the BBC's charter but hinted that any subsequent renewal might be of a 'non-exclusive' type and that provision should be made to permit an element of competition.

A vigorous debate ensued over the next few months in both Houses, with the Lords providing a backbone of resistance to Conservative proposals. Harry Hopkins argues that the challenge to the BBC monopoly was regarded by many as 'a head-on challenge to tradition, hierarchy and British received values' (1964:405). Defenders split across party lines and included *The Times*, some of the bishops, numerous university vice-chancellors plus various members of House of Lords. In a major debate in the Lords in May 1952, Lord Reith argued that the introduction of advertising to a broadcasting system untainted by vested interests and private profit was tantamount to a death knell, likening it to the introduction to Britain of smallpox, bubonic plague and the Black Death.[4] The spectre of Americanisation haunted the debate throughout: many old-fashioned Tories refused to subscribe to the new ethos of enterprise, believing that the government's proposals were synonymous, in Lord Hailsham's words, with erecting a golden calf in addition to the established Church.

In spite of these forebodings the outcome was a typically British compromise that according to a report in the *Manchester Guardian* 'testified to the continuance of our insular hypocrisy' (Hopkins 1964:407). The White Paper of 1953 proposed a scheme for a public corporation that would own the transmitters and hire them to a new group of commercial companies. To be granted a licence, companies had to be British owned and controlled and there had to be adequate competition between them, which seemed to rule out the possibility of any individual or company becoming a major shareholder in more than one company. Each company could bid to be the sole provider of commercial TV services in one of the designated regions and would have to provide 'proper proportions' of regional material. The companies would make the programmes, transmit them via the corporation's facilities and collect revenues from advertising to cover their costs; there would be no sponsorship and the company, not the advertiser, would be responsible for programme content and broadcast output. The system would be supervised by another public corporation, the Independent Television Authority, 'an ITA Uncle for a BBC Aunt' (1964:407), headed by 'great and good' public figures selected by the government and equipped with a notional annual budget of £750,000 of public money. This novel solution calmed the reservations of those opposed to commercial broadcasting, solving the thorny problem of sponsorship and ensuring that a sufficient mechanism of control was in place to 'safeguard this medium of information and entertainment from the risk of abuse or lowering of standards' by conforming to 'the highest standards of advertising conduct'.[5] The BBC had to accept that unless they learnt to compete and to hold the attention of a mass audience as well as minority groups they would be unable to fulfil their remit to inform, educate and entertain. The Act finally became law on 30 July 1954.

Television Act of 1954: creating the ITA

Looking back, it is clear that while the BBC held the monopoly, television was a middle-class indulgence like fee-paying private schools and holidays in Spain... Once the 'commercial' set were in, with their friendly accents and salesmen's blarney, the public took an entirely new interest in television.

(Altman et al. 1962:43)

During the passage of the Bill through Parliament all references to 'commercial' television, with its pejorative connotations, disappeared from debate and discussion and were quietly replaced by the term 'independent'. The regulator of the new sector, the Independent Television Association (ITA) was given a limited period of existence (initially ten years) after which time it would be subject to parliamentary review and renewal. In contrast to the almost totally permissive character of the BBC Charter and the BBC's right to editorial control, the ITA was given a restrictive brief with the aim of limiting any 'potential offence' that commercial programmes might cause to any individual or group. Political satire, for example, was virtually banned on the basis that material 'which contains any offensive representations of or reference to a living person' could not be shown. Any religious service or propaganda relating to matters of a religious nature could not be broadcast without approval. The ITA had the right to vet programme schedules and scripts in advance of transmission, to require companies to keep records for post-broadcast examination, to forbid certain types of programme and regulate advertisements. It was charged with the task of ensuring that 'independent' programme companies continued to be British owned and controlled and 'that programmes were predominantly British "so far as possible" in "tone and style"; that they did not offend against good taste or decency, incite to crime or disorder, or be offensive to public feeling; that accuracy and "due impartiality" be observed in the presenta-tion of all news and in particular in any items dealing with matters of political or industrial controversy; and that no expression of their own opinion on such matters be allowed from any of their Members or officers, or of any director or officer of a programme contractor' (Sendall 1982: 33). Terms such as 'high quality', 'good taste', 'due impartiality', 'due accuracy' and 'offensive to public feeling' are, of course, ambiguous and open to a range of interpretations. Thus programme makers and production com-panies such as Granada became involved in negotiating particular cases with the Authority as part and parcel of the ongoing day-to-day business of production and transmission.

Other aspects of the Act dealt with the nature and kinds of advertising that could be broadcast and the length and timing of advertisements. It was forbidden to broadcast adverts for certain products (anything connected with sexual or bodily functions was prohibited although personal hygiene products such as soap, toothpaste and shampoo were permitted); certain treatments such as smoking cures could not be promoted but cigarettes and alcoholic drinks could be. Adverts may not be accepted for personal services, whether those of a dating agency, a money lender or a fortune teller. In order that people did not suffer too much inconvenience or frus-tration from the programming breaks, adverts were allocated a maximum amount of time in any one hour and spaced regularly, following a pattern laid down by the Authority. Parliament thought it necessary to ensure that that direct sponsoring of programmes was illegal, but in certain cases sponsored documentary films were permitted provided that their function was to inform the viewer of issues unrelated to the sponsor's interests or products (Sendall 1982:99). Finally, the British Actors' union Equity took steps to ensure that 'proper proportions of British material' would be shown. No less than 80 per cent of programmes had to be British; and in order to prevent the new programme contractors from starting their service with a surfeit of old movies, films could not be transmitted which had been on general release at home or abroad before the date of the first commercial broadcast licence (Sendall 1982:106). This latter clause was one that Sidney Bernstein played a part in drafting after a series of meetings with representatives from the creative and technical unions led to what became known as the 'Gentleman's Agreement'. The details were never published, although the discussions came to govern what was termed 'proper propor-tions' of British material (Moorehead 1984:214).

As well as mollifying commercial TV's critics, the creation of a public 'watchdog' that owned the transmitters proved to be of benefit to all involved in the enterprise. The advertising agencies were happy because they had no overheads to fund; the costs of setting up the system did not have to come from their coffers. Prospective programme contractors were happy because although they were expected to provide high quality programmes to meet their local (regional) remit and reflect the character and culture of their regions, it was understood that these were expensive to produce and could only be provided through 'network operation', i.e. linking up for the purpose of putting out the same programme at the same time through all the regional transmitters. This latter proviso enabled the Big Four companies to maximise their production capacity as well as giving them a window in the London area. By the end of the 1950s the networking agreement was so successful that it undermined the notion of competition between the companies, a point that would be of considerable interest to the next government enquiry into broadcasting, the Pilkington Committee.[6]

The ITA's first major task was to build the transmitters and select the companies who would run services in each region. To encourage competition between the companies, two contractors were appointed to areas with the highest population densities (London, Midlands and the North), one to provide weekday programmes, the other at weekends.[7] Given the set-up capital required and the need to run at a deficit until viewing figures were sufficiently attractive to advertisers, only groups with large financial resources were encouraged to bid for these particular contracts. The London weekday contract went to Broadcast Relay Services/Associated Newspapers (later Associated-Rediffusion), the London weekend and the Midlands daily contract was offered to the Associated Broadcasting Development Group, the company originally incorporated in 1952 by former BBC head Norman Collins (later Associated Television, ATV); the Kemsley Press/Maurice Winnick Group was awarded the weekend contracts for the Midlands and the North (later re-allocated to ABC Television) and Granada the weekday contract for the North. Fourteen contractors in total contributed to the first ITV network, all of whom had strong connections with existing British businesses; most had media-related interests such as newspapers, cinemas and theatres.

Each of the Big Four companies who won the main contracts became known for their own distinctive styles of programming. ATV had variety and entertainment interests. With Val Parnell and Lew Grade at the helm it became known for light entertainment, its flagship show *Sunday Night at the London Palladium* presenting top British and International variety acts for the duration of its 12-year run (1955–67). ATV also developed ITV's first long-running twice weekly 'medicated' soap, *Emergency Ward 10* (1957–67), an information based drama that followed the lives and loves of doctors and nurses working in the admissions ward of a busy general hospital. ABC Television had existing interests in film production and exhibition and an

American shareholder, the Hollywood film production company Warner Bros. It is perhaps most remembered for inviting Sidney Newman, head of drama at the Canadian Broadcasting Corporation, to run its drama department in 1958. Newman developed the *Armchair Theatre* slot (1956–69), frequently introducing plays by young unknown writers written especially for television; by 1960 *Armchair Theatre* was both a ratings and a critical success. Newman then moved to the BBC, where he ran the controversial *Wednesday Play* series (1964–70). ABC was also known for making popular drama series that would appeal to the American market; *The Adventures of Robin Hood* (1955–59) was an early export success. Associated-Rediffusion had perhaps the least distinct identity of the Big Four although it did produce one of the most well-known early police series, *No Hiding Place* (1959–67) and the popular 'window on the world behind the headlines' current affairs series *This Week* (1956–68).

From the outset, Granada set itself the objective of providing high quality popular programmes that would surpass even the BBC's threshold of quality and standards. The company was against cultural segregation and sought to mix its more popular programming with innovative drama, hard-hitting investigative documentaries and pioneering coverage of political events. It quickly earned itself a reputation as the most socially conscious of all the commercial companies.

Sidney Bernstein and Granada

We did not quite foresee how much Granada would develop a character which distinguishes it most markedly from the other programme companies and from the BBC. (Kenneth Clark, Chair of ITA 1958 quoted in Sendall 1982:122)

Granada TV has a distinctive signature: a firm, not inelegant flourish. Many of its programmes are seen throughout Britain, and most of its ideas are copied by the other contractors sooner or later. (Altman et al. 1961:46)

From its inception Granada was recognised as a commercial television company with a difference. As a product of the entrepreneurial vision of the music-hall impresarios and cinema exhibition chain owners Cecil Bernstein and his charismatic brother Sidney, Granada was moulded in their image. Sons of an émigré family of uncertain origin, the Bernstein brothers shared with the founders of the Hollywood movie industry their Jewish background and migrant status, their parents arriving in England from Sweden in the 1880s and becoming involved in a range of business interests. Bernstein senior owned several music halls and cinemas, nascent precursors of the Granada cinema chain developed by Sidney and Cecil during the 1920s and 1930s. Sidney's interest in films extended far beyond the commercial exhibition of Hollywood and British movies; a committed socialist, he was a founder member of the London Film Club in 1925, the first private film society to show films without censorship. An ardent fan and friend of Soviet filmmaker Sergei Eisenstein, he was instrumental in bringing the film-maker and his film *Battleship Potemkin* (USSR 1925), banned from public exhibition in Britain, to London for a private screening at the Film Club. Eisenstein also delivered a series of talks on screen space, setting, camera work and editing introducing his innovative filmmaking techniques to a generation of young British filmmakers.

Sidney's political affiliations were no secret. At the age of seventeen, he joined the Labour party; at the age of twenty-six, he stood as a local councillor for Willesden Green, winning the seat from a Liberal to become one of the youngest county councillors in the country. He remained a councillor for five years before diverting his energy away from conventional politics to the anti-Nazi campaigns that were an increasing feature of his life throughout the 1930s. During the Second World War, Sidney was invited to become a member of the Films Division at the Ministry of Information (MoI). He is credited with, among other things, using his connections with Hollywood-based British filmmakers such as Alfred Hitchcock to ensure that film propaganda about the British war effort reached the American public successfully. In the post-war period, Bernstein's continuing involvement in the UK film industry led to him becoming an adviser to the British Film Institute. In 1953 he was a member of a government committee of enquiry into how to ensure a sustainable UK film industry that led to formation of the Eady levy, a box-office subsidy on cinema attendance that provided support for the beleaguered industry.

In 1948, Sidney and Cecil made their first application to the Postmaster General for a licence to operate a closed television system in their cinemas; the plan was to televise West End shows at the end of their runs and show them for one night only on provincial screens, creating the opportunity for a non-metropolitan audience to experience first-class drama (Moorhead 1984:197). This was the beginning of a business interest in television and its relationship to the film industry that would soon become a major preoccupation, although at this time, as a long-time admirer of the BBC, Sidney Bernstein remained opposed in theory to the idea of commercial television and submitted evidence to the Beveridge Committee in defence of public service broadcasting.

By 1953, it was obvious that the introduction of commercial television was inevitable. A large advertisement in *The Times* announced an apparent about face from Granada: their intention to apply for a licence to run a TV station. Sidney Bernstein defended Granada's decision in a letter to Labour spokesman Herbert Morrison: 'This does not indicate any change of feelings about commercial or sponsored television; I still think the country would be better off without it. However, if there is to be commercial television in this country, we think we should be in, and this may very well be useful one day' (quoted in Moorehead 1984:215). Shortly afterwards, a formal letter of application was sent to the ITA. Granada's submission was apparently uncontentious; the company had a known track record of proven success in the entertainment industries and ample resources to tide them over the initial loss-making period until advertising revenue became buoyant enough to cover production costs. It was only when Kenneth Clark, first chairman of the ITA, published his autobiography in 1977 that the Conservative government's true sentiments about Granada were revealed; there were numerous objections to the contract based on the suspicion that Sidney Bernstein was a former member of the Communist Party (Moorehead 1984:218). Clark knew Sidney from working with him at the MoI and threatened to resign if Granada was not awarded the licence. The objections were duly withdrawn although Bernstein continued to be regarded as a subversive character by many Conservatives, his adversaries accusing him of creating employment for 'Jews, Communists and Queers'.[8] In October 1954, the contract was finally secured; Granada Television Network Ltd was to provide programmes in the North (Monday to Friday) from 3 May 1956, initially transmitting from Lancashire and, because of technical difficulties, from a second transmitter in Yorkshire the following November.

It was through their involvement with the film industry and the MoI that the Bernsteins met many of the people who would later form the core staff at Granada. It is a particularly neat irony that at the very time Michael Balcon's film company Ealing Studios was sold to the BBC in 1955 and 'infiltrat(ed) the conqueror' with its own particular brand of realist drama,[9] another media enterprise emerged with a similarly charismatic, left-leaning chairman at its helm. Sidney Bernstein's young men, similarly to Michael Balcon's in the 1940s, were a hand-picked bunch of high flyers who shared Bernstein's political perspective as well as his vision and passion for the new medium. Foremost among them was Denis Forman who joined Granada in 1954 ostensibly as personnel officer (see his comments on this in his opening memoir), Reg Hammans from BBC Engineering, and Silvio Narizzano from the Canadian Broadcasting Corporation who joined as Senior Drama Director. Michael Balcon at Ealing suggested who might constitute the studio's construction staff, while Forman was responsible for recruiting renowned documentary maker, Harry Watt.

Forman began his working life in the Films Division of the MoI, which he joined in 1946. Through his work he came into contact with many of the current luminaries of British film culture including John Grierson, Harry Watt, Humphrey Jennings and Basil Wright, all of whom were associated with the British documentary movement of the 1930s and 1940s. He also met the Bernsteins, Sidney and Cecil and learned of Sidney's role as adviser to the MoI in wartime.

Forman left the Ministry three years later to take up the post of Director of the British Film Institute which he describes as a 'dim and sleazy' organisation, in need of a thorough makeover. Under his guidance, the Institute rapidly gained credibility; its official journal *Sight and Sound* was relaunched with Gavin Lambert as the editor, assisted by Penelope Houston. Cecil Bernstein was involved with Forman in the attempt to create a National Film Theatre, which started life in a rented cinema built for the 1951 Festival of Britain. His experience as programmer of the Granada cinema chain was invaluable to the fledging Film Theatre; and membership grew rapidly in response to the screenings presented by the *Sight and Sound* team guided by a standing committee chaired by Cecil.

Forman was involved in the campaign for Independent Television from its inception; he was first aware of Granada's views in 1950 in a statement the company presented to the Beveridge Committee which he describes as 'hard line Reithian stuff' (Forman 1997:49). Although Bernstein modified his views, he remained committed to the principles of broadcasting enshrined in the BBC's constitution but hated their unimaginative and stuffy presentation, particularly of news and current affairs. In the formative stages of development of the commercial network, Sidney played a major role in setting up Independent Television News, a non-profit making cooperative jointly owned and managed by the ITV companies, rather than allowing the ITA contract it to an independent news organisation such as Reuters. From the beginning, ITN set out to extend the subject range and alter the presentation techniques of British television news by encouraging its presenters to develop their own individual styles, although they were not allowed to make changes in emphasis or alter the meaning in any way. By the late 1950s these innovations attracted more viewers to ITN than BBC news although the BBC continued to be regarded as the most authoritative source of news and information (Paulu 1961:93).

Like the other large contractors, Granada had to meet both regional and national remits in its programme planning and production. It began as a Manchester-based company run from London while the first purpose-built TV studios were built on a site in Manchester's Quay Street. The initial capital outlay was around £1 million, much of which was spent on the new studios. An integral part of the plan were two 'Travelling Eye' vans (outside broadcast units) that would 'show the north to the north' for the first time. The vans were equipped as mini studios on wheels; powered by generators, they could transmit sound and vision signals directly to Granada's transmitter. As opening night in the first week of May 1956 drew near, Sidney Bernstein was determined not to make it a 'white-tie civic' ceremony such had been held for the other openings in London and Birmingham. He wanted to launch Granada Television in the same way that he launched his cinemas by introducing all the people, from the builders upwards, who had contributed to getting the station on air. Following this, the comic Arthur Askey sang some songs and the Lancashire star Gracie Fields, an old friend of the Bernsteins, was presented on film from Texas wearing a ten-gallon hat. A boxing match live from Liverpool and a filmed play, Blue Murder, was followed by the news. The evening ended, somewhat anachronistically, with a tribute to the BBC and a statement about how Granada advertisements were 'a trustworthy guide to wise spending'.[10]

During the first week's transmission, with the studios still incomplete, the distinctive pale blue 'Travelling Eyes' came into their own, transmitting eight programmes in five days. The biggest coup was to cover the triumphant return of Manchester City from Wembley bearing the FA cup, proof, if it was needed, of Granada's commitment to the north and of the company's determination to earn its regional credentials. Early programmes included Look at Life type films for the network such as A Visit to the Walker Art Gallery and Cheshire Cheese in 1956, as well as the more confrontational Youth is Asking. Granada also imported a number of quiz show formats from the USA such as Make Up Your Mind, Spot the Tune and Black and White. The (still running) popular current affairs series What the Papers Say began in November of the same year.

By early 1956, the three operating companies were having difficulty attracting sufficiently large audiences to stimulate spending from advertisers; it was estimated that they lost more than £11 million during the first eighteen months of operation. Granada, as the last of the Big Four to go on air, was hit hard by the failure to quickly build advertising revenue. In order to save the company money and ensure it would not be vulnerable to aggressive take-over bids, Sidney Bernstein made a secret pact with Associated-Rediffusion. The details of the deal were never revealed in full; what is known is that for four years, in return for a high percentage of the net income from advertising in the north, A-R would pay Granada the costs of producing all the programmes that were networked between them. This guaranteed A-R a supply of popular programmes and, by saving the cost of expensive network productions, the Granada group was protected from the threat of external control.[11] Almost within weeks of the deal, the financial tide began to turn; advertising revenue increased from a trickle to a flood. As the money poured in and profits rose, the sudden change of fortune prompted Roy Thomson of Scottish TV to comment that 'running a commercial television station is like having a licence to print money' (Black 1972: 55). The *Daily Mail* TV critic Peter Black observed that the companies 'were like men who had drilled for oil in their back gardens and found the largest gusher in the world' (1972:169).

With the company's finances secured for the next four years, Granada was able to concentrate its energies on completing the studios and making programmes. By January 1957 Granada had overtaken the BBC as the most popular channel in the north and was making innovative in-roads into all aspects of programme production. In April 1957 the company televised their first major football match, the home leg of the European Cup semi-final between Manchester United and Real Madrid. Although some of the productions continued to be London based such as the lavish light entertainment variety show broadcast from a studio in the Palace Theatre, King's Road *Chelsea at Nine* (1957–65), and *Zoo Time*, built around the animals in London Zoo, many of the programmes had a regional orientation. Almost from the start, Granada was interested in commissioning new drama and actively sought to produce single plays that were challenging, innovative, topical and close to the lives of their northern audiences. Sidney Bernstein's years as a theatre producer in the 1930s and his partnership with Alfred Hitchcock in Hollywood in the 1940s had given him very clear ideas about the place of drama on television. He wanted to ensure that Granada productions had a strong northern orientation and a staunch social message; to this end, writers with regional roots and voices such as John Finch, Alan Plater and Jack Rosenthal were encouraged. With Canadian Silvio Narizzano at the helm as head of drama, one of the first of these productions was *Shooting Star* (Oct 1956), an adaptation of a novel about corruption in the football industry. This was followed by the first televised performance of John Osborne's controversial stage play *Look Back in Anger* with much of its bad language left fully intact. In spite of dire warnings from other commercial producers, it proved a huge success. Granada was one of the first companies to develop a competition for new drama writers; in 1957 they broadcast 18 single plays to the ITV network, the following year 24 (3 slots a week were available at this time). Among them was the first televised production of *Death of a Salesman*, by the American playwright Arthur Miller.

Much of their series output, however, was more formulaic; *The Army Game* (a popular comedy series) began in June 1957 and ran for 153 programmes. Denis Forman developed two successful series in 1959–60,

Knight Errant written by Philip Mackie and *Family Solicitor* starring Geoffrey Palmer in his first major television role. *Skyport* was a popular series
based in an airport which revealed the behind-the- scenes work of airline
staff in the days when flying was still considered a luxury out of reach of the
majority of people. *On Trial* was a series of 'factual dramatisations' of
famous trials.

The ITA described Granada's major achievements of 1960 as 'documentary dramas'; *Police Surgeon* (ABC), *Deadline Midnight* (ATV) and Granada's
twice-weekly *Coronation Street* were all considered authentic, accurate reconstructions of everyday life that attempted to show life as it was, 'warts and all',
stripping away dramatic artifice and creating, with the help of more mobile
cameras, a sense of realism and immediacy. Only five months after its launch
in December 1960 *Coronation Street* was fully networked, becoming Britain's
top-rated TV programme by the end of 1961, a position that remained
unchallenged until the BBC's *EastEnders* came on air in 1985. Granada continued to make convincing, hard-hitting dramas throughout the 1960s;
Villains, began in 1964 and made on outside broadcast tape, 'dealt realistic-
ally with the ugliness of crime and the criminal', paving the way for Robin
Chapman's controversial political drama about London gangland *Big Breadwinner Hog* (1969). The same year Norman Swallow and Denis Mitchell
won the coveted Prix Italia for documentary; *A Wedding on Saturday* (1964)
was considered a breakthrough in the use of mobile videotape at the time.

In addition to pioneering drama documentary work, Granada quickly
developed a controversial reputation for its political journalism. In 1957 it
covered the Trades Union Congress (TUC) annual conference in Blackpool, followed by in-depth moment-by-moment coverage of the Rochdale
by-election in 1958. Until this time, serious political journalism on television was governed by the BBC's stance on impartiality, in part due to
nervousness around questions of influence and the anxiety that television
might be used as a political tool to manipulate voters' opinions. The BBC's
attitude towards coverage of political issues, at this point the benchmark
against which ITV was judged, is made explicitly clear in their 1956
handbook: anything that could be considered likely to influence electors in
recording their votes should be excluded. The BBC interpreted its role as an
impartial imparter of information very seriously; the fourteen-day rule or
'closed period' prohibited reference to any candidate or party in an election
period lest it be accused of endorsing their views. By-election coverage was
therefore considered impossible; not only did the BBC have to remain
impartial, but the Representation of the People Act (1949) stated that the
costs of 'presenting to the electorate the candidate or his views' were
chargeable to candidates' election expenses'.[12] In contrast, Denis Forman

believed that 'in a democracy the most important time to expose the voter to the full force of political argument was in the run-up to an election' (Forman 1997:135). After discussions with legal experts and with the ITA's permission, Granada screened two programmes in which the candidates appeared live discussing the issues of the election among themselves and with journalists (Sendall 1982:351). Following Granada's example, ITN reported on a by-election in its news bulletins for the first time. A National Opinion poll suggested that the programmes helped voters to decide (Trenaman and McQuail 1961:14n):[13] the exceptional turn out of the voters and favourable response to Granada's coverage affirmed Forman's convictions and justified the calculated risk he had taken. Kenneth Allsop of the *Daily Mail* proclaimed '[T]he televoter is born ... Rochdale has changed the nature of democratic politics ... Television is established as the new hub of the hustings'.[14] Michael Parkinson, at the beginning of what would become an illustrious television career, was one of the link people who covered the event, setting a precedent for Granada's full-scale coverage of the general election the following year in *Marathon* (1959).

Outside broadcasts on local themes and topics formed an important part of the regional remit, occupying around 15 per cent of all programming. Cheap to produce, local programmes provided training opportunities for Granada's trainee producers; as some of the following accounts testify, this type of local programming was considered by many of those who worked on it 'exceedingly boring'. Nonetheless, showing the north to the north was completely new and BBC did nothing quite like it. In 1959 Tim Hewat and Jeremy Isaacs developed a documentary series called *Searchlight* which focused on aspects of contemporary life. During the course of the series, they refined the use of location filming techniques that later became synonymous with the pioneering current affairs programme, *World in Action*. Hewat was a veteran of Granada's trainee producer scheme; a former journalist with the *Daily Express*, like many trainees he began in local programmes before graduating to co-produce the ground-breaking *Granada Goes to Rochdale* and *What the Papers Say*. *World in Action* sought to provide in-depth analysis of a single issue made around arresting visual footage without an on-screen reporter. Denis Forman purchased the title for £100 from British documentary producers John Grierson and Stuart Legg for a show they failed to launch in the USA. The British version was modelled on 'Mirrorscope' the serious four page fold-in which the *Daily Mirror* produced for several years (Forman 1997:133). In an article from the broadcasting journal *Contrast* in 1961, David Robinson described Hewat's style as dedicated to the Mirror-Express technique: 'What matters most is impact. He has a flair for the pictorial gimmick' (BFI 9 1981:93). *World in Action* was to become one of Granada's most respected programmes, noted for its uncompromising investigative journalism. As well as pioneering current affairs series, Granada produced a number of reports tackling controversial issues of the day such as venereal disease, the contraceptive pill and the campaign to decriminalise homosexuality.

Granada also had its share of problems in these early years. Quiz shows involving prizes of household goods or money were one of the most popular forms of commercial television. In 1959, one of the contestants on Granada's new quiz *Twenty One* won the largest amount of money to be paid out by a show, £5580. Newspapers claimed that the show was rigged, basing their story on the accusations of a less successful competitor who claimed he was given leading answers to questions as well as prepared in advance to answer questions he could expect to be asked. In an attempt at damage limitation Granada issued libel writs against the newspapers that carried the story and launched an independent enquiry, but pressure mounted as other competitors came forward with similar tales. In America, scandalous stories of quiz show rigging were proved true; Granada dropped the lawsuit and stopped the show, reverting to more serious forms of which the best known, *University Challenge,* started in 1962, and continues (on BBC 2) to this day.

In spite of these teething problems, the Bernsteins' attempts to give Granada programmes 'a distinctive signature' synonymous with their northern base have been judged by history to be at least partially successful, not least because of the imaginary construct of 'Granadaland' situated the north in the public consciousness. 'Granadaland' was the term coined by Sidney to describe the disparate northern identity of the areas of Lancashire, Yorkshire, parts of the Midlands, Cumbria and North Wales that could receive the Granada signal. Although many of the programmes made by Granada were eventually made in Manchester, the Bernsteins (and many of their employees) were southerners. Initially they had hoped to be allocated one of the potentially lucrative London franchises, but accepted the North with good grace. In a speech at the London School of Economics in 1959, Sidney claimed that Granada had applied for the Northern region because:

> the North is a closely knit indigenous, industrial society; a homogeneous cultural group with a good record for music, theatre, literature and newspapers not found elsewhere in this island, except perhaps in Scotland. Compare this with London and its suburbs: full of displaced persons. And of course if you look at a map of the concentration of population in the North and a rainfall map, you will see that the north is an ideal place for television. [15]

The account demonstrates Sidney Bernstein's talent for public relations, but like much of the programme production and publicity material generated by the company, Denis Forman had a hand in it, although his name rarely appeared on anything. 'Granadaland' was wholly Sidney's invention, but the absence of credit for any of Granada's talented staff in any of its publications characterised the company's ethos, summed up by the words of the *Observer* in 1959 as one of benevolent despotism.

Granada and ITV at the millenium

The battle for ratings between ITV and the BBC has been an integral aspect of British television since the first ITV companies began transmitting their more commercially orientated programmes in the mid-1950s. Unlike the development of other terrestrial broadcasting systems, where one of two possible models tended to dominate – public service broadcasting funded by a licence fee as in a number of European countries or commercial television funded by advertising as in the USA – the British initiated a hybrid system characterised from the outset by a unique commitment to public service principles. The Television Act of 1954 ensured that BBC and commercial television could co-exist with equal access to the airwaves. The commercial companies were controlled by an independent regulator (later to become the Independent Broadcasting Authority, the IBA) who ensured that 'proper standards of taste and decency' were upheld in programme content and 'due impartiality' observed in the coverage of news, current affairs and political events. The nature of this regulatory arrangement is often described as a peculiarly British compromise: competition between the ITV companies was avoided, with each having control of a particular area and contributing to the national independent television network. The result was a system dubbed by many of its critics a 'comfortable duopoly', where both the BBC and ITV reaped the rewards of a strictly controlled broadcasting environment with limited access to the airwaves.

Attempts to break the duopoly's stranglehold on British television began in the 1970s, gathering momentum throughout the 1980s as cable and satellite became viable commercial options. A review of the broadcasting climate was instigated by Margaret Thatcher's government in the late 1980s resulting in a White Paper, *Competition, Choice and Quality* which recommended, among other things, that the existing ITV franchises should be re-allocated to the highest bidders.[16] The 1990 Broadcasting Act introduced a 'lighter touch' regulatory framework, replacing the IBA and the Cable Authority with a new agency, the Independent Television Commission (ITC) that would license and supervise all areas of the newly liberalised commercial sector. Applicants for franchises would have to pass a quality threshold and satisfy the ITC that they could meet programming requirements; franchises would then be awarded to the highest bidder. The BBC would continue to be the 'cornerstone of public service broadcasting, although funding by the licence fee would eventually be abolished' (Bonner and Ashton 1998:372).

The bidding process reorganised the commercial sector; as well as opening up opportunities for new companies, it intensified the competition between companies and demanded that all franchise holders farm out 25 per cent of their programme production to independent producers. Granada was one of the sixteen companies to be awarded a franchise, but not without cost to its internal organisation. Following a controversial boardroom coup in 1992 the company lost many of its key staff; a new management structure seeking to create more competitive programmes for less money closed departments and disbanded their creative teams. The award-winning current affairs series *World in Action* was a later casualty of this more competitive environment, ending an era of probing investigative journalism that had developed a worldwide reputation.

As the only survivor of Britain's original Big Four commercial companies, by the year 2000, Granada had become a major player in a highly competitive international media marketplace. On any night of the week, around a third of all viewers watching television watch one of the seven ITV franchises now owned by Granada plc: Granada Television, London Weekend Television, Yorkshire Television, Tyne Tees Television, Anglia Television, Meridian Broadcasting and Border Television. Granada plc now earn half the annual advertising revenue generated by ITV, the seven companies covering over 60 per cent of UK homes. The company sells programmes to more than 120 countries worldwide, maintaining production operations in five countries. Granada's production operations make around 9000 hours of original programming each year for ITV, BBC, C4 and various satellite channels, including some of the most popular television programmes in Britain; *Coronation Street* has held a premier spot in the ratings since it was first networked in 1961. Granada has interests in pay-TV channels and a range of Internet and new media ventures, although the failure of ITV Digital in 2002 severely dented confidence in this area of the Company's operations and left it financially vulnerable.[17]

In a television environment driven by ratings and an entertainment imperative, Granada has continued to win awards for the high standards of its work. At its inception Granada established a reputation for quality programming which it continues to maintain, receiving awards at the beginning of 2001 for the drama series *Cold Feet*, comedy awards for *The Royle Family* (made for the BBC) and two major awards for its contribution to Special Educational Needs. Granada won six awards at the BAFTAS in 2000 and sponsors an award for developing new talent in writing. The company also collected honours at the Royal Television Society's Sports Awards for its regional sports programming and at the British Soap Awards with *Coronation Street* and *Emmerdale* claiming seven of the sixteen categories. It is through programmes such as these that ITV continues to command more than 30 per cent of the television audience, maintaining its share in spite of increasing competition from satellite, cable and digital channels and the publicly funded BBC.

Commenting on Granada's short but eventful history in 1981, Ed Buscombe noted that television was unmindful, even careless, of its past. At that time the history of independent television still remained to be written, with much effort expended on the BBC but its complementary 'other', the ITV network, a largely uncharted domain. Since then, the history of independent television has received formal historical treatment but it has taken the initiative and commitment of three former Granada employees to begin the task of providing what Buscombe termed 'the raw materials ... on which a history would need to work'. The remainder of this book is a testament to these early years: the stories form a unique informal archive of the development and character of a distinctive broadcasting venture. The memories cover all aspects of the company's production portfolio including drama, light entertainment, current affairs and sport and all aspects of its operations including casting, make-up, camera and vision mixing, engineering and public relations. These records provide invaluable commentary on the organisation and management of the day to day running of Granada, its technological challenges and innovations and its creative contribution to both the form and content of British television programming. They are also highly entertaining and great fun to read.

Notes

With thanks to my colleagues Professor John Corner and Peter Goddard for their helpful comments on the text.

1 Figures are taken from the *BBC Annual Report* 1959–60 and the *BBC Handbook* 1960.
2 Although there are no directly comparable figures, from his assessment of the information available in 1959 Burton Paulu concluded that there were more light entertainment programmes available on ITV during peak viewing hours, 'an impression which is confirmed by even casual viewing' (1961:136).
3 From H.H. Wilson (1961) *Pressure Group: The Campaign for Commercial TV*, in Smith 1974:111–13.
4 House of Lords debate 22 May 1952 quoted in Smith 1974:103.
5 Cmnd 9005,1953, paras 6–10 quoted in Smith 1974:108–9.
6 The Pilkington Report, published in 1962, was severely critical of ITV and demanded that the ITA exercise greater control over the companies.
7 The ITA deduced the probable value of an area by multiplying time on air by its population (Black 1972:74).

8 See his son Colin Clark's account of this incident below, pp. 36–8.
9 Charles Barr (1993) argues that the BBC not only took over the film studios from
   Ealing in 1955, but their style of drama too; policiers, such as *The Blue Lamp* became a
   staple of BBC drama series in the 1950s, many of them made by ex-Ealing personnel.
10 Quoted in *Granada: The First 25 Years*, BFI Dossier 9, 1981:31.
11 Black (1972) provides the fullest account available.
12 For a fuller discussion of this point, see Goddard 2001.
13 Trenaman and McQuail's book was the result of a Granada-sponsored research project.
14 *Daily Mail*, 14 February 1958, quoted in Briggs 1995: 238.
15 The formation and management of a television company' presented at the LSE in 1959
   and reprinted by Granada television (Paper no. 251).
16 *Broadcasting in the '90s: competition, choice and quality. The Government's plans for
   broadcasting legislation* (HMSO Cmnd. 517), November 1988.
17 Source www.granadamedia.com, visited July 2002.

References

Altman, Wilfred, Denis Thomas and David Sawers (1962) *TV: From Monopoly to
    Competition – and Back?* Institute of Economic Affairs, London.
Barr, Charles (1993) *Ealing Studios*, Studio Vista, London
BFI (1981) *Granada: The First 25 Years*, Dossier 9, British Film Institute, London.
Black, Peter (1972) *The Mirror in the Corner*, Hutchinson, London.
Bonner, Paul and Lesley Aston (1998) *Independent Television in Britain Vol. 5: ITV and
    IBA, 1981–92, The Old Relationship Changes*, Macmillan, London.
Briggs, Asa (1995) *A History of Broadcasting in the UK Vol. 5: Competition*, Oxford
    University Press, Oxford.
Forman, Denis (1997) *Persona Granada*, André Deutsch, London.
Goddard, Peter (2001) 'Political Broadcasting in Britain: System, Ethos and Change',
    in J. Bartle and D. Griffiths (eds) *Political Communications Transformed: From
    Morrison to Mandelson*, Palgrave, London.
Hopkins, Harry (1964) *The New Look: A Social History of the Forties and Fifties in
    Britain*, Secker & Warburg, London.
Moorehead, Caroline (1984) *Sidney Bernstein*, Jonathan Cape, London.
Paulu, Burton (1961) *British Broadcasting in Transition*, Macmillan & Co. Ltd, London.
Sendall, Bernard (1982) *Independent Television in Britain Vol. 1: Origin and Foundation
    1946–62*, Macmillan, London.
Smith, Anthony (1974) *British Broadcasting*, David & Charles, Newton Abbot.
Trenaman, Joseph and Denis McQuail (1961) *Television and the Political Image*,
    Methuen, London.

CAPTAINS
OF INDUSTRY

A tremendous place to work

Lord Birt of Liverpool

In 1966 Richard Everitt was asked to take time out from producing and directing drama programmes to run a course for production trainees who were fresh from university. Among the intake that year was John Birt. The piece which follows is based on a conversation he had with Richard Everitt when we requested a contribution to this book thirty years later.

When I was at Oxford and decided I wanted to work in television I had two thoughts in mind – either the BBC or Granada Television. I picked on Granada rather than any other commercial company because in my last year I'd married and my wife and I, unusually for students, had a flat with a television so I watched quite a lot. There was one series in particular, Margaret Morris's *D. H. Lawrence* which I thought was absolutely marvellous – a really accomplished piece of programme making. But over and beyond that it was clear to me that Granada was a centre of real creativity.

I also applied to the BBC and got through to the last nine for their General Trainee Scheme. Selection was very different to the Granada process. It was very philosophical and invited me to think about things which I had never in my life thought about. I remember one question in particular which was, 'What would happen if I was presented with a poll which showed overwhelmingly that the British people were racist. How would that inform my attitude to programme commissioning?' Rather a good question but I had been a film maker at university, interested in drama, fascinated by the cinema and I was a scientist. It wasn't the kind of question I was used to. It's now the kind of question I deal with day in, day out. It wasn't at the time so it wasn't an interview which played to my strengths. I knew after I'd finished that I hadn't done very well and wasn't surprised subsequently to be turned down. I sometimes wonder if I had gone into the BBC what I would have done.

But the selection process at Granada could not have been more different. I was first of all interviewed by Mike Wooller who was very keen to understand you, learn what you had done and what made you tick. Then the short-listed people were sent up to Manchester for a two-day assessment. My memory of it is fairly vivid. It was a bit rough and ready: we were all herded into a committee room and then taken upstairs individually for interviews. I think I was interviewed by Denis Forman, David Plowright and Julian Amyes.

The atmosphere of the board was friendly, jolly, amusing, creative. They were anxious to give you a chance to shine. I can remember being thoroughly engaged by this. It was a combination of that plus the sheer exuberance of the people I met when I was there: their creativity, their interest, their humanity which made me very keen indeed that Granada should offer me a job.

The last hurdle at the end of the two days took the form of being ushered into the presence of Sidney and Cecil Bernstein for a five-minute interview. They didn't ask us about broadcasting at all. In my case I was asked what my father did and how I'd been brought up. It was very much, 'What sort of a young man are you?' I was thrilled when I was offered the job of Production Trainee along with eight others. Denis Forman mentioned that the salary of £1000 per year was sufficient for a single person but he was aware that I was the only married trainee so if I got into any financial difficulties I should let him know. Jane, my wife, was an artist and tried to get a job in Manchester but found it impossible so at one stage I found we were really hard up. I returned to Denis reminding him of what he had said and asking him for a modest rise. 'We couldn't possibly do that,' he said. 'You're all trainees being paid the same. It would be quite intolerable if one of you were paid more than the others.' We solved the crisis by taking Nick Elliott in as a lodger.

I had made a fictional movie at Oxford but in my last year went through the painful process of buckling down and studying for my degree. For the first time in my life I started reading a serious newspaper and I can remember becoming very interested in the Rhodesian crisis. This was my first awakening in terms of reading a paper and getting involved in current issues. Anyway, one of the exercises on the Granada course involved us having to do something journalistic. I can remember as a group we didn't have much to offer but because of my limited knowledge of one subject I was able to do reasonably well on UDI in Rhodesia. So at the end of the course when I, like everyone else, wanted to be a drama director – and my final exercise was a drama which I had written and directed – I can remember being told that I was going to to go to *World in Action* and my chronic disappointment. I did two *World in Actions* as a researcher, the second of which was the famous programme about Mick Jagger which I prompted at the time. I turned up on *World in Action* at a time of pretty heady change with people like Gus Macdonald coming in. We were going to try to do things differently by incorporating the documentary styles of people like D. A. Pennebaker and the visual styles of directors like François Truffaut. We tried to turn *World in Action* away from being a rather tabloid programme – certainly very journalistic but a programme based on words – ironically given what I eventually came to stand for when I moved to LWT – to one using many more visual images to create an impact (see note p. 30). An example of this was when I brought Mick Jagger face to face with the Establishment in a country garden on a beautiful summer's day in Essex.

He was flown in by helicopter which was very much a stunt designed to underpin the fact that he had long flowing hair and wore an open loose shirt. He sat in this lovely English scene with the editor of *The Times*, an ex-Home Secretary, the Bishop of Woolwich and so on. Although the subject matter wasn't very substantial in terms of content, in terms of form the programme was powerfully symbolic and propelled my career rapidly through Granada. David Plowright sent for me and asked if I wanted to be a producer or director. I chose the latter so was immediately promoted to trainee director during the course of which I had the idea for *Nice Time* with Andy Mayer.

Andy had been President of the Cambridge University Footlights so we were always talking about comedy ideas. The basic idea of *Nice Time* was to use real life to entertain which was in some ways seminal. Lots of television forms came out of it. For example, we would find twenty people who were George Formby impersonators and put them together or we would find the world's worst male and female singers and put them together to sing 'Cinderella Rockefeller'. The writing team was from *Monty Python* and *The Goodies*. Pretty well everybody involved with the writing went off to have a successful career. Before I'd finished the course I'd directed the pilot and was then made producer of the actual show so my time as a trainee director was extremely short-lived.

Denis Forman loved *Nice Time* and took a keen interest in it. On one occasion I was summoned to his office because he said he had a terrific idea for the programme. 'I want you to build a luxury house for a hen,' he said. 'I want you to take the best possible advice about what makes a hen happy. I think you'll find it'll work extremely well.'

'Yes sir,' I replied.

So I went back to the production team and told them we were going to build a hen house. Andy and I took advice and built a house which had a plentiful supply of all things a hen would like. Not only food and drink but comfort and opportunities for entertainment. When we duly introduced the hen – an extremely frightened hen – to its house on a live programme, all it did was flutter around in a panicky way and shit all over the place. Then it collapsed and died!

On a more positive note *Nice Time* fostered a great deal of new talent in front of the camera: Kenny Everett appeared for the first time on television and an unknown Germaine Greer who was writing a book at the time. It was eventually to become one of the seminal books of the twentieth century, *The Female Eunuch*.

Other things were happening at the same time in Manchester. I remember somebody saying, 'Come to a party. George Best is going to be there.' After *Nice Time* we always used to go off and drink in the Brown Bull which brought together a demi-monde of what I imagined to be the sub-criminal world and the world of show business. It was the sort of place where you could drink after hours if you were invited. Everybody would be thrown out at 10.30 except for this group and the *Nice Time* gang. Then we would have a good time into the wee small hours.

After producing *Nice Time* David Plowright called me in one day and said that Jeremy Wallington and Leslie Woodhead were going to stand down as editors of *World in Action*. Jeremy was going to become an executive producer and Leslie was returning to documentary making so he would like me and Gus Macdonald to be the editors. I was amazed – I was 24 when that happened to me. I had been trained as a drama director, I'd researched two editions of *World in Action* and suddenly I was the editor of Britain's most watched current affairs programme.

I remember being surprised more than anything else. We had youthful confidence whether misplaced or not. We thought we could do it in a different way. We certainly had to do a lot of learning on the job: Gus and I had no experience as managers. We hadn't been around broadcasting that long. We had a team which was much older and more experienced than we were so it was a bit rough at the beginning, but I think we learnt quite quickly. The very first week the new series was broadcast, Northern Ireland exploded and frankly we were not really equipped by our experience to handle difficult editorial matters. I only hope that we had a lot going for us in terms of verve and imagination and energy.

There's no doubt the people who ran Granada were interested in creative talent. They husbanded it. They took a great deal of care of it ... They talked to everybody endlessly. Long, long conversations with people like Denis and David. Very creative people. LWT was very much – 'You're a bright young man. Sounds like a good idea. Go off and do it.' They left you alone to get on with the job. I was given a great deal more autonomy at LWT than I was at Granada. What I was given at Granada was a huge amount of care and attention and I had the most enormous affection for and trust in Denis and David. I saw them as creative people and never as remote managers.

Actually there's some strong parallels with the BBC. They were interested in innovation, risk taking, doing new things and working with new people, but they weren't reckless. They had a good balance between wanting to do new things and making sure they were done properly. The facts had to be right. *World in Action* had a great reputation for being accurate. Anything that was said had to stand up to any kind of scrutiny. Above all an atmosphere where creativity was really valued and encouraged. It was a tremendous place to work.

There were two downsides about Granada which I discovered when I went to LWT. One was that Granada, if anything, had too many able and creative people working for it so it was quite hard for anybody to get their programmes on air. Now with the slightly different perspective of a senior manager I think they probably had more people than was good for them in each of the areas. But it was a benign fault.

The second thing was that there was a feeling of a commune: you worked as a pack, as a group. At LWT the tradition was very different. Each individual would be given the power and the authority to go off and make a programme. Afterwards the management would tell you if you'd done it right. Cyril Bennett or John Freeman would say 'We think you've failed' or 'we think you've succeeded but there are weaknesses.' So you got a candid appraisal. There was more autonomy at LWT and there was a fraction of the programme staff than there was at Granada. You had space to move.

Though I loved Granada I did find it a bit constricting. I wasn't looking for a move but I was headhunted by LWT and offered a lot more money and more opportunity. So it was with considerable regret and not a little thought that I considered whether or not I should make the move but in the end I decided I would.

John Birt left Granada to make factual programmes at London Weekend where he and David Elstein formulated the 'bias against understanding' criticism of many current affairs programmes. He became Head of Features and Current Affairs at LWT, and later Programme Controller. He moved to the BBC in 1987 and eventually became Director-General.

The dottiness of it all

NICK ELLIOTT

Nick Elliott, Controller of Network Drama, ITV

Only a crazy scattering of memories remain with me of Granada in the late 1960s and early 1970s. In the public arena I remember for some reason the Aberfan disaster of 1966; the drug riots and rock and roll of 1968; Manchester United winning the European Cup in the same year; the election of 1970 (when we were on strike and Mike Apted, Mike Newell and

I worked as butlers on Lord Derby's estate on the East Lancs Road) and the surprise defeat of Harold Wilson; decimalisation in 1971.

Many of my private memories, I realise with alarm, seem to have some connection with drink. But they were the days when drink – like meat and smoke – were more acceptable, especially at Granada; and the Film Exchange, the Grapes, the Brown Bull or the Stables bar you could enter alone and always either meet or make a friend. Bill Grundy was in most of them. I remember working with him as a callow producer of about 24 and he regularly kept me drinking vile claret until well after four in the afternoon to test whether one was still capable of getting *Scene at 6.30*, or *Newsday* or *Six-o-One*, or whatever the local rubbish was currently called, on air. And I remember a famous evening when Derek Granger punched Bill on the nose for being excessively crude. And I remember rolling home after many of those wonderful impromptu late-night drinking sessions – even, I'm ashamed to say, driving the car and bouncing off the odd stone wall on the road home to the Peak District.

Whatever my ambitions and achievements in fields such as drama and documentaries it was Local Programmes that was to become my lot. I remember Brian Moser taking a call for me from Denis Forman when for a few weeks in 1967 I was enjoying the heady pleasures of working in 1960s London on *World in Action*. 'Denis has rung. That'll mean he'll want you to go North to produce *Scene at 6.30*. They always try to get the new people to do that!' And, indeed, Local Programmes it was to become. While my flatmate John Birt was helicoptering Mick Jagger and Marianne Faithfull, from prison to meet the Bishop of Woolwich and Rees-Mogg in a blaze of publicity, I was organising yet another story on 'mag stripe' (do you remember magnetic stripe film stock where sound and picture were not in sync?) with cameraman Ron Bowey, in Bury, or Rawtenstall or Newton-le-Willows. Long after the days when cameramen on *World in Action*, indeed on all other film programmes, were running around with hand-held Eclair cameras we still had some ancient thing which could never be lifted off its enormous tripod and its most exciting moment was a slow pan across a northern landscape to Brian Trueman or Chris Kelly standing with a mike.

But live television on a shoestring, five nights a week in Studio 4, also produced some of my funniest memories of those days. There were terrible cock-ups, like the time the OB scanner at Blackpool broke down and the expected long interview with economists Kaldor and Ballogh (remember them?) did not materialise, leaving Bob Greaves with about seventeen minutes to stretch out an interview with a probation officer that had been planned to last ninety seconds.

And there were those jokey items that always flopped, like the idea of tracing the German world record holder for collapsible umbrellas only to find that the man in the London studio wasn't German at all, but Peter Jay, the very serious economics editor of *The Times*, who was supposed to be explaining the devaluation of the pound. Or the St Patrick's Day item when a drunk Irishman passed out and keeled over live in front of astonished Lancashire eating its tea. Or there was the time when a parks keeper, live on air, kept insisting that his boss was a child rapist and would not withdraw his allegations however many times he was invited to. I remember the grim face of Barrie Heads, who was in charge, as I left the Studio 4 gallery. We knew it was going to cost – and it did.

People in Local Programmes in those days included PAs like Judy Finnigan and Judy Daish (now respectively the superstar and the top literary agent), Sue Woodford (now Lady Hollick) and John Flanagan (now a top drama writer). The boss was Mike Scott. And in the early days, when we usually had live music, and groups like The Beatles and The Animals played on *Scene at 6.30*. There was Johnnie Hamp, Derek Hilton, and later Rod Taylor. And usually directing these groups was old Dave Warwick, who loved to humiliate young producers like me in front of the Studio 4 crew. 'Sorry lads, the producer has again forgotten to ask what instruments the band play!' Mind you, the crew in Studio 4 were, like the film crew, not in the first flush of youth and not exactly keen to break new ground in studio techniques.

But many of the friends I made in those years – John Birt, Andy Mayer, Andrea Wonfor, Carol Wilkes – remain old friends today. And when at an occasion, such as Mike Wooller's memorial concert, I met up with those old Granada names and faces – Denis Forman, David Plowright, Derek Granger, Mike Scott, Barrie Heads, Dick Everitt, Joyce Wooller, Mike Cox, Gerry Hagan and others – the happiness of my first six years in television (1966–72) and the dottiness of it all comes flooding back and I'm extremely grateful.

A kind of happy magic

SIR DENIS FORMAN

I enlisted with Granada in 1954 and retired from all forms of active service almost forty years later, which in my case amounts to exactly half a lifetime. When I arrived at Granada's London office in Golden Square there were only five people there before me; the triumvirate of Sidney and Cecil Bernstein plus Joe Warton, who together had successfully built up Granada Theatres, Victor Peers, who had been Sidney's staunch associate during his sojourn in Hollywood as a partner of Alfred Hitchcock, and Reg Hammans, a top flight engineer from the BBC and the only person who brought any sort of experience, knowledge or informed judgement to the creation of the new television company.

Sidney told me to go to Joe 'to settle things' and so I arrived at his office with a ten-page draft contract drawn up by the lawyers of the Film Institute where I had been director. Joe looked at it for a few minutes, then looked up and said 'Do you want this thing? The pay is 3000 pound.' (He never used the plural.) Well no, I thought, I don't really want this thing. I trust the Bernsteins, so what the hell, in for a penny, in for a pound, or rather 3000 pound, and from that day on I never had any form of contract, letter of agreement or written understanding with Granada.

Nobody quite knew what a person of my sort should do. My first job was chairman of the furniture committee (and this incidentally was to be the only official title I was to hold until I became Managing Director). My main activity was to range through the second-hand furniture shops around Tottenham Court Road with an old Granada hand, Charlie Stringer. He gave a sharp intake of breath each time I bought a chair or desk for a pound or two over the rock-bottom price because I thought it looked slightly less hideous than the more basic article. Or rather I thought I had bought it, for I would later discover that Sidney had put a stop to all payments until he had satisfied himself that there was nothing cheaper on the market. I was soon to discover that Granada was the company that Never Knowingly Overpaid.

After a while I found I was doing the recruiting for the new company. Nobody told me to do this but when somebody wanted to take on a sound engineer or a researcher they would send them round to me to sign up. The average pay was £10 a week, £5 the minimum and I never went above £15 without consulting Sidney and Cecil. Then I began to take on programme staff and here on a lucky day a bearded Scot, one Kenny McCreadie, entered the office and expressed his desire to be a lighting supervisor. He was signed up in a trice and since I had taken a liking to him I asked, 'Any more like you where you came from?' (He worked in a small television unit run by the Rank Organisation). 'Might be,' he said, and a day or two later in walked Mike Scott, Mike Wooller and Joyce Wooller. 'Aha,' I said to myself, 'now we are really moving.'

But recruiting did not take up all of my time and I was insistent that I wanted to get on the programme side. Sidney agreed, and from then on Eddie Pola, a song and dance man known in the trade as Twinkletoes, would introduce me to all comers with 'This is Denis Forman, he is in charge of serious programmes,' which sounded impressive. There was only one snag: there were no serious programmes. But I soon began to set that right and when we moved to Manchester, *Youth Wants to Know* (later, *We Want An Answer*) was launched, soon to be followed by *What the Papers Say* and *Under Fire*.

Meanwhile Barrie Heads had arrived, working first as a researcher on OBs and then as the producer of News and Current Affairs. He was followed by Tim Hewat, Derek Granger, Jeremy Isaacs, Philip Mackie, and later by people like Howard Baker, Michael Cox and others. People began to recruit on their own behalf. Very early on Barrie persuaded the then Equestrian Correspondent of the *Yorkshire Post* to work on *Northern Newscast*. I discovered his name was David Plowright. Bill Grundy began to read the news. The arrival of *Coronation Street* caused a high influx of talent including Harry Kershaw, John Finch, Jack Rosenthal, Peter Eckersley. By now Julian Amyes was training the best young British drama directors to take over from the Canadian mafia of Silvio Narizzano, Hank Kaplan, Al Rakoff, on whom our early success in drama had been founded.

Later still came the production trainees, amongst whom were Michael Apted, Alex Bernstein, John Birt, Andrea Duncan (later Wonfor), Nick Elliott, Mike Newell, Jonathan Powell, Leslie Woodhead – all to become famous figures in British television. In addition, the training courses spawned producers, directors and heads of departments, and so on, in spades. There were also enormously talented people who found their own way into Granada, like Margaret Morris and Peter Wildeblood.

With the last wave of 'old Granada' recruits came Ray Fitzwalter, Gus Macdonald, Brian Lapping, Steve Morrison. The founding father had hired other like-minded persons who in turn repeated the process, and so was built that unique mix of enthusiasm, impudence, hilarity, dedication – and often inebriation – that was to dominate the Granada community in the 1960s and 1970s. We made one or two half-decent programmes during my time in Granada, but we also had our full quota of cock-ups and flops, usually mercifully obscured by the glittering halo that circled around our successes. In particular I recall *Judge Dee*, as probably the worst television drama ever seen on British television, for which as impresario, executive producer and script editor I was totally responsible.

But in truth it wasn't the programmes that made Granada unique – it was the people. Somehow we managed to create a lively and adventurous community that was touched with a kind of happy magic, the memory of which will last until we remember nothing at all.

GRANADA AND THE NORTH

What was the secret?

Colin Clark

Why was it such a success? What was the secret? What was the catalyst? What made Granada so different from all the other new ITV companies? What was the secret of its extraordinary *esprit de corps*?

I think it was Manchester. It was the north. It is hard to remember just how remote Manchester was in the 1950s. There was no shuttle flight up from London every hour. It was even, in those pre-STD days, quite hard to get through on the telephone. The idea of opening a television station so far from London seemed ridiculous. How could you get broadcasting staff to go and work up there. They were all based in London, at the BBC. How could you persuade a top journalist or an important politician to travel for four hours on the train. Where would they stay? What would they do in the evening? There were at that time no grand hotels or fancy restaurants in which to entertain them.

Of course we knew what wonderful people northerners were. Tough, direct, call a spade a bloody shovel and all that. And we knew the expression, 'Where there's muck, there's brass'. We had invented that phrase to explain the curious fact that some people in the north were a lot richer than us, even though we lived in London. But it never occurred to us that we should actually go to the north to have a look.

I should have known better. I had spent two years as a pilot in the RAF and we were always being sent to one remote airbase after another. We dreaded being so far from the bright lights, but we soon discovered that the further the camp was from London, the better time we had. Yorkshire and Inverness were our happiest postings. There the camaraderie would increase dramatically. We worked together, drank together and made friendships that lasted for the rest of our lives.

It would be nice to think that Sidney Bernstein – visionary thinker that he was – had seen this possibility when he applied to be the northern contractor for the new commercial television network, but alas he did not. He applied for the London area just like everyone else, and when he was given the north, he simply set about running it from the south as much as he could. But the programmes had to be made in the north, whether any-one liked it or not, or he would have lost his licence. So all the programme makers had to live in Manchester.

Actually Bernstein was very lucky to get anything at all. When the Tory government learned that a socialist was one of the finalists, Lord Woolton summoned the Chairman of the Independent Television Authority to his office. 'Sidney Bernstein is a communist,' he said. 'Now we don't want a communist running our new television network, do we?' 'Certainly not,' replied the chairman – who also happened to be my Dad, and who loved Sidney. 'You have a copy of his Communist Party membership and all your secret service files on my desk tomorrow morning, and I will see that he is disqualified immediately.'

You would have thought that having connections like that, I would have no problem getting a post at Granada, and this turned out to be true. I had met Mr Bernstein when I was working for Laurence Olivier at the Royal Shakespeare Theatre, and he had told me to call him if I ever needed a job. Six months later Olivier left for the USA and I called Golden Square to see what was available.

'You must call Simon Kershaw in Manchester' said the secretary.

'But Mr Bernstein offered me a job personally,' I wailed.

'I'm sure Mr Kershaw will see you very soon.'

I called the Manchester studio at once. 'Now look here, my name is Colin Clark. Mr Bernstein offered me a job six months ago when I met him in Venice, and now I'm ringing to see what there is.'

'Very well,' said an amiable Mr Kershaw. 'Come and see me at 11 a.m. tomorrow.'

'Here in London?'

'No. Here in Manchester.' And he hung up.

I went on the train and I spent a pretty miserable night in the un-modernised Midland Hotel. 'I've had a word with Mr Bernstein' said Mr Kershaw, 'and we are prepared to offer you the post of trainee assistant floor manager at a salary of £12 10s 0d per week, to work up here in the north of course. You can start today if you like.' I was a 'gofer' again, for less money than I had earned in the theatre and two hundred miles from home.

'And you won't last a week' said Jack Martin, the production manager, who had come in to watch the fun. 'There are no nightclubs up here.' And I agreed with him. But what he overlooked was that Granada was a family, a group of relatively young men and women who were united by a single aim, which was to produce, from Manchester, the best television programmes they possibly could. I met the same spirit some years later when I helped to start up Channel 13, the educational station in New York; but it is incredibly rare. Most people in television spend their time jockeying for promotion and power. Ratings become the only criterion of success and any idea of excellence is thrown out of the corporate window.

At Granada we were a team. There was no rigid hierarchy, no inflexible 'pecking order'. Everyone wanted to make a contribution, even the stage-hands. We were pioneers, and although we were almost all from the south, we began to feel immense pride for the north. I made friends with a young man called Tony who was working in the promotions department. For a while he lived in my little house in Cheshire and helped with the interior decoration. He used to roam round the pubs of Salford in the evenings, absorbing the local colour. Then the north worked its magic, and the programme which Tony devised has been at the top of the ratings ever since.

It was *Coronation Street* which really put Granada on the map, but like a christening present in a fairy story, it was a curse as well as a blessing. It was not long before the accountants realised that they had the proverbial licence to print money and that is a temptation no one can refuse. The real Granada had to go. It was really very naive of us to imagine that it could last. Television stations are big business – even an educational television station like Channel 13. Big business exists to make money and that means the lowest common denominator wins every time.

Characters like Sidney Bernstein and Denis Forman are anachronisms. However strong, they were too intelligent to survive for very long. In the brief period of their reign, a few lucky people were given the chance to learn all they needed to know for their whole career. I was very fortunate to have been one of that happy band.

A square peg

MARJORIE GILES

Whilst serving in the ATS during the Second World War there was a campaign to find 'square pegs in round holes'. I was perfectly happy driving ammunition trucks, but the powers that be thought that being tri-lingual, I would be better employed with the Allied Military Government AMG(OT).

Just over a decade later with academic qualifications in social sciences I experienced the reverse policy at Granada. Hidden talents were being investigated and I spent many years floundering from quiz games to politics via every other possible avenue other than the social documentaries I craved. It was to be only five years before my retirement that I finally found my niche with *This is Your Right*.

Granada's remit suddenly included religious programmes after the 1968 franchise changes. Pat Lagone was my producer, and we were instructed to come up with ideas. Pat was London-based, and I found myself living in a London hotel during the week, returning to Manchester at weekends. This involved complicated domestic arrangements: I was a divorcee, but my sons had reached a reasonably self-sufficient stage, I had a daily help, and supportive parents living nearby.

One of our first commitments was to attend a religious conference at Canterbury. The problem was that at that time no one had any idea of what we were going to produce. As yet no religious advisers had been appointed and our brief consisted of attending the conference, taking notes, plying everyone liberally with drink, (for which we were given a generous budget) and not divulging any plans. This was easy: we didn't have any! We too were plied with drink as the other companies tried to discover what Granada's plans were, hoping to catch us off guard. Inevitably, much time was set aside for general discourse between the various independent companies and their advisers. Pat had insisted on a pact between us: as a lapsed Catholic she didn't want to spend time with the Catholic advisers from the other companies and they were to be my province whilst she concentrated on entertaining the C of E and other denominations. I had fun, for the Roman priests were a jolly lot who enjoyed their food and drink, and I therefore found myself regaled with splendid meals and lots to drink. Poor Pat had a miserable time in the company of dreary though well-meaning non-conformist teetotallers who insisted on eating in the university canteen.

Back at the ranch, it was crunch time: we had to come up with an acceptable format for a 'non-religious religious' programme. We spent countless hours, usually over a bottle of Scotch, deliberating ideas. By late evening we had usually come up with some magic formula only to find the following morning when sober, that it was a lot of rubbish. When we did put forward a proposal, it was invariably knocked on the head. The day dawned when we finally cracked it: we were to use the knights and dames of the British theatre to perform the writings of famous theologians. We were told to go ahead with a pilot programme, and Sir John Gielgud was duly engaged to perform the passage 'For Whom the Bell Tolls' by John Donne. John Gielgud asked to read the lines rather than recite them by heart and insisted on London rehearsals at the Oval rather than in Manchester. When we finally got to the Manchester Studios, the 'set' consisted of a lectern in front of black drapes. The director shot it artistically with fancy lighting and unusual angles. Gielgud's sonorous voice declaimed the passage splendidly, and Pat and I felt duly elated. We travelled back to London by Pullman together with Gielgud and had drinks and dinner, only to find when the bill came, that neither Pat nor I had any cash, and our guest was not best pleased at being asked to foot the bill, though we assured him the sum would be added to his fee (£1000!).

When the pilot was viewed by the powers that be, Cecil Bernstein vetoed the format: he was convinced it would prove a massive switch-off, so it was back to the drawing board. The next idea was to use actors to perform Bible passages. Thinking of pleasing Cecil, we chose the *Song of Solomon*, and had a scantily-clad, nubile Wanda Ventham being fed grapes and apples by Ralph Bates and Jerome Willis. At the next viewing it was Denis Forman who objected: his Presbyterian clergyman father would have a fit to see religion thus trivialised. Yet another format had to be found. By that time my unnatural lifestyle had caught up with me. I never relaxed in the evenings and I had no recuperation time at weekends which perforce needed to be spent dealing with domestic matters.

I was suffering from blinding headaches and went from one specialist to the other to discover the cause: neurologists performed brain scans, my spine was X-rayed, my eyes were tested, and so on. The eventual conclusion was that I was on the verge of a nervous breakdown. In today's climate, I would have been signed off sick. As it happened, I had an invitation to spend three months in Australia, so I applied for unpaid leave. This was turned down, so I simply resigned, giving one month's notice. During that time a format was finally accepted, and *The Rain on the Leaves* hit the screens in June 1968.

I had a splendid time in Australia and my headaches vanished. When I returned however, I was in dire need of a job, but no one would give me one! I was to spend two years in the wilderness before being re-employed on a freelance basis. It was Douglas Terry who took pity on me and gave me a job; unfortunately it was London-based and carried no allowances. Happily my elder son was by that time at Brunel University and had a room in Ealing, which I was able to share. Then Janet Wadsworth was instrumental in getting my series *It's Fun to Read* accepted, and I finally achieved producer status. From that moment on, my assignments were always in education, for which, needless to say I had no qualifications: all the other producers were ex-teachers.

I finally found my niche with *This is Your Right* in 1978. Described as The Citizens Advice Bureau of the Air it covered all kinds of social issues. The presenter was Michael Winstanley, a Liberal peer, who was also a GP. By that time, of course, my background in social sciences was well out of date, but my sentiments were still in place. For the first time in my television career I felt completely confident. I had great freedom since none of the 'bosses' ever bothered to watch it. As long as I kept within my budget, which, needless to say was very tight, and didn't make any waves, I had total freedom. The programme highlighted and explained current legislation, and viewers were invited to write in with their problems. At times we had as many as 1500 letters in a week. These were answered by a team of twelve experts and sorted by a very able and dedicated office staff, headed by Carole

Townsend, who also dealt with telephone queries. The success of the programme was due to the immense popularity of Michael Winstanley who never lost the common touch and inspired great confidence. The programmes were aimed at that sector of the public which found it difficult to deal with the authorities, did not have the means to consult solicitors or accountants, and who did not know their rights; most of the letters were addressed to 'Dear Doctor' or even just Michael. Winstanley had direct access to MPs and the programme carried much weight and even succeeded in changing legislation. However it was not highly regarded among television people: it was not networked for a start, though this was through choice. None of the other Independent companies were prepared to invest in the kind of back-up Granada provided, and we did not want to devalue our work, nor could we have coped with letters from the entire country. There was no glamour attached to the job, I was therefore safe from predatory colleagues.

As I was nearing retirement, I was asked if there was anything else I wanted to produce, as I had by then been with Granada for five years. I declined. This did not however stop me from being thrown in at the deep end once more. Paul Doherty, the Sports producer was in Italy covering the World Cup and I was asked to stand in for him at Charnock Richard for a show jumping event. The programmes were to be directed by Eric Harrison, and I was therefore in a safe pair of hands, and merely a figurehead. I was invited to a press conference in a 'getting to know you' exercise, and found myself talking with Liz Edgar. Making conversation, I asked her whether she was riding herself. She replied,

'Oh, yes, forever'.

Facetiously, I asked, 'Does that mean you intend riding for ever and ever amen?'

'My horse is called Forever, you fool!' came the sharp reply. By the end of the three assigned days, I was a lot wiser and I can now view show jumping with insight.

On the way to my retirement party, I met Sidney Bernstein in a corridor. Long gone were the days when his commanding figure strode through the building, followed by a respectful retinue, with Mr Pook obligingly lending his bowed back for Sidney to rest his notebook to enter comments, and people vied with each other to sit with him in the canteen. He was now a sad, solitary figure sitting alone in the canteen, where I would always join him. He stopped to talk with me and asked where I was going. On being told it was to my retirement party, he said rather forlornly that no one had invited him. I told him he'd make my day if he were to join me. As he arrived at the designated committee room, a senior executive asked crossly, 'What's he doing here?' to which I replied sharply, 'I invited him.'

He was the architect who had supplied the foundations on which we had all built our hopes and dreams. Sadly, some people have short memories, don't they?

Best and worst

GEOFF LANCASHIRE

It was the best of times, it was the worst. ... Well, at least, it was one of those times calling for a circumspective look at life – like what the Hell was I doing in this madhouse? The 'how' and the 'why' were far easier to answer. I'd been ghost-writing for newspapers when circulations, fuelled by the scrapping of wartime newsprint rationing, had soared and twinkled brightly before sputtering and slipping into freefall. The titles were *The Sunday Empire News*, *The Sunday Dispatch*, *The Sunday Chronicle* and the *Sunday Graphic*. Kaput went my contracts and *finito* my glittering career. Now I was employed by an ITV company with nine days and nine and a half hours to go before going on air.

My knowledge of ITV according to my very youthful lights, was that the first company, Associated-Rediffusion had staffed itself with the disenchanted and disaffected from the BBC while the second company, ATV, seemed to have peopled itself with a sort of razzmatazz crowd. But in the seven months (three months of ATV) certain objectives had been achieved – ITV was not going to hold a sort of Radio Luxembourg position to the BBC; viewers warmed to and actually enjoyed commercials. Jeremiac press predictions were soon cast aside and favourable reports crept in ('As good as the BBC' or 'Of BBC quality') but somehow this reportage wasn't good enough. What many of us wanted to read was 'different from the BBC' or 'better than the BBC' but how could Granada follow A-R and ATV and make any significant impression when available staff had already been trawled into the A-R and ATV nets. It didn't even have a decent set of initials, for heaven's sake, but was named after some exotic Spanish city. It was unquestionably the most foolish assumption I've ever made – and I was going to be proved so monumentally wrong.

I'd been assigned as a continuity scriptwriter to Central Control (Presentation and Promotion Departments were designated later). My office was in Quay Street – Phase One of the TV Centre and the first building in Britain expressly designed for television. The building seemed to be packed with very young men and women working at a frenetic pace – clutching clipboards and wearing stopwatches like Victorian pendants. They also seemed fluent in a TV newspeak and communication was peppered with 'racks, pos-negs, tee-ex's telecine'. Clearly, if I was going to join Granada's brat pack I would have to undergo a rite of passage – and so it was that I discovered Telecine wasn't to be found lurking in a wire in-tray on top of a filing cabinet. In those nailbiting days before opening transmission tapping into a shimmering skein of memorable characters helped matters. First and foremost, for me, I forged a friendship with my co-continuity scriptwriter, Jack Rosenthal. Jack's humorous wisdom and generosity of spirit was a constant solace and later, I believe became a valuable resource for characterisation in his playwriting career. A few weeks later Jack joined Granada's ludicrously talented all-stars of the Research Department.

To underpin Granada's first days on the air, the company hired some CBS people to help expedite matters. The senior transmission controller was Tim Kiley – an ebullient bundle of energy ('Morning folks! A new day! A new challenge! A new opportunity!) who lived in a clean and wiry live-for-ever frame. Tim Kiley returned to CBS and became director of their prestigious *Coast to Coast* documentary. The other memorable American was David Low, the Production Manager. David had a stocky, Broderick Crawford build, which gave the impression of wanting to sag under the stress of an adventurous past. He also had an endearing custom of playing a violin after lunch in a style, which might be described as bravura, but falling a few lessons short of Menuhin. A marvellous oasis of sanity. David Low also returned to CBS and his post of Production Manager was filled by Carl Robert who, I don't think played a musical instrument but definitely played a mean hand of poker.

The other senior transmission controller was Joyce Wooller – cool, self-assured and self-contained. The three station announcers, John Reid, Bob Jones and Norman Somers – irreverently named her Nellie Wooller which seemed an entirely inappropriate sobriquet for Joyce who had the poise of a Givenchy model and serene, confident looks that induced not a lecherous stare but a stammer. She scared the wits out of me – but I still like to think that 'Nellie' was a very high compliment.

It is almost impossible, nowadays, to fully appreciate the potency of Outside Broadcasts (OBs). They had the immediacy of the here and now which viewers found irresistible. Granada had designed and built two teams of OB units under their own title, *The Travelling Eye*, and planned on producing fifty OBs in the first month – then a record for a single TV company. It would also mean that the only completed studio (Studio 2) could be dark for part of the day thus allowing sets to be struck and set-up for the night's live shows – *Spot the Tune, Make up Your Mind, Youth is Asking* and so on.

Of course, not all Outside Broadcasts went as smoothly as Programme Planning intended. One of *The Travelling Eye* shows from the Manchester Ship Canal was called *Barton Bridge* – a swaggering piece of high Victorian engineering guaranteed to bring a lump to John Betjeman's throat. It was a movable aqueduct carrying the Bridgewater Canal over the Manchester Ship Canal and when a large vessel was navigating the latter the Bridge could be swung open. The OB was going to show just that ... a large ship passing as Barton Bridge opened. All right, so it wasn't exactly Neil Armstrong slow-mo hopping on the moon but in 1956 it was still dramatic stuff.

The OB opened on a strip of arrow-straight water with the ship the merest blip on the horizon. Now the Blue Riband of the Manchester Ship Canal is not one of the most eagerly sought after maritime trophies and even the least nautical of us realised that some time would have to elapse before ship and bridge met. 'Hank' Lewenhak had shown foresight in having 'an ace in the hole'. The production team had booked an old seafaring man to sing a shanty as the ship passed by. They must have got him from the Joseph Conrad school of extras – white cap, knitted jersey, Ronsealed-mahogany complexion and the far-focused eyes of a man long at sea. He even carried a squeeze-box concertina.

With the ship still distanced, 'Hank' cued the ancient mariner. Now Ship Canal shanties are at something of a premium but our man was rich in shanties of the 'Heave ho, my hearties! A wet sail and a flowing sea' variety. So, he went on for verse after verse after verse until 'Hank' Lewenhak couldn't stomach any more of 'white waves heaving, heaving high, my boys' and yelled, 'For Chrissakes, stop him! Somebody interview him! For Chrissakes!' The squeeze-box was mercifully silenced and a desperate interviewer launched into some despairing questioning like, 'That's a nice Jersey you're wearing. Aye. What kind of colour would you say it was? Navy blue. Oh, really? Navy blue?' as this was the main thrust of the interview we never got to the question we all wanted to hear – what was a gnarled old Cape Horner doing sitting on a canal bank singing sea shanties ... five miles outside Salford? But the exercise had worked. The ship had inched its way to Barton Bridge which duly swung open – though it might have been better if the Ship Canal pilot hadn't decided to join in the fun by releasing the steam-valve ... setting off a thunderous blast which had the cameraman hanging on to his equipment and the old mariner flattened to the Canal Bank.

Another watery tale concerns a further *Travelling Eye* broadcast – The Roses match from Old Trafford. I was watching in central control as the show started. It was clearly going to be a washout as the weather was Manchester Monsoon with the proverbial stair rods of rain bouncing off the empty stands and forming Olympic-size pools in the outfield. Start of play would unquestionably be delayed ... by two months at least by the look of it. The director had been reduced to sweeping the desolate stands – but when he reached the Warwick Road end he stopped to pick out a solitary spectator sheltering under a large black umbrella. The sound mixer commented, 'There's always one, isn't there? Just look at that silly bugger.' As the camera zoomed in on the spectator, vacuum flask by his side and sandwiches on his knee, Jack Rosenthal entered Central Control and with an anguished look at the screen, groaned, 'Oh, God, it's my Dad.' It should be said that Jack's Dad, Sam Rosenthal, had been a noted opening batsman in the Lancashire League – so who were we to comment? Maybe, Sam's wistful expression was conjuring up, perhaps, a brighter day and a batsman striding to the crease ... well, it was always possible. ...

In the next twelve months I became a fanatical Granada adherent, a dyed-in-the-wool Granada man. It was no longer a case of 'as good as' or 'better than!' ... Granada had become TV's new leader. Its approach to documentary programme making had become the benchmark for all companies – and its drama department had had a reliability and competence unmatched by any other station. In my years as a freelance working sometimes for A-R, ATV, TWS, Thames and BBC I was referred to and proud to be so, as 'The Granada scriptwriter'.

Festival time

ANDY MAYER

There has always been a temptation for incumbent franchisees to behave like medieval barons when it comes to feeling a little possessive about their territory. Nowhere was the baronial tendency more pronounced than in Granadaland. This was the nation state declared by the Bernsteins in the early days of their occupation of the north of England.

Over the years the company's presence in Manchester became more and more solid and the TV centre, with its strange helter-skelter tower sat firmly just off the back end of Deansgate like the local mill. Having a major TV company was important to the city as its industry declined and holding Manchester hostage was important to Granada as the ITA put increasing emphasis on regional identity.

The opportunity for a most vivid demonstration of mutual identification occurred in 1973. The mayor and corporation had discovered that in this year the city charter would be 100 years old, and plans for a centenary celebration were afoot. In charge was a committee. Naturally Granada sat on the Festival committee and it was expected by Manchester and assumed by Granada that the company's contribution would be significant. Manchester is home of the Hallé and Denis Forman, keenest of music lovers, planned a splendid evening of music and song at the Free Trade Hall as the jewel in Granada's festival crown. At the TV centre there would be more music and dance. Those privileged to attend would promenade the city's streets between the events.

This was all very well and fine, but fears were expressed that to some Mancunian folk the plan might seem remote and elitist. It would never do for the Monarchs of Manchester to seem remote from their subjects, and so a Granada street festival was added on, to entertain the posh guests as they moved from Studio 12 to the Free Trade Hall but more importantly to keep the rest of the punters happy.

I was appointed producer of the People's Festival and, with the help of Clarissa Hyman, street performers were ordered from all over the country. Stilt walkers, jugglers and rock bands would be on hand. Eric Ward, the famous escapologist, would dangle in flames from the jib of a crane encased in a straightjacket. Hermione Demoriane would dance in her underwear on a highwire above the crowds. The Great McCabe would leap upon eggs with his hobnailed boots and never break a shell. Professor Bruce Lacey would present his notorious jelly lady. 'She's naked and she's edible.'

All the arrangements were swiftly made. Tony Brill and Geoff Tarn joined as administrators and Peter Plummer was signed to direct the movie of the event. But as the day drew near I began to fret. Ad Hoc research indicated that the citizens of Granadaland neither knew nor cared about the treat prepared for them and intended on the night (a Thursday) to pop off home at 5.30 as usual, for tea and a bit of telly.

I put it to David Plowright, then Programme Controller, that it would look shaming if the emperors of Granadaland threw a party and nobody came. David agreed. Something had to be done, but what? It came to him in a flash. We've got a TV station! Mike Murphy and Norman Frisby of the press office set to work and within hours fanfares began to beam out across the northwest touting Thursday's attractions. Maybe people would turn out after all?

Came the night and at 5.30 Crown Square, the ground zero of the festivities was empty and quiet. It seemed the message had not got through and that Eric, Hermione and McCabe would dangle, dance and leap unseen.

By 6.30 the square was packed. By 7.30 I was ringing the police for help. We were amazed. It had never occurred to us that the powerful medium we sold to advertisers might actually work.

Luckily the crush eased around 8 p.m. Disaster was averted and Manchester had a night to remember. The evening had two incendiary highspots. The first featured the Great Blondini in The Coffin of Death. This was a deceptively simple stunt in which Blondini (aka Eric Costello) climbed into a plywood coffin lined with explosive and blew himself up. He had purchased the act in a Liverpool pub from a Captain Dynamite who had somehow lost both his arms and was unable to light the fuse.

When Blondini climbed into the coffin and Mrs Blondini urged the crowds, mostly youths, to stand back, few obeyed, assuming with northern scepticism that the bang would be small. Inside, Blondini lit the fuse and pulled the rug over his head. The explosion broke glass in the Law Courts, a hundred yards away.

When the smoke cleared, the awed and dazed audience ran forward and carried the semi-conscious Blondini (bleeding from both ears) shoulder high.

The evening ended with another bang. I had arranged a firework display from the roof of the TV centre, during which a rocket launched from the top of the tower turned and, like a cruise missile, whistled with pinpoint accuracy into the rooftop air conditioning plant, setting the building on fire. The happy crowd cheered gratefully as fire engines raced to save Granada from itself. It seemed a fitting end to a display of benevolent paternalism.

A handful

MICHAEL PARKINSON

What struck me most initially about working at Granada was that it was a lot like working in an art gallery. It was the only office I have entered to have a Francis Bacon in the entrance hall and a John Bratby mural in the canteen.

They were the best of times. The fact is that none of us knew what we were doing. Coronation Street was produced by a Canadian. There was a great sense of artistic freedom running concurrent with technical ignorance and it made for a stimulating environment.

I still believe that the writers, producers and directors brought together at that time – I am talking about the 1960s – were the most remarkable bunch of people I have ever worked with. The exciting, stimulating experience of working with people like David Plowright, Barrie Heads, Peter Eckersley, Tim Hewat, Leslie Woodhead, Michael Apted, Mike Newell,

Johnnie Hamp and many, many more, has not been surpassed in my long career. I also think Denis Forman was a wonderful overseer of what must have been a handful.

I liked Sidney for his eccentricity and loved Cecil who when I left Granada put an arm round my shoulder and said, 'There will always be a light burning for you at Granada.'

I don't think anyone working for the company at that time and into the 1970s will ever forget the experience. We were part of a unique enterprise and were one of the most important cultural factors in the cultural revolution of the 1960s.

That alone would make working for Granada an exceptional experience, but it was much, much more to do with being based in Manchester and having that special point of view which was different.

In retrospect

JACK ROSENTHAL CBE

The day before yesterday – or possibly in the spring of 1955 – Granada Television was a small green hut in the middle of a derelict Manchester bombsite. It was occupied by Granada's sole member of staff, Jim Phoenix.

A couple of miles away, I was a junior copywriter in an ad agency. There I read in a trade paper that something called Granada TV planned to go on the air a year or so hence and that this Mr Phoenix was getting a hundred letters a week applying for jobs as 'anything from typists to transmission controllers'. I wrote to him saying I hoped he didn't mind letter 101, but was there anything that I, too, could apply for?

He interviewed me in the green hut and in his rich, Deryck Guyler accent he told me his official title was Northern Administrator. I glanced at the weeds and rusty scrap iron outside the window and asked him what there was to administrate. 'Well, for now, a cup of tea,' he said. 'D'you take sugar?' and put the kettle on the primus stove. He suggested I apply for a place on the Granada Graduate Scheme (officially to 'Get To Know Granada'; in reality to work as a Pretend Trainee Manager at Granada Theatres, dreaming up ways to cut the weekly budget – by 10 per cent a week – every week).

Over the years, Jim became not only the best Northern Administrator I ever had but, like so many future Granada colleagues, a mate and a mentor. A man to look up to, in both senses. A year later, 10-foot executives seemed compulsory at Granada, cast, no doubt, in the leonine, charismatic, dynamic, beautifully-groomed image of Mr Sidney himself — a real giant of a man.

I did as Jim suggested, but also, so's not to tempt Providence, I applied to Vantona Textiles for a job as a shirt salesman. One Friday morning two letters arrived, one from Vantona offering me £8 a week and one from Granada offering me seven. A harrowing weekend of agonising followed – after all, in those days you could spend 19s 11d and still have change from a pound – then I made the big sacrifice and plumped for Granada.

Just as Jim was the only employee, it seemed I was the only member of the graduate scheme. Maybe I *was* the graduate scheme. After nine months of getting-to-know-Granada, Clapham Junction, I was back in Manchester. And times had changed. The green hut had gone, in its place was an office block and, across the road, were the world's newest, shiniest state-of-the-art TV studios. And Granada wasn't just me and Jim any more. There were now hundreds of upstart Johnny-come-lately typists and transmission controllers and everything in between, muscling in and milling about as if they owned the bloody place.

The Personnel Department had no idea what to do with me. So they hid me away in the Buying Department. I lasted a day. The only purchase I made — and I hope every lady and gent who's ever worked at Granada is grateful — was a few dozen toilet-roll holders. Chrome lacquer finish.

The next morning, now administrating the north at full pelt, Jim moved me into the Research Department run by Barrie Heads. I wasn't the best researcher in the world. But when I was eventually nudged sideways into Geoff Lancashire's Promotion Department, I was replaced, not by one researcher, but two. One was a slip of a lad called David Plowright, the other a young scallywag called Jeremy Isaacs. Maybe I hadn't been as lousy as I thought.

Over the next few months, I began to think Granada was the most exciting place on earth. It probably was. The corridors bustled with Bright Young Things, clipboards clutched in hand and stopwatches bouncing on bosoms. The air clanged in a Babel of colliding accents — Cambridge, Cockney, Canadian, Kensington, with the odd bit of Ardwick thrown in. The canteen shimmered with legendary, yellow-corduroyed whizzkids of West End stage and Silver Screen discussing Life and Art over their cordon bleu lunches, watched over by New Masters originals hanging on the walls. Phones rang everywhere. Typewriters clattered. Shrill voices from one office yelled, 'But that's how we always did it in Toronto.' From another came the sweeping strains of a violin being played by a director who wasn't to be disturbed because he was 'thinking'. And the excitement went on well after home time. The New Theatre pub across the road throbbed and bulged and crackled with passions and ideas and anecdotes. But mostly with passions. Like a sort of Mancunian Club Med with clothes on. Everyone threw parties for everyone else. Romances began and ended. 'Songs For Swinging Lovers' had a hell of a lot to answer for.

Throughout all this euphoria I had one niggling worry — although it shouldn't really have been mine at all. It should've been Mr Sidney's up there on the sixth floor. My worry was that — what with Opening Night only three months away, then two, then suddenly next week — did anyone have the faintest idea what its programmes were going to be? And, if they had, did anyone actually know how to make them? And if they did, what the hell were we going to show the next night? let alone for the next forty years. And had any of this even crossed Mr Sidney's mind?

On the day before opening night, I was buttonholed outside the third-floor lift by an hysterical-looking Production Designer.

'Jack!' he yelled, 'You'll do! Where are you going at lunchtime?'

'Down Deansgate.'

'Good! Got any money?'

'A couple of quid.'

'Right! Go to a stationery shop and buy some green cards, 12 by 9. For captions. Apparently they have to be green. And 12 by 9. I think they have to be 12 by 9 ... And green.' And he blundered off down the corridor.

I spent a sleepless night.

The day of opening night dawned, as I half-suspected it might, and Mr Sidney called every single employee into the canteen for a pre-match pep-talk.

'If you don't like Granada's way of doing things,' he said, 'just tell us and we'll think about your way. If we reject your way, that's it, hard luck, we'll do it our way. And don't bother mentioning it again.' He smiled ominously. 'If any of you are unhappy with that, you can leave right now.' No one moved a muscle. This was Getting-to-Know-Granada in one easy lesson.

Afternoon came. The studios suddenly seemed quieter, apart from the occasional spinning sound of my toilet-roll holders. Everybody said 'Good luck' to everybody else. And then it was evening. And, at last, a black-and-white version of a green caption of some-size-or-other somehow appeared on the nation's TV screens. An announcer's voice uttered, for the very first time, 'From the North, this is Granada.' We were on the air. With actual programmes.

The next morning, we arrived at work to find a postcard sellotaped on the office door of every employee. Hand-written by Mr Sidney. 'Thanks,' it said. 'It was a wow.'

To be fair, in retrospect, I don't suppose Jim and I deserved all the credit.

How to rise invisibly to the top

Jim Walker

To understand why we rave about the 1960s revolution you need a taste of the 1950s. For instance, my first job after College was in Gateshead Public Library, burning books.

I had to burn books that weren't as popular as Pearl S. Buck or Catherine Cookson and therefore didn't deserve their shelf space. The first book I had to burn was *The Ragged Trousered Philanthropists*, but I couldn't bear to destroy it and took it home instead. For this I was severely bollocked.

If you reached up to take *Ulysses* or *Sons and Lovers* from the shelves, you found yourself holding a block of wood with a label to indicate that the Library Assistant would decide whether or not you were mature enough to read the real thing. I allowed anybody to read anything and was bollocked.

Fortunately, I met Richard Kelly in a Newcastle pub and became a radio broadcaster on *Voice of the People* and *Voice of the North*. Richard invented the vox-pop and it's impossible to convey the shock of hearing Geordie accents coming out of the Rediffusion wooden wireless set which had hitherto spoken only in the voice of Whitehall and the occasional cockney comic. It was like seeing your granny suddenly reading the News on the telly.

Came the day when the BBC authorities in their luxurious offices in St Peter's Square in Manchester ordered us in our slum studios over Woolworth's to invent a title for a Saturday morning magazine programme hosted by Bill Grundy. In Yates's Wine Lodge we conjured up a list of twenty-five titles, some inspired, some silly. One of them was *Trouble at T'mill Probe Decision Shock*. The authorities rejected all twenty-five and dreamt up their own title – *It's Saturday*.

On the first edition we discovered an astonishingly successful racing tipster in Sheffield. For three weeks in succession he gave out winners and was wildly popular. But the authorities thought it was vulgar and stopped it. And I of course was bollocked.

As the 1960s differed from the 1950s, so Granada differed from the BBC. I was lured to Quay Street even though it meant a drop in wages from £38 to £36 a week and even though BBC colleagues warned that GTV was infested with backstabbers. It was bruited darkly that to get into Granada you had to be Jewish, Communist or queer. As a gentile father of two I could only suppose I qualified as a Red.

When I asked Mike Scott, Head of Locals, why I'd been poached, he said it was because I had a Lancashire accent. In all honesty I confessed that I was from Newcastle, 200 miles away to which he replied casually, 'Well, you know, northern.'

Nick Elliot made me a presenter of a programme called *Octopus*, a sort of budget-free *Tomorrow's World* made in Studio 4, which was so small that it later became a store-room. After three weeks the rumour was that *Octopus* was on its last leg.

I was promoted to producer of the daftest programme ever devised. It was called *Campaign* and presented by Chris Kelly. The idea was that, instead of exposing an issue and passing on, we should shake it every week, like a dog with a slipper. The first episode complained about the shortage of nurseries in Rochdale and public lavatories in Stockport. So did the second. And the third, and the fourth. By then I was ready for a change and so I imagine were the viewers, if any.

Now-famous figures wafted along the corridor. ... Anna Ford, Gus Mac-donald, the gloomy John Birt.

Because I'd worked for Harry Evans on the *Northern Echo*, Scottie made me a News reporter – a Zapata-moustached character with shoulder-length hair popping up in the colour studio with pre-learnt pieces to camera or on black-and-white film shot by our one and only crew.

Once again I was on the screen, and oh, the glory of it all! As I was pushing my little boy on the swings one Sunday, a kid pointed at me and shouted to his friends that I was on the telly. This was the pinnacle of my life. It had been worth learning Latin declensions, swotting through Nietzsche and sweating over Balzac. 'Yes,' I replied modestly, 'I'm Spiderman.'

To prove it, I swung myself high in the air and, misjudging the moment, let go of the chains. As I felt the pain of the tarmac bashing my canteen-bloated body, I heard the kid cry out in awe: 'It *is* Spiderman!'

After the glory, the money. I was made News Producer. Every morning I listened to the local radio bulletins over breakfast. On the train I read all the papers and tore out the regional stories. Other passengers must have thought I was crackers, tearing up newspapers in a frenzy from Marple to Piccadilly.

The Film Exchange was the overpriced boozer in which I advised a young radio writer called Alan George not to go off teaching in the Gilbert and Ellice Islands. He ignored my advice but came back two years later to write under his own name, Alan Bleasdale.

The best thing about the FE was that it had a back door on to Artillery Street. By clinging to the wall you could approach GTV late in the tipsy afternoon, without being spotted by the Sixth Floor. This became known as the Ho Chi Minh Trail (see Roy Shipperbottom's contribution. *Ed.*). It was during one such lurch along the Trail that I conceived an item for a programme called *Reports Action* (once again, a potty title imposed from on high). Presented by Bob Greaves and Anna Ford, later replaced by Joan Bakewell, the show drummed up volunteers to clear canals, carry kidney donor cards, foster children and so on. Volunteers rang in to rows of 100 telephonists, a format much followed since.

My brainwave was that we should stop people smoking by sending out free samples of every known cure. As a non-smoker, how was I to know that millions of desperate addicts would reach for their telephones? Lines throughout Britain were jammed for a day and a half. We put out dozens of promos begging smokers to send postcards instead of telephoning. The government gave us a grant to pay for the postage. Still the telephones wouldn't stop. Granada was jammed. Denis Forman jokingly called Bob Greaves a 'saboteur'.

The national newspapers were half-paralysed and could only write stories about *Reports Action*. In spite of all this nice publicity and in spite of an independent survey that proved we'd saved 10,000 people from smoking, I was, as the producer, quite rightly bollocked. Even more strangely, we had a strike – against me, Jim the lifelong Bolshie! *Reports Action* telephones were manned by 100 trained volunteers from organisations like the Samaritans and Age Concern. But Granada's secretaries and typists saw the opportunity to seize an hour's double-time answering these telephones on Sundays and called a strike. Not the noblest cause, in my view, stopping a do-gooder programme. Many people ring up to 'volunteer' because they're in trouble themselves – lonely, unstable, even suicidal and not all secretaries can deal with that. Mercifully, the strike only blocked one show out of five in the series.

In the 1980s, Granada fell victim to the Thatcherite plague. There suddenly appeared racks of identical grey suits who spoke of 'management's right to manage'. There was no mention of producer's right to produce or performer's right to perform.

Whereas in the past we would submit ideas upstairs to be accepted or rejected, now ideas were handed down, in great detail, from on high. I was forced to produce Granada's part of the *Telethon*, the embodiment of American vulgarity. I protested to no avail. Nevertheless, thanks to the inspired madness of my co-producer, Martyn Day, and the 27-hour long professionalism of Richard Madeley and Judy Finnegan, I actually enjoyed it and Granada triumphed over every other region. All the producers were later invited to Buckingham Palace to meet Prince Charles. I'm proud to say that, as a republican, I declined to shake the royal mitt.

I was next instructed to make a series called *New North* which would show that the northwest was enjoying an economic boom. I protested that the viewers would simply look through their windows and dismiss this as a blatant lie. The 10 per cent of the population who were living on dole money would see the series as a sick joke. Mostly, the northwest was a rain-swept, derelict dump. Nevertheless, the series must be made. I was only obeying orders.

One episode showed how the filthy Leeds–Liverpool canal would soon be transformed into a sort of spaghetti-shaped Venice. Another urged us to appreciate our delightful nuclear installations – more than any other region. The uranium spun merrily at Springfield near Preston, power stations purred at Heysham, Trawsfynydd and Wylfa. No mention was to be made of the waste debouching from these reactors and from Sellafield, all of which make the Irish Sea the most radioactive in the world.

At the end of the series I asked Personnel to put my lump sum in a Tesco bag, and let me take early retirement with a good pension. I think I got out just in time. From what I hear, the word freelance no longer bears any relation to freebooter or freethinker. It means you have the freedom to starve yourself and/or your family between short-term contracts. And to get those contracts you have to do a lot of 'networking' which I gather is a kind of genteel crawling.

So, to all the Media Studies undergraduates who are obliged to work for almost nothing in television today I have this single piece of advice: never make a programme. That way, your work cannot be criticised, you'll never be bollocked and you'll rise invisibly to the top.

Goodbye Granada, the fun ran out and so did I.

Door-to-door salesmen

CLAUDE WHATHAM

When we all moved up to Manchester before the opening, Sidney gave all the directors a short lecture which has stayed with me. He said that now we were up here in the north it mattered very little if our work was praised by the *New Statesman* critic or not. We shouldn't feel satisfied if we had just produced a programme that we knew would be praised by the cultural section of the community. There was no special value in doing productions for people who were already converted. It was the others who were important.

He said we were door-to-door salesmen. We had something to sell and we had three minutes to get our foot in the door and grab their attention. We had to say in the first three minutes of the programme, 'Hey! Look at this! Isn't it great! Bartok! He's fantastic!' We had three minutes before someone said, 'What's on the other side, Mother?' We had to use every trick in the book to do that. It didn't matter how brilliant or sensitive or cultural it was if they turned it off. We were *never* to lower our sights but we were showmen and our job was to get an audience.

He believed in variety – and variety to Sidney meant just that. He put on a variety show from the Chelsea Studios called *Chelsea at Nine* in which the top American comics could appear on the same bill as Marcel Marceau, Menuhin and Bessie Smith.. At first the ratings were lamentable but he slowly forced them up until they were good.

That is probably the main difference between television then and now. Then they put on the shows they wanted to put on – and made people want to see them. Now they try to work out what people *might* want to see – and give them that.

THE
GRANADA
EXPERIENCE

The light in Denis Forman's eyes

GRAEME MCDONALD OBE

I'd never been further north than Hampstead and I knew precisely why when I saw Stockport for the first time from a train taking me to a programme directors' board in Manchester. I had been recommended to Granada by several directors who, secretly, wanted me off their backs as a young know-all account executive with a commercials firm for which we worked, 'TV Advertising'.

Joyce Wooller was there to welcome me and introduced me to the other members of the board. Tim Hewat, I remember, was characteristically aggressive and dismissed my volunteering of *West Side Story* as the best show I'd seen that year as a 'brave try'. One of many wounds he was later to inflict on me! To my surprise, I got the job – or rather a statutory union trial contract of eighteen months.

So there I was in Water Street on a snowy Monday morning to meet with Joyce Wooller once more and learn that my supervisor was to be her husband Mike Wooller. Mike was a wonderful man who tolerated all my blunders with great good humour as, indeed, he did for the rest of his life.

We were first allowed to direct the Welsh-language programme *Dewch I Mewn* with which Granada went on the air each Monday as some sort of sop to viewers on the Welsh borders of Granadaland. It was a hazardous assignment waiting to understand words in English that you used, say, to cut to a photo of Stanley Matthews. The show always ended with a musical number usually involving a camera shot through the strings of a harp! An overrun was conveniently accommodated by putting the station on the air early – a decision made with great élan by Granada's chief executive, Denis Forman. Later in life I remembered this with a great feeling of power when I pulled the strings of a Channel as Controller of BBC 2.

Denis, the man we all looked up to, watched over us trainees and the light of pride in his eyes only dimmed when we displayed some crass ignorance such as my inability to direct an OB of cricket from Old Trafford through my shocking lack of knowledge of the number of balls in an over. Luckily, rain stopped play on this occasion and I could indulge myself taking shots of pigeons playing in puddles over which I superimposed the score so far. I was never assigned to sport coverage again and wasn't that surprised.

Next, the big time, *What the Papers Say*, a network programme I loved because one couldn't prepare for it. The script came up with the presenter on the morning of transmission and there followed a mad scramble to assemble blow-ups of quotes and photos. The aim was always to have more cuts than in any other director's week, whatever the effect might by on the viewer. My producer was usually Jeremy Isaacs whose main concern then was that I got the last caption with his name up before we went off the air so that his mother in Glasgow would know he was alive and well.

Alongside this early work we had to direct the late news, a chore only because we couldn't socialise too much. I often took refuge with Paddy Owen who ran the Central Control Room, Granada's link with the network from where programmes were cued and routed. More power to wonder at. There was, I recall, an ominous red telephone on the control desk for emergency calls to the network. It never seemed to be used, however, rather like, I always thought, Will Hay's telephone in *Oh, Mr Porter!*.

Another network programme I enjoyed, once I had mastered the (to me) complex rules of the game, was *Criss Cross Quiz* whose possessive deviser was always to be found in the canteen after a recording, bemoaning the fact that he had to spend a night a week away from his wife in London for his thirty minutes of fame.

The show that replaced *The Army Game* was *Mess Mates* which attempted to pull the same trick in nautical terms but somehow lacked the same magic. Three actors were its mainstay and so were on long-term contracts: Archie Duncan, Sam Kydd and Ronald Hines. As their luck would have it, when the actors' strike occurred in 1962, these three were all that we had to permutate. Twin cousins, ghosts, anything and everything we could think of were devised to keep the ball in the air and the network contribution going.

So now, by reason of my new-found adaptability to deal with adversity, I was suddenly deemed to be a drama director and it was back to Manchester. Not for me directing the newly-devised *Florizel Street* (later called *Coronation Street*) about which a contemporary director Howard Baker and I said 'We'll eat our hats, if it ever took off.' Instead it was *Railway Police* for me. Now, can you imagine viewers rushing home to watch something called *Railway Police*? Well, of course, no one did so it was a short-lived series but it did teach me the new-found if cumbersome skills of outside broadcast drama. There wasn't a shunting yard in the British Railway Northern Network that we didn't use but nevertheless the fickle viewers stayed away in droves.

A far more formative experience was to be under the tutelage of Philip Mackie whose drama series for Granada seemed to me wondrous. Real plays, real actors and an encouragement to use the studio to its full potential. Having acquitted myself reasonably well with this master I was assigned to the other luminary at Granada then, Derek Granger. Derek, former theatre critic of the *Financial Times* was both the producer of *Coronation Street* and the Bernsteins' touchstone for drama, a role he later brilliantly fulfilled with his series *Country Matters*, and *Brideshead Revisited*. So who was I to demur when I was given a new series to direct, that he had partly devised: *Bulldog Breed*? After all, Derek, it appeared, combined both the common and the Midas touch. But, in fact, *Bulldog Breed* bombed and there was nothing more salutary than working on a series that the network terminates. Nowadays we'd have been shunted to a later slot. Yet another major lesson in TV life.

Generous as always, however, Derek recommended me to Julian Amyes, producer of an upcoming production of J. B. Priestley's *Dangerous corner*, I decided to make the production claustrophobic à la *Huis Clos*. So I devised with the designer a totally enclosed set in which I would shoot the action from two directions and prayed they would knit. Unfortunately they didn't and I therefore committed the cardinal sin of 'crossing the line' many, many times. I asked Julian if this worried him and he said forlornly it was now quite common in foreign films. Sadly I never worked for Julian again but, later, at the BBC our roles there were happily reversed.

I now had a nasty feeling that after this episode Granada couldn't quite place me. The light in Denis Forman's eye seemed more than a mite dimmed when he considered me as a director, and so the role of producer loomed. What better than *Cinema*, Granada's exploitation of the movie industry it knew so well through its cinema chain? And there at its centre was Derek Granger suddenly transformed into a film-loving presenter. Derek was, on screen, his usual ebullient self, always reminding me a bit of Donald O'Connor in *Singin' in the Rain*. But Derek soon tired of the lime-light and went back to his first love, producing, and Mike Scott, Granada's man for all seasons, became *Cinema*'s new presenter.

Mike brought to the role a superb knowledge of Soho restaurants to retire to after viewings but no knowledge whatsoever of films however famous, actors however starry or directors however prestigious. But he learnt fast and wrote colourful and apparently informed scripts and so we all had a good time.

Nevertheless, despite this glorious existence, lunching in London and recording in Manchester, I felt I had fallen into something of a backwater and knew, in my bones, that Denis Forman's eyes had probably dimmed over completely in my regard. I had explored every avenue Granada had generously offered this promising recruit and had been found wanting in them all. Rescue came though from the most unlikely source.

A favourite canteen companion was Gerald Savory, a theatre playwright famous for his stage hit *George and Margaret*. He had a splendid knowledge of plays and the theatre generally and Granada had harnessed him to replace Philip Mackie who had gone off to create more drama magic at Yorkshire TV. Gerald and I became great buddies and I was stricken when he too jumped ship to become Head of Serials at BBC TV in London.

I paddled along with *Cinema* and the odd drama assignment at Granada until, one day Gerald Savory rang me from the BBC to ask me if I would like to join him there as a drama producer. I could hardly wait to gain my release from Granada whom I hoped I had served well though perhaps in the end ultimately disappointingly. When he saw me, Denis Forman's eyes at last lit up brightly again either because he was to be shot of me or, I prefer to think, in happiness for me and my new future. I hope I have continued to earn that pride.

Why I eventually went north and stopped worrying

CHRISTOPHER MORAHAN

In 1958 I was wooed by Harry Elton, wine and all that. He was a friendly Canadian working for Granada, and out of the blue he telephoned me to arrange a meeting. And that time I was working at ATV directing *Emergency Ward 10* – Harry wanted me to come to Manchester to help start *Coronation Street*. We parted on good terms, he went north, and I stayed in the south to complete 80 *Emergency Ward 10*'s over two years. We had just started a family and didn't want to move, just to be in the same routine, making two episodes of television every two and a half weeks. Perhaps that was my first mistake with Granada, not going north then. However, I was flattered, and tucked away the idea for a later day.

You see, Granada did have a very strong appeal – Sidney Bernstein was a new legend – stories were already current in TV about the pictures of Barnum in every office, about Sidney patrolling the building looking to see if the pencils were sharp, about the art collections, and of course there were the programmes, particularly those directed by Silvio Narizzano. We were all mad about television then and those of us who weren't directing plays were desperate to do so.

I had the good fortune to be in the right place at the right time, finding myself floor-managing *Ward 10*, episodes 2, 4, 6, 8 and then directing episode 13 on 1 April 1957. So I owed a great deal to Bill Ward at ATV for giving me my first break. But it didn't stop us looking at how other people did it – which brings me back to Silvio and Hank Kaplan at Granada; to Peter Graham Scott and John Moxey at A-R; to Ted Kotcheff, Phillip Saville, Charles Jarrott and Alan Cooke at ABC. They were our role models, and we used to stay home to watch their work – maybe babysitters were expensive – if video recorders had been invented we might have recorded the plays (perhaps never actually to look at them, as so often happens now). But then they were live, actually taking place there and then in Manchester or wherever. And we talked about them the next day.

About three years later, in 1961 or 1962, I made a research trip to Manchester for a play I was to do for ATV about a father and son who worked in the abattoir near the Salford bridge, and I took up Harry Elton's invitation to drop in should I be nearby. It was a marvellous day. Mike Scott was my guide and mentor – I saw the paintings, I saw *The Street* in the studio, and best of all, I was invited into one of their script conferences. Harry Kershaw was there, and Harry Driver (so far there seem to be an awful lot of Harrys), and the talk was good, not showy but anecdotal, true to life, the lives of the characters coming out of their own roots, stories they wanted to share with their audience. That day I learnt an important thing about Granada – the audience was their equal.

I decided to leave ATV's staff shortly after, perhaps influenced by my visit, and I wrote to Granada to ask whether I could direct some plays for them. The reply was swift, yes, I would be welcome as long as I started on *The Street*, that's how everybody started in Manchester. I didn't go north. Was that my second mistake?

However in 1967 I was invited to Manchester by Mike Scott to spend a couple of days talking to the Trainee Director Course which he was running about a series of plays I had recently directed for the BBC. It was a stimulating time; and I reflected that I hadn't been asked by the BBC equivalent to talk about these productions, even though they had been for the BBC. I learnt another thing about Granada – it was not parochial. Then in 1970, I was finally asked to go north by Peter Eckersley, Granada's Head of Drama, to come and do some plays. Over the next two happy years I directed plays in Manchester by John Hopkins, Donald Howarth and Alun Owen. Apart from the fierceness of the taxi drivers, I was made at home at once, Peter was a fine producer, he had the backing of the chieftains, he liked writers (he was encouraging Jack Rosenthal at the time, and Arthur Hopcraft – *The Mosedale Horseshoe* had been made, and Michael Apted had just filmed *Another Sunday and Sweet FA*). The plays I did were largely in the studio but the atmosphere there was good, the chips in the canteen on Friday huge, the bar at the Film Exchange full every evening.

I had missed the particularly productive years of Philip Mackie's reign as Head of Drama, marked by his special wit and sense of style. It was over a period of about ten years, from about 1965, that a number of distinguished heads of Drama at the BBC and in ITV had been given trust and encouragement by their controllers to pursue distinctly individual work – Mackie and Eckersley at Granada, Sydney Newman at the BBC, and Peter Willes at A-R and later Yorkshire. I never came in contact with the senior management at Granada at that time but it seemed their confidence in Peter was wholehearted. There was a caring for quality and a sense of the particular character of the organisation in Manchester that was quite palpable. Was it overstaffed? Did people drink too much? Probably compared to today's norms and correctness. But it was lively, and good things were done. Those who worked there had a sense of continuity, and future possibilities seemed endless.

For the next four years I never went near the place, except to sneak into Manchester to visit a BBC location – in my new capacity as Head of Plays for the Corporation. Of course I went on watching Granada programmes – particularly the splendid *Country Matters* produced by the masterly Derek Granger, acutely jealous of their quality. In 1977 I went to the National Theatre (NT) for four years and it was during that period that I worked for Granada once more, directing Alan Ayckbourn's *Bedroom Farce* as part of a three-play deal with the NT. The scheme fell through after a year, due to insurmountable difficulties over scheduling, though I suspect that neither of the organisations had great faith in the arrangement. Peter Eckersley had died, and David Plowright, the Controller of Programmes at GTV, assuming also the responsibilities of Drama Head, was beginning a gradual re-emphasis away from single plays towards series – a movement common throughout ITV. An era was coming to an end.

While I was in Manchester, doing Alan's play, I learnt of another project, which interested me hugely. There were plans to produce a series based on Paul Scott's *The Raj Quartet*. I had never been to India, but had recently read the novels, and learnt a great deal about the life there from my wife's family – which had served in India for generations. I was considering what to do when I left the NT and the possibility of working on such a vast project was very challenging. I asked for my name to be put forward as one of the two directors. David Plowright agreed. During my last months at the NT, I was asked to undertake an analysis of Granada's experience in India while filming the nearly perfect *Staying On* (directed by Silvio Narizzano, my early Granada hero) to see what could be learnt about the best way to execute a project of much greater scale and was invited to take on the producer's role in addition to directing half the series.

Our Executive Producer was Denis Forman also Managing Director of Granada TV. Denis had fathered the project from the start, working closely with Ken Taylor, the writer, on the form and style of the adaptation. Denis knew India well since serving there in the army towards the end of the war and after. He had many Indian friends, and had returned often. Most importantly he shared with Paul Scott a distrust of the conventional English upper-class view that our mission in India to rule had been a sacred one. Denis, like Scott was sceptical. Perhaps here too I discovered for myself something of Granada's particular character – no doubt it stemmed from the Bernstein family, but it was magnificently embodied in Denis and David: there was a strong sense of non-conformist, alternative, un-London view which I found very stimulating.

So early in 1981 I had gone north with a vengeance. For the next three and a half years I commuted between Manchester, Delhi, Bombay, London and Simla. The details of making *The Jewel in the Crown* (as it was now to be called) are probably not the stuff of this memoir – suffice to say that throughout the period, Jim O'Brien, who joined me as the second director, and I received support and constructive criticism of such an order that it allowed us to do our best work. Notwithstanding a fire which destroyed our Manchester studio, exhaustion, bad stomachs and sunburn, late snow in foothills, rain in Kashmir, we finished on time and budget. Granada, by now even more confident because of the success of *Brideshead Revisited*, just completed, made the crucial decision to fund our project without contribution from any co-producer, a commitment unimaginable in our present climate. All creative decisions were made by us, with no third party involved; it was staffed nearly 100 per cent from Manchester; Denis had insisted it should be made by those who had given years of service to the company. 'They deserve to go to India,' he said. Paternalistic? Maybe, but it worked.

In 1987 I went once again to Manchester, to direct a film of Elizabeth Bowen's *The Heat of the Day*. I was surprised to see Bob who had been our standby chippie in India (and had doubled for Tim Piggot-Smith on several occasions) in uniform at reception. It was marvellous to meet again; we had been through so much together – I was only sad he was no longer working as a craftsman.

It was good to work for Granada in its pomp. I doubt if we will see the like again.

Come the revolution

JEREMY PAUL

After several years working with other, often less congenial companies, I climbed aboard the Granada showboat for *Country Matters* and was lucky enough to find Derek Granger at the helm. A writer had to be at the top of his form for Derek but the air of relaxed enjoyment was totally sustaining –

as were, in those days, Granada expenses. To come and watch work in progress and stay at the Midland Hotel was one of the joys of a writer's life.

I have two stories about the Midland. The first involved Derek, and both took place in the French Restaurant. I was up for my adaptation of A. E. Coppard's *Crippled Bloom* which starred Joss Ackland, Pauline Collins and Anna Cropper: and Derek took all four of us to dinner there. Or he intended to. Joss had just bought an expensive roll-top sweater which he was extremely proud of. We were blocked by the maitre d': 'Ties only, please.' Our equally elegant producer-host blew his top. 'Would you have the nerve', thundered Derek, 'to turn away Lord Snowdon if he were standing here?' Snowdon at that time had made the roll-top the very height of fashion, wearing it fearlessly on most royal occasions.

The maitre d' refused to budge: it was a house rule, and if broken, no matter by whom, it would 'upset' the other diners, the good burghers of Manchester and their ladies. Derek was apoplectic. He vowed to take away all of Granada's custom and he looked as if he meant it. The maitre d' was completely unfazed by this dire threat (which might well have capsized the Midland), and the upshot was dinner for five in an unassuming little Italian restaurant round the corner.

Some years later, I made a serious miscalculation on Granada's generosity. I was up for a *Sherlock Holmes* story I had dramatised and begged Jeremy Brett to let me pay for a dinner at the French Restaurant. It was virtually impossible to pay for anything with Brett but I had the edge on this occasion. 'Granada will be paying, so I insist.' Brett agreed. He wasn't eating much at the time, a few lettuce leaves and a carrot. Frustrated by his frugality, I forced him to choose the wine. I left the bill at the desk next morning without glancing at it. Six days later I received a very stern note from Granada Accounts. Would I please send by return a cheque for £70 for a bottle of Chateau – consumed in the French restaurant on said date? It's just occurred to me that I haven't worked for Granada since.

Country Matters was daringly imaginative in concept and execution and wouldn't be done today. The *Sherlock Holmes* years were happy and fulfilling for any number of reasons, but the mood had changed. This was not the fault of our producers, Michael Cox and June Wyndham-Davies, who were stalwartly committed to the writers and protected us from much that was going on. The passion was still there, but where was the deep-lying joy? Not etched in the faces around us. We were carrying Granada's flag through most of the countries of the world. But each new series had to tough it out against the money.

This familiar but justified bleat once flew back in my face. I wrote a script which had Holmes and Watson pondering a case through the late-

night streets of Whitehall. We knew shooting in London was difficult –
most probably it had to be Liverpool – but the sequence was important, I
felt, for mood and quality. Cut it. Right then, could Granada afford a bath
for Holmes? And perhaps a samovar, with Watson drinking tea? Play it all
in a cloud of steam. I like to think it was my shaft of sarcastic wit that came
up with this bright idea, but it may have been June. I was not too pleased
when several well-meaning friends said later, 'Did you do that one ... can't
remember the story, but that one with the marvellous scene with Holmes
in the bath?'

Expediency creates art. Does it really? Not very often, and only then if
you fluke it. There used to be anthology series. They gave writers and
directors a freedom to tell a variety of stories which audiences lapped up.
Then someone announced, 'Nobody wants this any more.' Who was this
person?

Well, the new times are with us now. Tastes change, and viewing habits
move on, as they must. But the spirit of the old days endures for those with
a certain memory. And I suspect many of us, within these pages, will be
drawn back to the gut feeling that Granada had something quite special
that was prized from its grasp. And would like it back, please, come the
revolution.

Yesterdays

BRIAN TRUEMAN

I'd been acting, since my short-trousered start in the BBC's Home Service
Children's Hour, for eleven years. A 'semi-pro' through school and university, I'd emerged from two years' National Service full of hope and armed
with the Equity card I'd had since I was seventeen and for which professional standing my sponsors had been Ewan McColl and Violet Carson. An
appropriately odd couple for the career that lay ahead. For now, like most
young actors, I found myself resting as much as acting. A fat TV part for
Peter Dews ... nothing. A live commercial for ILA shirts from the neonatal
Granada ... nothing. Then my ex-journalist brother-in-law told me that
Granada was looking for a part-time newscaster (the BBC 'read', ITV 'cast')
to take some of the workload from Bill Grundy's shoulders.

One Monday evening in 1957, I sat on the edge of a desk and read/cast
through the yellow pages of a news-script watched by the News Editor, Barrie
Heads, his deputy, David Plowright and the sub-editor, Terry Dobson. And

at 5 o'clock the day after, I was the new Northern Newscaster in a tiny room on the north face of Granada, facing the Globe and Simpson building with the Water Street traffic buzzing by.

I sat behind a desk in a wildly green shirt – because a white one would have flared on screen and, for the same reason, with a bright orange face. Ahead of me a small Vidicon camera and its operator. Behind me, a *Northern Newscast* logo hung from a couple of nylon strings. I only had a commercial break to get into the chair while the previous programme's cast and impedimenta were removed. Since the show had been *Popeye* shorts, introduced by actor Gordon Rollings, a potted palm and a parrot in a cage left as I came in. We often went on air with the logo swinging gently from side to side and I stopped drinking the water once I found that the parrot had usually been at it first.

There was no floor manager; instead a lightbox on the desk told me to start, wind up and stop. Numbers 1 to 10 indicated which stories to read once the main items had been covered. The supplementaries were all differ- ent lengths so that the programme's running time could be manipulated. The news ended. 'Good night, Nos Da, Ecky Vah!' I said, phonetically. That was supposed to be English, Welsh and Manx. I'm sure the English was right.

The inauguration seemed to have gone well. There was only one sug- gested improvement: because the of the characteristics of the Vidicon's tube, I should raise my head from the page more slowly – otherwise my eyes got left behind, to join me half a second later.

At first, there was no film in the news, just a few stills so the newscaster didn't need a monitor. The cameraman, who had no viewfinder, did. When the news began to include black-and-white, silent film, Bill Grundy and I had the problem of matching commentary to the picture when all we could see was the back of an off-air monitor. A second monitor was, apparently, impossible so I got them to screw a large mirror to the bottom of the tiny studio's door. We got the image back to front – but we got it. Years later, there was some debate among John and Jill-come-latelys as to what the mirror was for. Some guessed an obsession with trousers, others that the studio had been a dressing room for height-challenged performers.

And then there was sound! Steve Stevens, a gargantuan freelance cameraman, bought himself an American Auricon sound camera. Big and heavy with a microphone like a small Hovis on a stick, it needed a 110-volt supply, so one of my jobs – apart from being the artiste – was helping Steve carry the 1 cwt plus ex-US Air Force transformer to the scene of the action. Together with lights, it consumed vast quantities of juice; Steve always carried a 3-inch nail to replace the 15 amp fuse in the unfortunate location's fuse box. When we left Manchester Central High School after a chat with the Head, the fuse box was smoking. I don't think the school burned down but if it had, *Northern Newscast* would have given you the whole graphic story.

At 20-stone, hairy stomach visible through gaping, grubby shirt, cigar clenched between the teeth, Steve was imposing in the badly-designed tower-block sense of the word. A good cameraman but a bad ambassador. And he tended towards the irascible. I was doing a piece to camera outside York Minster when a man walked down the steps behind me. 'Oi!' bawled our Mr Stevens. 'Get out of my shot! D'you think you own the bloody place?' The reply was a good deal more courteous than the question. 'No. But I'm on very good terms with Him who does.' It was the Dean. Steve growled; I grovelled.

I always knew what to ask in interviews: Terry Dobson, by then Deputy Editor to David Plowright always insisted on giving me a typed list of questions since an actor, university graduate and, worst of all, non-journalist couldn't possibly have the nous to think for himself. They were always the same questions:

1 How does your scheme/idea work?
2 What are the chances of it going through?
3 Have you had any reactions so far?
4 How much will it cost?
5 And what of the future?

It seemed to work in any situation. It probably still would. Right, Mr Blair ...

Then life speeded up so much it blurs. I became, in turn – and without dropping the previous roles – a chairman, voice-over, character actor for daft late-night magazine shows and frontman for longer and longer film reports. Meanwhile, most of my Sundays were occupied with providing character voices for Radio 4 comedy sit-coms in shows with Ken Platt, Ray Allen and, for donkeys' years, Jimmy Clitheroe in *The Clitheroe Kid*. Mike Scott always referred to it as 'The Clitoris Kid' but then he would.

He, Mike Scott that is, became Exec. Prod. Local Progs and decided to lose the nightly magazine, substituting 'themed' nights in its place. Nick Elliott produced an Arts show despite his communication skills which produced guidance like 'What I want is a sort of ... well, not exactly that but having a ... it's got to have more ... I mean, if I say it's somewhere between ... or, anyway, around ... you know ... All right?' I gather it didn't do him any harm.

And on Tuesday evenings, my commission was to produce and present a series of 20-minute, idiosyncratic documentaries of interest to 'Granada-land' as the aspirations of Mr Sidney – aka The Fiddler on the Roof (because of his penthouse atop GTV's main building) – were persuading him to call it. I grabbed a quick holiday before I began the task and while I was away,

Cecil B. for Bernstein ordered it to be called 'It's Trueman'. Which it wasn't: it was other people. We made 32 films in a year. Two researchers leap-frogged fortnightly subjects. For the most part the Desperate Duo were the foul-mouthed, chain-smoking, affectionate, fierce, clever, alcohol-tolerant, vulnerable, loyal pianist Diana Bramwell – who was wonderful – as was the other young, bright, honest, unassuming researcher Ashley Hill who is now Channel 5's Head of Scheduling. Lumme! Two editors – usually Brian Tagg and Alan Ringland similarly leapfrogged to alternative films. Only the director and I worked on them all and he, fortunately, was totally devoted to film and a good friend. Barry Clayton stalked about like Von Stroheim with lights on, was loud and totally tactless, claimed, not infrequently, to have 'dreamt the movie!' during the night and was a terrific director. He needed to be. We were allowed a two-day shoot and a three-day edit per film so it was just as well that he knew what he wanted, could see how all the bits he shot went together as he shot them and seemed to be able to use 398 feet of every 400-foot roll. Thirty-two films and none of them crap. Several, as when what we set out to shoot wasn't really there, were bullshit – but never crap.

Eventually, after I'd produced and presented – thanks to another wonderfully loyal team, a brilliant architect and a patiently long-suffering family – *A House for the Future*, I'd had enough. David Plowright, by then Programme Controller, indicated that my future lay in fronting the local magazine show for the umpteenth time and I left for an even more freelance life with anyone who'd let me do what I wanted to do for money.

Increasingly, that meant writing animation film scripts for Cosgrove Hall Productions who, as Brian and Mark, I'd got to know when they were graphic artists with Granada. Having yet another change of life came at just the right time. There was a lot more sanity in the lunacy of the adventures of a one-eyed mouse and a vegetarian vampire duck than in the unpleasantly evolving 'grown-up' telly.

And out of the past comes a question: what of the future? Today's television is over-stocked with people who have no loyalty to their companies, their departments or their colleagues. They get no loyalty from them, either. Executives zig-zag from one company to another in search of status and pay. Never mind the quality, feel the quids. As with so many at the top of commerce, industry and politics, being *numero uno* is everything. Doing anything worthwhile – least of all serving the populace – is nothing. And benevolence? What's benevolence?

Now and then, those of us who were lucky enough to be in the business, in or out of Granada between 1960 and Mrs T's assassination job, run into one another. When the subject of our mutual past arises, we talk of 'The Golden Years' – silly old sods. But they were.

Once were giants

Herbert Wise

The earliest event was the interview. Denis Forman, behind a not very imposing desk at Golden Square. To my amazement, he took me on, there and then: what insight, to be able to spot talent so swiftly! I was thrilled.

Then there was the raw building site in Manchester, all rubble and bricks, to be the first purpose-built TV studio in Britain. Exciting!

Later, a meeting of all staff in a room like a lecture theatre somewhere; Denis Forman (Arts), Eddie Pola (Light Entertainment), technicians, engineers, cameramen, and eight of us, the original programme directors (Jimmy Ormerod, Bill Gaskell, myself, and five others – can't remember their names), but no SLB; and a guy named Guy Nottingham – an American – who was to run the training course. At that meeting, I, a Herbert till then, when asked by Guy 'Is there a Herbie Wise here?' became a Herbie, which has stuck ever since.

I had spent some of my previous five theatre years running a major repertory theatre and was utterly dismayed at that meeting to be allocated to Outside Broadcasts – Sports and Features for instance. Such talent and experience as I possessed lay in the drama field – so why was I on OBs? I tried to get the decision reversed – to no avail. I was devastated. It was a crucial decision for me, for it affected my whole relationship with the company which became one of attrition.

To leave? I considered that foolish: I was delighted to be in TV, and with Granada in particular, a company I believed in and had great hopes for. So I stuck the OB course – run by another American – Dave Lowe. I had some control-room practice – how easy it seemed when watching others, how difficult to do it oneself – all live of course, in those days!

Having spent three months training me I calculated that, if I were to refuse to sign my contract at the end of the course unless I were moved to studio production (my first step towards drama!), the company would not kick me out. It worked! I was in Studio. But at a cost: the company was, not surprisingly, absolutely livid with me. Yes, I was in studio – doing a quiz game, about valuing objects. I knew nothing whatsoever about quiz games but I adapted.

My debut as a TV director was anything but promising. It was in the first week of Granada's transmission – a Thursday – and in order to get the maximum publicity we were valuing a horse among all sorts of other objects. Running the quite complex rules of the game was quite demanding of the compere. We rehearsed in the morning for the evening's live transmission and stopped at lunch time as another programme rehearsed in the only studio we had open at that time. The compere and I had lunch at the New Theatre Pub (soon to become famous/notorious) after which I went back to my office.

It is difficult for directors nowadays to imagine the apprehension, fear and terror a live show like that induced in one. And not only in me.

I was back in the studio ninety minutes before transmission. I waited for the compere to turn up. He was not only late, but was plainly drunk. He, poor man, was even more terrified than I was, and Dutch courage was a great temptation. Anyway, not hopelessly drunk, but enough to convince me that he would be incapable of steering the programme, with its complex rules, confidently. Panic. Should the programme be cancelled? Call for the producer. Eddie Pola arrived; so did gallons of black coffee. The coffee went down the compere's throat, Eddie went down mine. No, we can't cancel the show. I was in trouble.

The show went on the air, live. The compere was sober enough to cope – just; he was also drunk enough for it to show. The last glimpse of him on the screen was his enquiring face asking the – off screen – floor manager, how many minutes left? In the control room, I was in a state. My vision mixer on my left, did something that displeased me. I hit her hand: 'Don't do that.' To my astonishment, she started to cry. I felt terrible.

I went back to my office. My assistant told me there was a message for me: Mr Bernstein wants to see you in his office first thing in the morning. (So I was in trouble. Back at my digs, Mrs McKay – the Mrs McKay – said 'Mr B's secretary rang to say Mr B wants to see you in his office first thing in the morning.' Thanks.) I did not sleep much that night contemplating my attenuated career in TV.

The next morning, I was early in my office. There was a typed inter-departmental blue memo from Miss Hazelwood, SLB's private secretary, on my desk: Mr Bernstein would like to see you ... At 9 o'clock I was on the carpet. So was Eddie Pola. SLB was furious. 'In the first week of transmission ! Drunk! DRUNK! Humiliation, etc etc.'.

To this day, I don't know how I survived. The Head of Programmes – yet another American – whose name escapes me now – wanted me out. I know, because he told me so. I don't know whether it was Denis Forman or SLB himself who decided not to give me the sack. But survive I did, and the next four years proved to be the most exciting years I spent in TV. But it took me a further two years to get where I wanted to be: Drama.

Some happier memories

A young man came to see me bearing a play which he asked me to read. On his return some days later I told him I did not care for it. He then tried to sell me an idea for a TV series about a street.

'A street? And what happens in that street?'

'Oh, everything about their ordinary daily lives, and so on.'

I told him I could not see the dramatic potential in the everyday happenings of people living in a street, and sent him away with the proverbial flea in his ear. His name was Tony Warren.

When we had our first union strike, we decided to hold it late at night; this only involved our telecine operator members, and in order to give them our moral support and to show our solidarity, all of us union members decided to turn up. As a result the line of our parked cars stretched up and down Quay Street and the side street adjoining. The strike was about being underpaid.

I shot the first few moments of a new series showing a Jewish boy, in close-up, chanting his bar mitzvah prayers in Hebrew. SLB gave directions for it to be reshot; it was considered to be too Jewish.

Working with Denis Forman on a number of programmes, notably the Sir Thomas Beecham concert at Lincoln's Inn Fields, and the conductor's subsequent interview with Peter Brook; and the six months' preparation and excitement leading to *The Verdict is Yours*.

Working with the late Philip Mackie – lovely Philip – on many dramas, still one of the best, if not *the* best of drama producers I have ever worked with. Never dominating, never imposing his will, always guiding, always evoking. Alas, there would be no room for someone like him in today's TV industry.

The Stables Theatre (described elsewhere in this book by Gordon McDougall). What a marvellous concept! What a glorious generous idea! To this day, I do not understand why it failed. It was an honourable failure.

What TV tycoon/executive/entrepreneur today would send its directors round Europe to observe, enquire into, and study TV in other countries, as SLB did in 1959? I went to Brussels, Warsaw, Prague and Amsterdam. Who, today, would think such a move productive? Alas, shareholders are considered more important.

Travelling in SLB's Rover. 'I don't use a Rolls, it's too ostentatious' – while he was dealing with the mail; and constantly dictating to his secretary no. 2. The flight in his plane to London, when he would read a newspaper, then spread it over his face and fall asleep instantly.

And Wilfrid Lawson, a marvellous actor, more often in his cups than sober, was playing a tramp in a play I was directing. After rehearsals Wilfrid

disappeared for a while, and when due on set about an hour before transmission was nowhere to be seen. Searchers in the building could not find
him. The situation was getting serious; finally I went out into the street to
find him. And there was this tramp, unshaven, in filthy clothes, string
holding his trousers up, sitting on the pavement, and laughing quietly to
himself. The doorman had refused to let him enter the building. I said, he
was a wonderful actor.

My last days at Granada and the events leading up to them were not so
happy. In March 1959 I told SLB that I would leave Granada at the end of
that year in order to work as a freelance. In June of that year I became
particularly concerned about an event, aspects of which related to what I
considered unwarranted censorship. The details are now irrelevant, nevertheless it offended my idealistic and passionate belief in artistic freedom
and, in my view, it needed to be exposed.

I knew a prominent journalist from my provincial theatre days and
confided the story to him, asking him to use it, but without revealing my
name. That may have been a coward's way out, and I make no excuses for
that, but this is what I did: I felt morally absolutely justified. The journalist
kept his word and when the story appeared, Granada was in an uproar.
Who was the 'traitor'? I kept my head down; but before long – maybe in
order to flush me out – I learned that one of my colleagues was suspected.
So I had to own up.

Shock, Horror! I was in trouble. Again. Deep trouble. I pleaded to be able
to talk to SLB to explain my motives – truth, artistic freedom, censorship –
but to no avail. In fact, no one would talk to me.

A miserable month went by. Then, one day, I was summoned to see
Victor Peers, the General Manager. To my amazement and relief, he told
me that everything was OK now, I was not to worry, it had all blown over.
Could I talk to SLB? No, he did not want to see me. I returned to my office;
I told my assistant the good news. She just looked at me. She said nothing,
just looked at me. On my desk was a note – the familiar blue inter-
departmental memo. It read: 'It has been decided that after the end of this
month your services will no longer be required.' It was early August.

I don't think SLB ever really forgave me. I did not work for Granada for
some years after that, not until Philip Mackie asked me to direct a couple of
plays in his Victorian series. I did not attempt to see SLB. I happened to
pass him in the corridor one day; I acknowledged him, and as he passed me
he just said 'Slumming?' and moved on.

Looking back over my long career, I have to admit that I have never been
happy in a paternalistic environment. And Granada was paternalism

personified; personified in the figure of SLB. On the other hand, SLB was a man of vision; he had a dream, and the courage and determination to realise it. And that dream was Granada.

Once were giants!

PRODUCTION
TRAINEES

Harmony in a pink shirt

MICHAEL APTED

I've noticed over the last couple of years that I've been dreaming a lot about Granada; me there now, me there in the 1960s, me with people I haven't seen for years, some I thought I'd forgotten. That time in my life seems to have assumed some kind of patina, become a kind of golden age. I think there are two explanations for it; one, because it was, and second because it represents a yearning for a life far away from the stress of holding together a career and any sort of sensible life in Hollywood. Of course, I conveniently forget the stress of being yelled at by Tim Hewat, or the strain of keeping Pat Phoenix and Violet Carson from coming to blows in a *Coronation Street* rehearsal room, or the youthful terror of trying to figure out whether I had any talent and the faintest chance of a career.

For whatever reason, Granada certainly left its mark on me. Some is tangible, for I'm already beginning to shoot *49 Up*, which began as a *World in Action* special in 1964 and has now involved me for 37 years. That says something about my stamina, but a lot more about the power of my connection with the company. Wherever I was or whatever else I was doing, I was always drawn back to do the series, back to Manchester where I began my working life. My hero, the Spanish director Luis Buñuel, wrote, 'our imagination and our dreams are forever invading our memories; and since we are all apt to believe in the realities of our fantasies, we end up transforming our lies into truths.' So what did those years in Manchester, 1963–70, mean to me?

My generation of production trainees could hardly have chosen a better time to join Granada, probably the best; the Bernsteins were very active, Denis Forman was Head of Programmes; Tim Hewat was running *World in Action*; Philip Mackie, Drama; Johnnie Hamp, Light Entertainment; David Plowright, Local Programmes and Mike Scott, Mike Parkinson and Peter Eckersley were producing and anchoring *Scene at 6.30*. It was intoxicating stuff for lily-livered boys straight out of college who'd never been further north than Birmingham. Under the dynasties created by Hewat and Plowright there was a genuine populist drive to talk about real issues in a language that everybody could understand – to be passionate and accessible, to care about what you were saying and not to talk down to the audience. It wasn't an accident that this was happening in Manchester, as it was part of a much bigger picture. Most of what was best in popular music, writing, art and sport was coming out of the north. There was a vigour and muscularity in the air and Granada was putting it on television.

It was dazzling to watch, for underneath there was a powerful humanity and willingness to take on a social and civic reponsibility which in today's world, and not just in broadcasting, has vanished.

What made it all so heady was a unique kind of harmony that existed between this brash, boozy, rather intimidating world and the sophisticated aesthetics of other, different men. It was the current affairs boys who expanded my view of the world; then it was Derek Granger and Julian Amyes who taught me my job. Derek – the first man I ever met who wore a pink shirt – showed me how to 'own' material, to inject my sensibility into a script and make it mine, yet never to let anything get in the way of telling the story. And I shall never forget Julian gently telling me how there was no right or wrong way to work with actors and crew, nothing you could learn from a book about how to direct, only the sense of what was best for you. That was the real journey, the real adventure in work – the discovery of self and there was a simple truth and dignity to it. Then there were the Granada writers, Peter Eckersley, Jack Rosenthal, Arthur Hopcraft and later Colin Welland, men of great talent and perception, with wit and irony in their work and lives. From them I developed a taste in material, a way to find drama and humour in ordinary, everyday life and we put together Granada's first films and some of the best work I've ever been associated with – *The Mosedale Horseshoe* and *Another Sunday and Sweet FA* among them. It was a time full of good lessons and great role models that opened up a world rich in possibilities.

The early training we were given was pretty much 'on the job'. There wasn't the time or the money for anything very formal, so it was just a matter of going to work and figuring it out as we went along. Blasphemy in an age of film schools, degrees in communications etc., but wonderful for us. We got to try our hand at everything: News, Magazines, Sport, Documentaries, Rock and Roll, Children's, Religion and Soap. We made horrendous mistakes – cutting to commercials during cricket coverage two wickets into a hat-trick was classic, and I plead no contest to broadcasting an entire live interview without sound, but people were kind and supportive and covered for us. It was a lot of pressure but we learned our business, found our strengths, discovered what we could do and what was beyond us. If we'd trained at the BBC we'd have been boxed up and salted away long before we knew who we were. I moved from documentary to drama because I wanted to give it a try, so I asked to do Mike Newell's holiday relief on *Coronation Street*. Julian Amyes said OK and it changed my life. There was a power and confidence in the building and a sense of people working to their full potential. It couldn't and didn't last, but it was a privilege to be there for some of it.

My long-term contribution has been the *Up* films and in some way their history dramatizes what being at Granada meant to me. *7 Up* had the clear, almost naive, political agenda that despite the radical social changes of the early 1960s, the English class system was alive and well, sustaining the strong and neglecting the weak and that the accident of birth brought power, riches and success. The message was powerful and popular, insightful and funny, specific but a bit parochial. When *28 Up* was finished, I was asked to show it in America but it felt a bad idea because how could they understand it knowing nothing of our schools, politics and culture? So its success was a great surprise until it dawned on me that Americans were seeing something quite different from what I'd intended: they were responding not to the polemic but to the humanity, to the resonance of universal stories about growing up, to success and failure, to dreams and disappointments, to ambition and compromise. And so it is with me and Granada – when I first left I was grateful for the work and the vision, but as I get older I relish the other things; the people, the memories and the values, and they are what stay with me. Maybe I'm being too romantic about it all, but then I go back to Buñuel, 'reality and fantasy are equally personal and equally felt, so their confusion is only a matter of relative importance'. So it doesn't matter if I embellish or edit or how rosy my spectacles might be; what counts is that the moments were there and I lived through them, and they gave me a foundation and an identity. In 1979 I made a choice to transplant myself to America and leave my roots. It was, and still is, exciting and challenging, but hard to be cut loose into an alien culture. Those pieces of Granada that I carry with me through my daily life are invaluable signposts when I need to remind myself who I am and where I come from.

En route to the Stables

GORDON McDOUGALL

In 1963 Mike Newell, Michael Apted and I moved into a semi-detached house with imitation lattice windows in Alexandra Park, Manchester. It was so damp that when you stood in front of the electric fire in the morning your trousers steamed. We were being paid £10 a week. The first Monday morning in September the three of us reported to the studios at 9.00 a.m. We'd been assigned to *Scene at 6.30*. Jim Crawford, the chief researcher, tried to make us feel less unwanted than we knew we were, while organising the day's programme. At eleven Mike Parkinson, the producer, walked in and straight past us, looking distinctly crapulous and murmuring: fucking production trainees, that's all I fucking need this morning.

Suddenly, after a lifetime in boy's schools and male colleges, we realised we were young and available. We went to the Cavern (and the Beatles came to the studios), we went to the Blue Angel in Liverpool and drove girls back to Manchester and felt apologetic and kissed a gentle, unconsummated goodbye. We drank with George Best in his nightclub. And, at work, we were trained by Julian Amyes who put the fear of God in us that dire consequences visited a fledgling director who asked a cameraman to track on an 8-inch lens or push his cable. If it works on paper, he would say, it may not work on the floor. If it doesn't work on paper, it sure as hell won't work on the floor. A dictum I've adhered to all my life.

Meanwhile Gordon Flemyng, who directed from the floor and not from the control box, was belying the theory with every show he very successfully managed to get on the air. Our training finished six weeks early and Apted and I were assigned to Granada's most exciting, macho programme, *World in Action*. Tim Hewat had won from Sidney Bernstein the concession that this one programme could be made from London and all on film. A special penthouse had been built for the production studio on top of the London offices. Jejune and terrified, we reported to the freckled Australian who was the most feared man in Granada. An alarming (though probably apocryphal) story circulated about Michael Parkinson's brief assignment to *World in Action*. Parky was supposedly despatched to Istanbul where, after a few days, he cabled, 'Story uninteresting, am moving to Tehran.' Hewat, the story went, cabled back: 'Generate interest.'

We were to make Tim's last edition of *World in Action*, a film he had always wanted to produce himself but had to hand over to others because he was leaving. *World in Action* was shot and edited between the Tuesday conference and the Monday transmission; this edition took four months to complete. It was to be about seven-year-old children and it was to justify Hewat's belief that we are predestined from our early experiences of life: 'Give me a child till he is seven and I will show you the man' an old Jesuit dictum, was to be its epigraph. That first day Tim took us up to the top of Golden Square. 'If I'm making this show,' he said, 'I start with the camera up here and twenty children down in the square.' Voice over: 'Here are twenty children, these five are going to be winners.' Zoom in. 'These fifteen are going to be losers.' Zoom in. 'Now we're going to show you why.' We smiled internally at the crassness of the style and spent four months making a programme which said exactly that.

My next assignment was to assist Silvio Narizzano who was making a series of Feydeau farces adapted by Philip Mackie, called *Paris 1900*. I had always wanted to meet Silvio because he was responsible for the greatest piece of television I had ever seen, *Death of a Salesman*, made by Granada in 1958. This was the first televisual experience in which one was able to realise the power of the medium to transport one in time, to superimpose a scene from the past upon the present. Yet, Silvio told me, this had been achieved in Studio 2, hardly larger than a shoebox, shot live, with the cameras having to move into the corner of the studio to shoot the captions for the commercials in the ad-breaks. My admiration for the days of steam television and the men who made it increased fourfold.

I returned to Manchester where, for reasons of union agreements, I could not be made up to director. I went out with Apted on the Moors Murders story and became part of the army of reporters tramping the damp moors outside Saddleworth trying to pick up titbits. As more and more appalling details of what had happened in that house and the one in Denton emerged, the conversations among the pack became thickly studded with the sickest jokes I have ever heard. It was the only way to get through the horror and it made me realise that for the most part we laugh at what we are most afraid of, as a mechanism of release.

Some years later, when a director at the Stables was having problems with a scene from *Christie in Love* in which a policeman digging up the bodies obsessively recites limericks, I was able to use this experience to shed light on such conflicting, and superficially obscene, actions. I had an idea for a documentary about the Easter Rising and Granada sent me with a writer to Dublin. For several days we interviewed the survivors and, had we had the foresight to tape the conversations, they would have made an extraordinary historical record. Sean O'Kelly, the previous president, told us on his deathbed that he had retrieved Eamon de Valera's fountain pen from certain English confiscation on the night before de Valera was due to be executed. In the Presidential Palace the following day, de Valera confirmed this: 'And he never gave it back ...' A group of foot-soldiers who had dug trenches in St Stephen's Green and fired at the Shelbourne met us in that famous hotel which they had never been inside and, for the first time in their lives, tasted Irish coffee. The piece later became a play which was performed successfully in many theatres.

For the next two years I spent a lot of time away from Granada on secondment. They were good enough to pay my salary while I gained theatre experience in weekly rep in Barrow-in-Furness and, in 1965, as assistant to John Osborne and Anthony Page during George Devine's last season at the Royal Court.

Back at Granada and made up to director, I was let loose on *Scene at 6.30*. It was shot live in a medium-sized cupboard called Studio 4 which was in use every day and sparsely serviced, so that cameras and microphones and even the facility to superimpose captions would often go down on air. Cool as ice on transmission, hours later over supper one would suddenly and inexplicably start to shake. Aside from a ten-item show which would finish rehearsal 20 minutes before air time when the producer would cut the two pieces you needed to get your cameras from one side of the studio to the other, we had to shoot live the first television versions of all the latest hit numbers: Substitute, It's Over, You've Lost That Lovin' Feeling, The Sun Ain't Gonna Shine ... Lionel Blair once disputed it was the same studio I had shot Dusty Springfield in the night before; I had to explain I'd used a forced-perspective floor. After eight months of this, I was offered the Artistic Directorship of the Traverse Theatre in Edinburgh, at that time the only theatre apart from the Royal Court specialising in new work. I think Granada could hardly believe that a person would quarter his salary and leave them for a 59-seat theatre. As with Roland Joffe, rather later, it made them view the departed in a new light.

In less than a year I was invited back to Manchester for talks. Denis Forman asked in what ways I would like to change Granada's drama. I'd been thinking on the train and concocted an idea in which actors and writers would work in theatre and television at the same time. I never thought they'd wear it and indeed it did get cut down from my original scheme. But within six months I had left the Traverse, we were negotiating a special contract with Equity, and Granada were converting the stables of the Liverpool Road station from a builders' yard into a theatre.

For eight months we met every actor in Britain with a view to casting the company. They all seemed to expect me to be middle-aged; Peter Plouviez, general secretary of Equity, sat opposite me in The Pontefract Arms after a contract meeting and said: 'How does it feel to be an executive of a major industrial company at the age of fourteen?'

The Stables Theatre opened in January 1969 and simultaneously the company began making television plays. I believe nothing like it has ever existed before or since. Mr Sidney hated the idea of the bar because he didn't want to own premises on which people drank, but apart from con-tributing hugely towards the budget, the bar was vital for bringing people into the building who would otherwise never have gone near the theatre. The former middle-weight wrestling champion of the world, Tommy Mann, came to the bar and stayed for the show. Soon he was doing the fights for *Dracula*, appearing in *The Cherry Orchard* and offering to put up money to save the theatre when it closed. The theatre attracted a company of actors who were to stamp their mark on television: Maureen Pryor, Maureen Lipman, Richard Wilson, John Shrapnel, Zoë Wanamaker. The first plays of Trevor Griffiths, Peter Ransley, Bill Morrison and a host of other important writers were performed there, attracting continuously excited reviews. 'There seems to be no end to the string of talented playwrights the Stables can discover in one year,' said the *Daily Telegraph*; and the *Guardian* said it was the finest company outside London.

The television side of the operation didn't work so well. 1969 was the worst possible year to start such an operation. Independent television's profits were being decimated by the levy, colour TV was imminent and the unions worked to rule and then struck for several months, and we had a company of twenty actors on salary who couldn't be laid off. At the end of the first year we had to buy back the actors' 'holiday period' of three months to catch up on the unmade television productions and consequently the operation went £63,000 over budget. We were offered the choice to close or to continue making small-scale shows in, of all places, Studio 2. We chose to continue, but these were exactly the sort of plays that needed to be cast with stars and didn't benefit from the work of a company.

It soon emerged that I had created Frankenstein's monster for myself. Scheduling twenty actors between thirteen theatre shows, twelve television shows and countless late-night and lunchtime pieces in a single year was a task for a sophisticated modern computer program; I had a perspex-covered board 6-feet square and four felt pens in different colours. It took a whole night every two weeks. I produced all the shows, directed seven theatre and two television plays in a year, and administered the whole enterprise. There was nobody but myself sandwiched between the Granada board and a company of twenty very ambitious and egocentric actors. Many nights of the week I would be in the 8th-floor flat till two o'clock discussing strategy and in the studios next morning at eight to deal with correspondence and rehearse. Granada very much wanted the Stables to use staff directors but we had no lead time to experiment with the new techniques we wanted to develop.

After a time it became clear that whatever you put into a sausage machine turns out sausages, unless you change the machine, and we never had time to do this. So the big company pieces didn't work on television because the directors couldn't find a new way of looking at drama under the pressure of having to get the show in the can. And the first company piece we did was the first play in colour in a Granada studio; the technicians were working to rule and it overran by an unprecedented three days!

After two years, Mr Sidney viewed the Stables television output and decided that, although much of it worked, it didn't justify the sums being spent on it. I chose *The Cherry Orchard* to be the last play in the theatre. I did it as a protest: the Stables Theatre was an expensive, desirable luxury that no one had the care or determination to keep in existence. I turned the whole theatre into an orchard. Cherry trees grew from moss on the floor up into the rafters. The audience sat on wooden benches and turned their seats to watch the action in different areas of the theatre space. Viewed as close as that, the play's unfolding became our failed dreams and aspirations, our insouciance and carelessness. At the close, the dying Firs lay on a couch in the empty theatre space as the sound of trees being felled came from just outside the building. Mr Sidney called me from some foreign airport to say it was the most moving show he'd seen in a theatre. 'You're closing it down, Sidney,' I said. 'I don't want to hear that.'

The chance to fail

Claude Whatham

Granada began for me at nine o'clock on a bitterly cold morning just after Christmas 1956. The central heating at 36 Golden Square had failed – which wasn't an auspicious start to the company's first production training course. The group of fifteen or twenty reserved (and to some degree suspicious) 'students' huddled together in silence in a freezing film preview theatre waiting for activities to begin.

We had all received the timetable. *At 9 o'clock Mr Sidney Bernstein would address the course. At 9.05 students would be divided into working groups. At 9.15 separate workshops would commence* ... it all looked a little too well organised to be true. But right on time a small bunch of executives moved purposefully into the theatre. Sidney Bernstein led the way. Imposing, immaculately dressed in a dark suit and startlingly white soft shirt, and looking vaguely like a Mafia godfather, he stood before the blank screen. His pugilist's face was unsmiling – but his eyes were unexpectedly kind. After an abrupt 'Good morning to you' his address was indeed brief and ended with this sobering valedictory observation. 'At the end of this course some of you will get very good jobs. Some of you not quite such good jobs. Some of you may not get a job at all. I wish you luck.' He then left at speed followed by Denis Forman, who had stood a step or so behind him in a distinctly military manner (with a concerned expression rather like an Adjutant on a CO's inspection) and all the other anonymous bigwigs trailed behind. Well the timetable got underway exactly as planned ... and at 9.45 I sat down to direct an Interview Programme – something I hadn't the faintest idea how to do!

Granada went into operation some six months after the opening of the

ITV Network, so most of the technicians and production personnel who were poached or were tempted to leave the BBC were already contracted to other companies. We were never entirely sure whether that was the reason that not one person on the course had ever directed or produced anything on television or whether it was some deep plan to change the shape of programmes. The Training Staff seemed to have been entirely recruited from Canada and looked rather thoughtful when none of the 'students' had any idea how to set out a camera script or, in most cases, understood the simplest technical terms.

There were two courses running concurrently. A Director and Producer Course and a Production Staff Course for Floor managers and Production Assistants. The directors came from many different backgrounds. I had originally been a stage designer; Peter Eton was a veteran radio producer – he produced (and was reputed to have 'invented') *The Goon Show*. He went on to produce *The Army Game* and *Bootsie and Snudge* for Granada. Another man from radio was Philip Jones, who went on to become Head of Light Entertainment for Thames Television. Theatre spawned Herbert Wise and William Gaskill. Bill Gaskill didn't last long. Sidney Bernstein once said to me, 'We had to get rid of him. I didn't think he was up to it ... I see he is now Assistant Director of the National Theatre ... we all make mistakes!' And then he laughed. Some of the trainee floor managers (FMs) soon moved over and became directors. Mike Wooller became a distinguished documentary producer and made (among many other celebrated programmes) *The Second World War* for the BBC. Peter Frazer-Jones went into light entertainment. Don Leaver became a leading director and producer in Drama.

Mike Scott was an FM for quite a long time. In the early days Granada pioneered the 'live' unrehearsed and unscripted studio shows (and a lot of their other output looked that way too!). The guest participants didn't enter the studio until just before transmission. It became the standard practice for the FM to 'sit in' for them during the camera rehearsal, and – if it was a question-and-answer format – debate some topic other than the programme subject with the audience. Mike was particularly good when the audiences were children.

When the time came for a local network evening news programme *People and Places* to be set up, Mike found himself elevated to the role of 'anchor-man'. He eventually became Programme Controller at Granada, and was also a very popular interviewer and presenter on the national ITV network.

Each 'student' had to produce one 15-minute and a final 30-minute show at the end of the course. Some were quite ambitious. I only remember one of my colleagues' efforts. Bill Gaskill produced Menotti's *The Telephone*. My

15-minute show was all right. My 30-minute show was a disaster. I didn't get a job there and then, yet I started directing live shows a week after Granada went on air.

During the very early days people were given enormous opportunities (and also the chance to fail). Some eleven or so directors produced almost the entire output of original productions for Granada during those first years. We did a lot of work. Most people had three shows or so on the go at the same time. A weekly 'chore' like *What the Papers Say* involved going to bed early the night before – and then preparing, setting up, rehearsing and transmitting 'live' the next day. At the same time they would be running a monthly production – perhaps a drama series like *Shadow Squad* (dropping the weekly chore during the production week). Then most people had their own personal project, which might take up to three or four months to prepare and research – a major documentary or a one-off 90-minute play. When this got near to a production date then of course the other shows would be reallocated.

There was a weekly directors' meeting chaired by Denis Forman at which there was a very free discussion about the previous week's output, which could be a chastening experience. Ideas for future projects would be thrown around. As there were really no separate departments like Drama, Music or Documentary, there was a lot of cross-fertilisation. You could be asked if you (as, say, a drama director) would like to have a go at jazz show as you might find a new approach. Sometimes it was a disaster. Sometimes it worked.

There was a modest flat on the top floor of the administration building of the Granada Studios in Quay Street. It was known as 'The Penthouse' and Sidney Bernstein used to stay there on his weekly 3-day visits to Manchester. It amused him to say that 'he lived over the shop'.

He gave small dinner parties for visiting celebrities – usually politicians, journalists or academics. A young director or another member of staff would often be invited. The talk was always brisk and informative. At the end of the meal Sidney would say, 'Nothing is quotable after ten o'clock', and the guests would know that nothing that was said would ever go out on the air from Granada – and there was also an unspoken agreement that confidences would be kept by the guests. The purpose was background information only. Sometimes people would arrive very much later after the meal was over. They might be a producer or researcher arriving back after the wrap on a production or fact-finding foray.

One night I shall always remember: Michael Parkinson, who was then a staff journalist/researcher, and another reporter, arrived ashen-faced. Over very stiff drinks they attempted to convey the horror of their evening. They had been present as the mother of one of the victims of the 'Moors Murderers' listened to the tapes of her daughter's screams as she was being tortured. She had to identify the voice as that of her child. I can't remember who the other guests were that evening but I do remember that the discussion – usually dispassionate and uninvolved, witty and argumentative – reached an extraordinary level of humanity, which was hauntingly relevant. Mike wondered if the British legal process that required an innocent person, the mother, to go through that ordeal and at the trial to sit through a recital of the injuries and sufferings, could still remain a whole human being afterwards.

Sidney was always very keen to broaden the experience of his young directors. He had three 'heroes': Alfred Hitchcock, Charles Laughton and Ed Murrow. When Hitchcock visited Granada he invited three fledgling directors to meet him for lunch. We, of course, were tremendously excited and waited for the great man in awe. I think Hitchcock was under the impression that we were all agog to hear about how *Alfred Hitchcock Presents*, an American series of mystery stories which Hitchcock introduced – but did not direct – was produced. He outlined for us – quite uncritically – the American production system: All the money and effort went into the script. The director only joined the team two days before the shoot ... his job was organisational. 'If he had any creative input into the show, well, that was just a bonus.' The production manager reported back every hour, on the hour, as to whether each page of script had run the estimated screen time, if it was over, then that amount of time was cut from the next page of script to be shot. 'Film that ended up on the cutting room floor was just a waste.' The director was not involved in editing the film.

The meal became more and more depressing. Questions became more and more scarce. Finally, someone plucked up enough courage to ask how long the 'shower scene' in *Psycho* took to shoot. 'Eleven days,' he replied. I don't think Hitchcock had quite the effect on us that Sidney intended.

DRAMA

Still haven't been paid

JIM ALLEN

For me writing became a political necessity. When I worked down the pit a bunch of us started a rank and file paper called *The Miner* and after we bought a typewriter on the hire purchase, big Joe Ryan who I'd worked with on the docks shoved it into my hands and said, 'You got us into this, you edit.' And so I was thrown in at the deep end. I'd learned to type with two fingers and was compelled to find the words to express the politics. For four years we published our paper and were a bit spellbound when we saw our names in print. Kicked from pillar to post by management, chased by police at different pits, and attacked by union leaders, we enjoyed every minute of it. Then in 1960 I was blacklisted and this led me into television.

I was working in the building trade as a scaffolder's labourer when my name came to the attention of Granada and I was invited to write a trial script for *Coronation Street*. In January 1965 it was transmitted and I still haven't been paid for it – although I did get a contract.

I forget how many scripts I wrote, but I stayed there for about eighteen months before 'I broke out'. I had seen and lived through much, and was eager to give expression to something more substantial than cardboard characters filled with self-admiration. With one or two exceptions, the actors were all working-class Tories acting like thirty-bob millionaires. When a new face joined the writers' team, he was looked upon as a threat, but in my case they needn't have worried because I had no intention of staying long.

The one writer who didn't give me the hard stare was John Finch, a bald-headed Yorkshireman with real talent and a great sense of humour. We became boozing buddies, and it was John who introduced me to BBC producer Tony Garnett. For a year I'd been trying to persuade Granada to commission me to write a script about 'the lump' – a brutal anti-union labour-only system of work in the building industry. My pleas fell on deaf ears and I was desperate when John suggested Garnett. In 1967, the BBC showed *The Lump* on the Wednesday play slot and it was a huge success. It was through Tony that I met Ken Loach, and together we made *The Big Flame*, a film about Liverpool dockers taking over the port. It was after that that I made my break from the *Street* and went freelance.

Writing for *Coronation Street* was a great learning experience. It taught me the grammar of television and the economy of language. It also paid the bills. Nowadays I rarely watch it. When I do, I find the characters lifeless and predictable, and the stories dull. Perhaps to spice it up, they should reconsider a suggestion I made when I was serving my time there. I suggested they pack all the characters on to a bus and send them on a 'mystery tour' to the Lake District. Then drive the bus over a cliff and kill them all off. In today's battle of ratings, that would be a winner.

Fruitful years

STAN BARSTOW

I was in and out of Granada quite a lot from the mid-1960s (when the late John Gibson and I made a documentary in a mental hospital for the Norman Swallow-Denis Mitchell series *This England*) to the early 1970s. They were fruitful years. For during that time I'd managed also to complete my longest and most ambitious novel to date, *A Raging Calm*.

Serial adaptations of classic novels had become an important part of television drama and interest was growing in contemporary texts. *A Raging Calm* was offered to Granada shortly after publication (and when no one had fallen over themselves to get to the film rights), but the Head of Drama, Peter Eckersley could find no place for it.

One of Granada's great strengths, however, lay in its stable of in-house producers – people such as Eckersley himself, Derek Granger, John Hamp, Gus Macdonald, Brian Armstrong, Howard Baker, Leslie Woodhead, Richard Everitt, Mike Scott and, later, Pauline Shaw, Michael Cox, June Howson and Bill Podmore – who were given a creative freedom which invigorated the company's output and sustained its splendid reputation.

It was to one of the most experienced of these, H. V. (Harry) Kershaw, that John Finch (whom I'd been helping in the early stages of his marathon serial *A Family at War*) showed my novel some eighteen months later. Using his clout, Harry somehow got me a commission to write a first episode and a treatment of the whole. We took it step by step from there and I had delivered the first three episodes by the time I had to interrupt the flow and make a journey to a Writers' Conference in Melbourne, Australia. Though there was no immediate pressure I resisted the temptation to stay longer. I was too afraid of events catching up with me and losing my impetus, to take a long holiday.

The rhythm of demands on my time over the next few months would show that I'd made the right decision. With Harry advising on every script, we met regularly to talk things through. Like John Finch, he had learned his trade on *Coronation Street*, first as a writer, then as producer, and the experience of working with such a professional television craftsman would stand me in good stead with my next job for another company. He was, as I wrote to his widow after his death, in 1992, 'one of the great journeymen of television, who helped to set standards and to maintain them. You simply felt better about the whole thing by knowing he was around.'

Tall and dapper, with a small moustache, Harry invariably dressed like the insurance salesman he had once been, in white shirt, sober tie and a grey or dark blue suit – it led to one of his best stories. Invited to speak to a Miners' Union weekend conference about popular television, and being a convivial chap, he went the night before and took a few drinks with the participants. At one stage their spokesman asked him, 'Tell me Mr Kershaw – when you speak to the meeting tomorrow will you be dressed like you are now?'

With some misgivings Harry looked down at his natty suiting and said, 'Yes, I will. Will that be all right?'

'It'll be fine with us, Mr Kershaw', the man assured him. 'There's some folk think they can come here and talk to us in any old gear.'

In the Film Exchange, the drinking and dining club favoured by certain Granada personnel at that time, Peter Eckersley said to me, 'I don't quite know what you and Harry are up to, but I'm sure it will turn out fine.' What we were up to, as it turned out, was creating the blueprint for one of the most successful drama programmes Granada had ever made. Brian Armstrong was assigned as producer, June Howson and Gerry Mill directed. Both were good at getting close in on actors and generating warmth. The strong cast was led by Alan Badel, Diana Coupland, Michael Williams and Frances White. We groaned when it was scheduled against the vastly popular BBC series *Colditz* but by episode three (of seven) it had pushed the prison drama out of the charts and moved into sixth place itself. An explanation was that, starting twenty-five minutes before *Colditz*, *A Raging Calm* had time to hook the women, who then refused to let their menfolk switch channels. Such are the wiles of programme planners.

The lost producer

DEREK BENNETT

Before the Executive Producer/Producer system was properly established, drama series in particular sometimes came about in an ad hoc way and either no one or, at the other extreme half-a-dozen people, seemed to be responsible. This was very confusing to young and inexperienced directors.

One early series – and this means the full horror of three cameras, studio-bound, live production, sometimes with a live commercial to happen in a corner during the break – was a dreadful thing called *Knight Errant*. Best forgotten, it had awful scripts, bad acting and a lack of control.

I had a phone call the day before I was due in the studio with one episode, asking me to attend a meeting that night with the Bernsteins, and several executives and producers, to discuss the series as a whole.

I was one of the young, inexperienced and confused directors, and probably arrogant as well. I couldn't see what many of the people present had to do with the series, even with drama or television, though their names were on the huge script distribution list, and when SLB asked me whether *Knight Errant*'s leading man had a hairy chest and if he had I wasn't to let him wear an open-necked shirt because many women were offended by hairy men I became a little hysterical. Eventually SLB laid down something to the effect that on no account were the leading man and his female assistant to give the impression that they were romantically or sexually involved. I became more hysterical, couldn't stop laughing, and pointed out that the next day I was in the studio with an episode in which the two characters went off for what was to all intents and purposes a dirty weekend on a yacht somewhere off the coast of France.

The result was like something from an early Hollywood scene of a studio or business conference. I swear people edged their chairs away from me and began to shake their heads. I couldn't resist mentioning that they had all received scripts some time before, had presumably read them and that anyway I had rehearsed the episode for six or seven days, had done the all important camera script and that we were in the studio in a few hours' time and due to transmit the day after.

There was much tutting and what did I think I was playing at and so on and I felt exposed and isolated. Suddenly SLB said, 'Leave the boy alone', and everyone shut up. 'I think Derek and I can sort this out', he said and asked them all to leave.

He poured drinks for us both and for the rest of the evening I passed some of the most interesting hours I'd had. He should have been a great film producer.

'Can we do so-and-so', he asked and if I said no, we didn't have the set, or it would be too awkward for the cast he would niggle away until we found a solution to most things. Led by him we managed, without making too many drastic changes or making it impossible for the actors, to improve the episode. He was totally supportive and appeared in the studio over the next two days to show the flag and smile encouragement.

Before that time he'd been a remote figure and though afterwards I had several disagreements with him – dressing downs standing in front of his desk like a private on a charge: 'I don't know what you thought you were doing last night Derek', and memorably: 'If I'd been his agent I wouldn't have let you shoot that scene that way.'

'But Sidney, his agent wouldn't have known how I was going to shoot that scene.'

'Don't quibble, if I'd been his agent I'd have known.'

I had enormous respect for him. The success of Granada and the warm feeling that those of us have who were there in the early days is largely due to him and the people, not particularly those mentioned above, who supported him.

We were lucky

JAMES BRABAZON

I never wanted to be a producer. Julian Amyes hired me to come and direct stage plays at the Stables and then transfer them to the screen. But after I was contracted it was discovered that the Assocation of Cinematograph and Television Technicians (ACTT) was in one of its negative moods. A lot of British directors who had gone to Hollywood when the Americans had a fit of Anglophilia were flocking back, chastened, when the fit passed, and they all wanted their old jobs back. New tickets were not on. But Granada had to pay me, so they had to find something for me to do. Producers didn't require a ticket, so a producer is what I became.

Being a director is fun, being a producer isn't. I mentioned to Julian Amyes that I didn't much enjoy being ground between ruthless directors and heartless accountants. He stretched his hand out to me – not in a gesture of sympathy but to show how it shook. 'What do you think they pay us for ?' he said.

But there were compensations. Indeed I often think the real reason people like to go filming is for the joy of looking back at a nightmare. The job itself is tedium and stress in equal measure. But there are great moments. So – looking back ...

There was a time when a Welsh schoolboy, plucked from his lessons for the *Childhood* series and rehearsing opposite Anthony Hopkins said, 'Don't worry if you can't remember your lines, Tony, I can prompt you. I learnt yours too, see.'

There was a moment when, in Sardinia of all places, we watched the skies at 3 a.m., at 4 a.m. and saw the wind had changed and the order was given 'Get the girls to make-up.'

This requires some explanation. We were in Sardinia because Denis Forman had been persuaded to let a bright and unconventional director called Carlos Pasini make a strange film about a despairing youth who walks into a painting by Hieronymus Bosch and has a life-changing experience. Among other things it involved three beautiful girls, hand-picked in Rome by the director, who had to appear naked in a sort of bower teaching the hero the delights of sensuality. We weren't sure of the views of the authorities about such goings on, so the scene was scheduled for the last day, a Thursday. If we were told to get off the island we could say, don't worry, we're leaving tomorrow anyway. Indeed we had to leave on the Friday flight, because the whole thing had been done on the basis of an excursion fare for the entire unit, and to miss the flight would have doubled the budget.

On the crucial Thursday it rained. Rained? A large cloud settled over the entire island and it poured endlessly from a black sky. The weather forecast was for no change for two days. All that was left was prayer and sleeplessness. At 4.30 the wind changed, the cloud thinned almost imperceptibly. Getting the girls to make-up was more of a decision than usual, because it meant all over, and if we hadn't been able to film after all the girls would not have been pleased – they were restive enough as it was.

At six o'clock the crew went out to the sodden location. The sun burst through. By eight o'clock the sun was blazing down and we were filming. The flight was not till the afternoon. We wrapped at lunchtime and made it with minutes to spare.

But despite all that drama and the beauty of the girls, the image which remains most vividly is that of four sturdy Granada crew members, most of whom had never before been much south of Stockport, patiently searching the ground while three ravishing signorinas (still clothed) pointed – 'There's one … You missed that one', and the Mancunians, no doubt breaching union regulations, plucked out hundreds of baby thistles that had sprung up after the rain exactly where the ladies were to plant their delicate bottoms.

That was a rarity, that film. Most filming had to be done within thirty miles of base. And coming from the BBC, from which thirty miles gets you pretty well nowhere interesting, one of the remarkable things about Granada was the variety of locations within that range. When we did *Childhood*, six films about growing up in Britain, I wanted as wide a variety of experiences as possible; so we had to find locations to represent Leeds, Ireland, Sussex, Wales and Devonshire. And we found them. And we found the children, almost all from local schools. That was very satisfying. Three of the directors of that series are now established in Hollywood – Michael Apted, John Irvin and Mike Newell. I'm not sure they really prefer it there.

Location hunting was always enjoyable, and often involved great scenery. We did go outside the range for *Spoils of War*, but that demanded a steelworks, and the only active one was on the Cumbrian coast the other side of the Lake District. So that was a refreshing drive. And one of the great moments was when we discovered a short fag-end of street just over a footbridge from the works and out of the way of traffic – a perfect place for our cast to live in.

After the BBC, there was also the joy of smallness. The film department was just a floor down and a corridor away, and basically was Stan Challis. That's how you get things done. If you wanted to know anything about anything, you went up one floor to Walt Mariner, a man of infinite resource.

Even at Granada, however, there was sometimes a gulf fixed between management and practitioners. I brought a director from London for a couple of studio shows, Alan Gibson. That in itself was not very popular with the crews, and when, about a quarter to six one evening, he embarked on an elaborate series of shots in which the fall of an actor was taken on fast mixes between three cameras, giving the impression of slow motion, they dug their heels in. Artsy-fartsy, was the verdict. And the result was that we went into overtime and that was very bad news and I was summoned to account for it to the management. When, however, I explained what happened, they showed not indignation but fascination. They really had little idea what went on in the basement.

But the truly remarkable thing about Granada was the people. London TV people talk TV. In my day at least Granada people talked everything else, and that's why their TV was fresh and real. And consider some of the people at the top. Peter Eckersley, head of drama, was a wit and philosopher. Denis Forman was a major music critic. You don't get them like that in other companies. I'm not saying that Granada was quite Michelangelo's Italy, but such men create an atmosphere of excellence, and it was felt throughout the company.

Age of gold

ROBIN CHAPMAN

No doubt about it, the 1960s really were a golden age for writers in television. Or should we say it was a black-and-white one? Sometimes I'm tempted to suppose that the coming of colour marked the end of the writer's ascendancy. But before that we had a lovely time. Rather as Elizabethan playwrights did in the 1590s. It too was an age of patrons. And nowhere more than at Granada, that most paternalistic yet enlightened of companies.

My first patron, although he never produced anything of mine, was Peter Wildeblood. He, generously and typically, bought my first television play even though I'm sure he knew he would never find a slot for it. But it earned me the magic sum of £250, gave me confidence, and turned me at one bound from an actor into a paid playwright – albeit an unpresentable one. My enemies of course say I've remained that way ever since. The play was called *The People's Friend* and the draft remains in my bottom drawer.

My second patron was Philip Mackie whom I first became aware of when Joan Littlewood chucked him out of a rehearsal we were doing of Brendan Behan's *The Hostage* down at Stratford East. Philip bore Joan no grudge and when in 1963 I enjoyed some success with my first novel he invited me to join Hugh Leonard and Michael Hastings to write a series of linked 15-minute plays for prime-time viewing called *Triangle*.

Yes, you may believe your eyes. This was the 1960s. The plays were wild, the acting, from a young resident company, pretty dire, and the direction, well, let's say it was experimental. All in all, even Dennis Potter would have been hard put to it to do worse than we did. Yet despite this, *Triangle* went out for seven weeks in a row at nine o'clock on Friday nights.

When Philip Mackie visited Theatre Workshop he was acting as a scout for Sidney Bernstein who had conceived the idea of setting Joan Littlewood and her company up at the Old Met (a huge, decaying music hall) in the Edgware Road. There she would provide a people's theatre for Central London and a TV people's theatre when her shows were televised by Granada. This rather splendid idea Joan turned down flat – Granadaland not being big enough for both Joan and Sidney. However the idea behind it struck a spark in me and informed the future body of work I was to make at Granada for my third patron, Denis Forman.

Denis had discerned a smidgin of virtue in one of the playlets I had written for *Triangle* and invited me to take part in a very strange project indeed called *The Man in Room 17*. In this mysterious room somewhere above Whitehall two mighty mandarins solved international or national crimes too complex for poor old plodding Scotland Yard. My first job was to create two eggheads. They were donnish, intellectually arrogant and skittish. Their chief delight was to make a mock of the crime they were to solve (to them it was always childishly simple) and play the Chinese game Wei-Chi. I called them Edwin Graham Oldenshaw and Ian Dimmock so that when at last we saw their initialled briefcases they would read EGO and ID.

After twenty-six episodes of this silliness I suggested that we make our two heroes rather more sensible, perhaps even credible? The notion was accepted and they became *The Fellows* at Cambridge. Here they were crimin-ologists examining the sociology of professional crime and the situation and structures they considered were examples of criminal behaviour rather than puzzles to be solved. Philip Purser in the Sunday Telegraph called *The Fellows* 'the most original, infuriating, thoughful, flippant, valuable crime series ever'. Which just about sums up the creative contradictions that writers could enjoy at that golden time.

Out of *The Fellows*, grew two further crime serials which were unique, I believe, in that they were not policiers but, instead, were told entirely from the criminal point of view. Neither played safe; both were truly bent telly.

The first was *Spindoe* in which a South London gangleader fought to regain his underworld fiefdom after a spell inside. Directed by Mike Newell with gritty realism it was also a highly literary gloss on *Macbeth* with a nod in the direction of Dashiell Hammett – in other words it looked like a B movie and sounded like something else.

Then came *Hog*, or to give this 8-hour serial its full title: *Big Breadwinner Hog*. Here, a young tearaway took on the criminal establishment only to win it all (mostly by sheer cheek and luck) but then, weighed down by success and an urgent need for respectability as cover, he became a grey-suited, featureless, boring, crop-haired executive of crime. Quite a come-uppance.

Like Hogarth's *The Rake's Progress* on which the story was modelled (hence the hero's name) the first episode was the despair of our elders. Anybody over 40 complained about the violence (as with Tarantino nowadays the action was underscored by verbal assault) and several MPs in need of an image-boost called for me to be put on trial for treason, sedition, glamor-ising crime, and inciting the already rebellious youth of Britain to grow their hair and not wear ties. The IBA had a respectable litter of kittens and hardly anyone noticed that the whole thing had been conceived from the start as a naughty but nice moral fable.

Spindoe and *Hog* embodied my hopes for a people's theatre on television accessible to all those millions who had not left their minds behind when they settled down to watch a thriller.

Such puritan – or should I say black-and-white? – idealism could not survive the advent of colour. From then on TV's drama celebration of the word declined. Higher costs and would-be cinematic production values both conspired to diminish the role of dialogue and the writer. And equally and inevitably safe adaptation came to be preferred to unpredictable originality.

But for one brief moment (well, let's say eight years or so) Granada allowed me to write sixty hours of original fiction in perfect freedom with not a script editor in sight. Sixty hours. That's almost three-quarters of a million words. Such patronage of the individual voice has always been a sign of a golden age. Let's hope another comes soon. We really do need some real telly again.

Primary television

Michael Cox

In any medium there is a particular excitement about working on material that belongs to that medium and no other. The most obvious example is, of course, musical composition: a symphony cannot be adapted from a painting or a sonata from a short story. These are unique forms of expression and the creative artists we admire most have usually chosen that personal path. They are not content to re-imagine someone else's vision; they are determined to present their own view of the world.

When I chose to make my career first in the theatre, then in television, I wanted to contribute to that process. I can't conduct a symphony or play or a sonata but I was fairly sure that I could organise the forces which are needed to bring plays to life. And those forces are considerable and very costly. It was probably Orson Welles who said that a painter needs a brush, a writer needs a pen but a film director needs an army. That is the heart of the problem for anyone committed to original work for the screen. In the jargon of the business, we are not talking small change, we are talking telephone numbers.

It is for that reason that the single, original play has always been an endangered species and has now disappeared from ITV altogether. There are television movies – strange hybrids, caught between the disciplines of two quite different forms – and there are dramatisations of novels in three or four parts. But – apart from the soap operas – the only original drama for television, the only bankable new work is either violent or sensational: cops, medics and politicians are the only characters on view.

It was not always so. Although Granada's commitment to drama first of all meant television adaptations of stage plays, there were soon a respectable number of original scripts in production. In the first few years, among a wealth of familiar pieces by Priestley, Maugham, Harold Brighouse and Arthur Miller, we began to see new work by new writers. Peter Nichols, Hugh Leonard, Clive Exton, Giles Cooper and Jack Rosenthal were among those who were encouraged by perceptive producers like Peter Wildeblood,

Derek Granger and Gerald Savory. The adaptations continued, often in the form of series: the short stories of Saki and de Maupassant, the Feydeau farces and the Victorian melodramas, all of them produced by Philip Mackie. The series was always relished at Granada – the audience were offered the security of a known quantity each week but, because each story was self-contained, were not frustrated by missing an episode of a continuing serial. Then in the late 1960s, there came a change.

Denis Forman had always regretted that the Bernsteins would not support his idea of dramatising *The Forsyte Saga*. He was told that costume pictures never made money and besides it would necessarily have been a serial. Then in 1967 the BBC tackled Galsworthy's novels in twenty-six episodes and brought the nation to a standstill on Sunday nights. He could not resist drawing attention to this at a drama conference and the point was made: the television audience would accept a serial, even if it was a period piece.

At the same conference, to which we all had to submit ideas as the price of admission, John Finch floated a notion with the working title of *Conflict* about the experiences of an ordinary family in the Second World War. That working title encapsulated the reasons for its eventual success. We all know that successful drama is about conflict of some kind; John's brilliant thought was to run two conflicts on parallel lines. We were to see the personal clash of emotions within a family against the backdrop of the most frightening confrontation of nations in living memory. The proposal won the day and was called – with winning simplicity – *A Family at War*.

I was lucky enough to be a junior partner in this enterprise and spent the next two or three years of my professional life working on a project which only television could deliver. The risk was enormous because success could not be guaranteed but the company decided to invest in a piece which demanded considerable resources and great faith.

In those days, television drama was commissioned in blocks which fitted the transmission calendar. A limited series of six episodes would be balanced with another of seven parts to make up the magic thirteen-week quarter of the year. *Family* was planned to fit this pattern. We knew at the start that we would make thirteen hour-long episodes but, if we were to continue, the next thirteen had to written in advance so that we were ready to continue. If the first thirteen were not popular, we could at some cost cancel the thirteen to follow and, in the early stages, there was the possibility of coming to a complete halt after twenty-six. That would have taken the story from 1938 to 1942, to the point in the war which Churchill called 'the end of the beginning'.

In the event, *Family* went the full distance and in fifty-two episodes took the story through to the end of 1945. It usually achieved the highest viewing figures and several times reached first or second place in the charts. It launched the careers of some young actors, like Barbara Flynn and John Nettles, who have gone on to great success. It pioneered some notable television techniques such as the production of whole episodes on location videotape. It opened up overseas markets for British drama, particularly in Scandinavia where it was enormously popular. But it was a gruelling show to do because the budget was never a high one and it was often made against time. Each episode took two weeks to rehearse and shoot and, to maintain a weekly transmission schedule, we often split the cast and made two at once.

Although other writers were involved, the main creative burden fell on John Finch. Although there were associate producers such as myself and Jonathan Powell, the main burden of juggling the figures and logistics fell on the producer, Richard Doubleday. Richard belonged to a vanished breed: he was a gentle, caring person who understood the imperatives of casting and direction, a man of great taste and good humour, but one who – almost literally – worried himself to death about the bottom line of a budget. He delivered the series on time and on budget but, sadly, he is no longer here to see his work repeated and enjoyed a quarter of a century later.

All of us who worked on *A Family at War* can look back and see that John Finch had created a new narrative form: the television novel. This was long before Frederic Raphael delivered *The Glittering Prizes* for the BBC or Alan Bleasdale celebrated *The Boys from the Blackstuff*. This was the original break-through which established the television playwright as a person with his own unique voice, recording the human condition but writing in a popular form just as Dickens had done in the previous century.

John has continued to write work of that kind, fiction which entertains but at the same time explains, through character and action, that the way we live now is a product of our past and the trials and triumphs of those who went before us. The most notable example is *Sam* – also for Granada – the 39-part story of a boy who grew up in the Yorkshire coalfields in the 1940s and emerged from the pits to fight the social and political battles that are still being fought today. I was lucky enough to produce that series – my favourite television assignment in thirty years – but that is another story ...

The programme committee and *Coronation Street*

HARRY ELTON

In the autumn of 1960 I screened the pilot of a proposed twice-weekly half-hour serial for the Granada programme committee. It was about the lives of people on a working-class street in Manchester. The committee didn't like it and *Coronation Street* was almost killed before it got on the air.

The programme committee reviewed everything affecting programmes at Granada. It decided what went on the air and what did not. It met weekly alternating between London and Manchester. Most of the members lived in London and had to come up to Manchester every other week to attend. Sidney Bernstein insisted on this because he wanted everyone to remember that Granada had a Manchester-based licence. The principal audience was in the north and he felt that it was essential for the senior people to keep contact. Sidney Bernstein was the chairman of Granada Television and his word was law.

It was always a tense moment after an audition tape had been played to see which of the committee members would be asked to express an opinion first. No one wanted to stick his neck out with what might turn out to be an unpopular view. I waited with apprehension and high hopes.

Eddie Pola was first. He was the American light-entertainment producer. He had stayed on and worked in Britain after winning the All England Charleston Championship in the 1920s.

> Jeez Harry that's a soap opera. You don't put that crap on at seven o'clock at night. That should play in the afternoon.

Victor Peers was Granada's general manager. He had a lifetime career in films starting with Alexander Korda. He remembered sitting at a card table set up in the desert paying out Bedouin tribesmen after their day as extras.

> Harry there is not a single thing I like about this programme. I don't like the settings or the characters and the way they talk to each other. Surely people watch television to be taken out of their dreary lives and not to have their noses rubbed in it.

Cecil Bernstein, deputy chairman, was Sidney's brother. Together they had built the hugely successful Granada cinema chain of motion-picture palaces. And now they were inseparable in the development of Granada Television. He was the popular showman of the two with a sure instinct for what the public wanted.

> Harry you've made a horrible mistake and we can't blame you because you are

a Canadian. That north-country dialect is a joke. It's the language of Old
Mother Riley and George Formby. No one will ever take it seriously.

Denis Forman had no title but acted as the programme controller. After a
distinguished war record he became Director of the British Film Institute
and inspired the creation of the National Film Theatre. He later would
become Granada Chairman and Managing Director.

Harry your show is neither funny enough on the one hand nor documentary
enough on the other. It falls between two stools. People won't know what to
make of it.

Sidney Bernstein was last. He was a millionaire socialist dilettante with a
genius for management and organisation. This programme was intended
to fill a slot on the network.

Harry when I get driven in from the airport I can see many houses that are
much nicer than those on your street. Is this the image of Granadaland that we
want to project to the rest of the country?

With a rare show of unanimity the committee had decided this programme
was not what we wanted to put on the air. Something else would have to be
created. But there was a deadline looming and I had nothing else in the
pipeline that could be ready in time.

From the earliest days the big four programme contractors (Rediffusion,
ATV, ABC and Granada) divided up the time-slots on a network so no one
of them had to fill out the schedule alone. The broadcasting act required a
total of 85 per cent British content. Although the most popular programmes
at that time came from the USA and fitted the 15 per cent allowable foreign
content, we had to produce storytelling programmes of our own. Based on
the size of our audience Granada was responsible for 40 per cent of the
evening schedule from Monday to Friday including two weekly half-hours
in the audience-building early evenings.

I joined Granada in January 1957. A Canadian with three years' American television experience, I had studied at the Royal Academy of Dramatic
Art for a year in 1952. Therefore, it was assumed that I must know something about things dramatic and I produced *Shadow Squad*, *The Verdict is
Yours* and *Biggles*. These programme series found respectable audiences
and allowed me to find and develop scriptwriters.

At the time of the dry run, *Biggles*, the current series, had to end in early
December. Faced with no alternative the committee reluctantly agreed to
let the programme go into the schedule for a *short, limited,* run but I must
find a replacement as soon as possible.

Although deliberations of the programme committee were confidential, word soon spread that 'they' didn't like it. I had a team of production people who were working feverishly to get the new show ready for air. Looking for a way to get some positive feedback for our efforts I arranged a screening for all the Granada staff in Manchester. Monitors were distributed throughout the offices and workshops. Everyone was asked to fill out a questionnaire. Most of them liked it very much! To be sure they were all northern people and Tony Warren had become a favorite around the studios. But responses to the casting, the sets and the scripts were very positive and we worked with renewed confidence and energy.

Tony Warren is one of the writers who emerged during the *Shadow Squad* series. He has the most remarkable talent for dialogue and character creation of any writer I have ever worked with. He was put under a modest contract to do a variety of jobs that helped him learn the mechanics of television and scriptwriting. He wrote one of the *Biggles* scripts. The series was about the jingoistic exploits of the Royal Flying Corps in the First World War. It was based loosely on the books of Captain W. E. Johns. That noisy, greasy world was clearly not Tony's cup of tea and he nearly had a nervous breakdown doing it. He pleaded to write about something he knew and I sent him off to find stories about real people who lived in the streets of Manchester and Salford.

He returned with the first script and an outline of several further episodes of a serial he called *Florizel Street*. The basic characters, dialogue and style were clearly established. This is what the programme committee saw. Only the name was changed to *Coronation Street* and the characters Ken Barlow and Albert Tatlock were added. This is what went on the air on 9 December 1960.

The first reaction to new programmes in those early days of commercial television came from the newspapers. They all had TV critics who rushed to judgement. They wrote that *Coronation Street* was a flop and wouldn't be around very long. In fact, at the start, it was not shown on the full network. 'Mr Television' show business, Lew Grade of ATV, decided it was not good enough for his audience in the Midlands and brothers George and Alfred Black, another pair of show business proprietors, refused to take it on Tyne Tees television based in Newcastle.

But a much more reliable measure of what the audience thought was seen in the weekly Nielsen television ratings. There were only two channels and very quickly an audience started to build in the north. That was understandable because the series was about the north. But almost as quickly it was building in London and Scotland and finding favour among the elegant retired people of Southampton. The programmes moved very quickly into the top ten, where they have remained for more than forty years. Lew

Grade's wife was from Manchester and saw it on a visit home. She persuaded her husband it was good. Five months after the programmes went on the air, the midlands and Newcastle completed the line-up. The programme committee was puzzled but pleased with the reaction and decided that it could stay in the schedule longer than they had originally intended.

Tony Warren wrote the first twelve episodes and indelibly put his mark on the Street. But clearly he could not continue to write two half-hours a week. Harry Kershaw, script editor, and Harry Driver, story editor, took over responsibility for scripts. They had both first worked on *Shadow Squad*. They assembled a group of writers that has constantly grown and changed through the years to keep the programme alive.

Why did the programme succeed in attracting an audience when it first went on the air in 1960 and why does it continue to hold a very large audience more than forty years later? I believe the key to the programme's popularity from the beginning was the writing. The genius of the early programmes was Tony Warren who established the characters, their relationships to each other and particularly their use of the north country dialect. These were the very reasons why the programme committee felt that it would not succeed. Clearly *Coronation Street* offered something to the television audience that satisfied a need. Something about watching twice a week helped their lives. And whatever that ingredient is has an appeal far beyond the north of England. It was the work of a group of people who were new to television at a time of great experimentation to find programmes that would be popular.

Serial storytelling has a long history. Charles Dickens wrote most of his novels in serial instalments that were published week after week in magazines. There are stories of mobs of Americans waiting at the harbour in New York to be the first to see the next episode of a Dickens story. *Vanity Fair* was also published in instalments. In the 1930s US radio daytime schedules were filled with different 15-minute serials. Soap manufacturers sponsored most of them and they were called 'soap operas'.

Serial storytelling was slow coming to television. Most of the dramatic programmes at that time were series. They had one or more of the same characters in each episode but the stories were different and so were the characters and settings. There were great advantages of scale in a serial format. It would use the same characters and sets as the story lines evolved from episode to episode. The actors could be engaged at a much more reasonable rate per individual episode. The audience could identify with the characters and become interested in their unfolding lives from week to week.

However in the late 1950s at Granada it was felt that no programme of any value could be created that would run on into the future with no clear idea of how it was going to end. What's more where could one find a writer who would work endlessly on such a programme?

I found the climate at Granada was not very warm to popular pro-grammes. The attitude was typified by the way BBC radio was structured at that time: the Light, the Home and the Third. The Light programme was filled with pop music, variety and banal quiz programmes. It was designed to go in one ear and out the other. The Home programme was just a little more challenging and if the audience listened very carefully they might learn something from a mixture designed to improve their minds. But the Third programme was for 'us'. It was for those who were intelligent enough and sophisticated enough to appreciate rigorous intellectual content.

After *Coronation Street* was well established on the air, members of the programme committee came to me one by one to say they were awfully glad they were able to help me in those early days (except Victor Peers who congra-tulated me and said he still didn't like a thing about it). But they paid little attention to it. From time to time I would hear, 'My wife's cleaning lady says the *Street* has gone a bit off. Are you having problems?' I felt my life would be vastly improved if I could buy up a handful of cleaning ladies in London.

After Tony wrote the first episode, I asked him to write an explanation of what his programme was about. Why should people watch it? What would they get out of it? He struggled and together we produced:

> A fascinating freemasonry, a volume of unwritten rules. These are the driving forces behind working-class life in the North of England. To the uninitiated outsider, all this would be completely incomprehensible. The purpose of *Coronation Street* is to entertain by examining a community of this kind and initiating the viewer into the ways of the people who live here.

Although the members of the committee did not see the point of this mission statement, I think the public clearly did.

Prudence with money

RICHARD EVERITT

Sidney Bernstein dedicated Granada's first night to the BBC and he created a BBC in miniature with its diversity of output and commitment, despite commercial pressures, to public-service broadcasting. Experimentation, risk, attention to detail and personal initiative were encouraged under tight budgetary control. The results were sometimes comical.

In 1960 I was assigned as Floor Manager to an eccentric Irishman, Chris McMaster, who was to direct a children's series *Biggles* adapted from the novels of W. E. Johns. The budget was minuscule but one script required a volcano to erupt. There was no Special Effects Department so he experimented at home. He made a model volcano out of clay, packed it with gunpowder extracted from 12-bore cartridges and lit the fuse. The resulting explosion required the attention of the police and fire brigade.

My appointment to trainee director in 1961 can be attributed almost entirely to my awareness of the company's attitude to budgets. When asked at the interview how I saw the style of studio drama developing in the next decade I replied, 'No scenery. Just black drapes and clever lighting.'

Further evidence of prudence with money came to light when drama was beginning to emerge from the confines of the studio. A thriller series called *The Odd Man* written by Eddie Boyd in 1964 had a scene on the top of some high-rise flats where two policemen were trying to stop a man throwing himself off, so it was potentially dangerous. I enquired about insurance cover. 'Don't worry', I was told. 'You can kill up to two actors under our standard policy. If you're thinking of killing any more we'd better take out extra cover.'

Eddie Boyd and I worked together again on *The Corridor People* (1966). He was a brilliant writer but very reluctant actually to put words on to paper. I had to resort to locking him in my attic at home with promises to feed him every ten pages. Although the series reached 16 in the ratings it received the following notice from Nancy Banks-Smith in the *Guardian*: '*The Corridor People* is as contemporary as a space shot. A send-up, a take-off. A spoof on sex, crime, death. Beautifully produced, way out and with it ... and I hate it.'

In those days series and serials (as opposed to plays) were rehearsed as well as recorded in Manchester. One exception was *The Man in Room 17* (1965) which was based on an idea by Denis Forman: two men solve crimes from a room in Whitehall without ever leaving it. Quite mad but it worked – fourth in the ratings. It was a totally schizophrenic production: one writer (Robin Chapman who was also the overall script editor) and director would work on the 'Room' scenes rehearsed in London while another pair would work on the 'Action' sequences in Manchester. The two parts only met in the editing suite.

Eight years later *Shabby Tiger* (1973) adapted from Howard Spring's novel by Geoffrey Lancashire, Adele Rose and John Stevenson provided a different challenge. The Manchester of the 1930s had to be recreated and that included real trams of the period so we went to the Crich Tram Museum in Derbyshire and built the façade of the street alongside the tram tracks. The scenery blew down in a gale but a bigger disappointment was when it was transmitted in New Zealand – we had a letter from a viewer saying we had got the number of the tram going from Ancoats to Piccadilly wrong.

A happier note was struck in 1986 when *Floodtide* a 13-hour serial written by Roger Marshall went on location to Paris. Film crews, like armies, march on their stomachs so a catering wagon was sent from Deansgate to the Champs-Elysées, the gourmet capital of the world, to provide them with bacon butties.

In 1971 Peter Eckersley, then Head of Drama, asked me to read a number of unsolicited plays which were piled up on his window sill. One was outstanding. It was called *Whose Life is it Anyway?* By Brian Clark. It was originally about 90 minutes in length but had to be trimmed to 60 minutes to fit the time allocated on the network. Ian McShane played the paraplegic who wishes to die against all medical advice. After it was broadcast Brian Clark restored the edited scenes, wrote a number of others and submitted a two-hour version to a theatre producer. He invited a number of eminent actors to play the part, all of whom said it was unactable on the stage because the 'hero' couldn't move. Eventually Tom Conti had the courage to take the part and it went on to great success in the West End, Broadway and as a Hollywood feature film. The title has entered the language.

However the budget allocated to a production is spent, it is important that it shows on the screen. For a play in the anthology series *The Victorians*, the designer had a large library set built at great cost. As the director I had chosen to play the scene in tight close-ups round a piano. Phillip Mackie, the producer, was horrified. 'Pull back,' he said. 'Show us the money dear boy – show us the money.'

However cost-conscious you are, however, actors can sometimes defeat you. In *The Fell Sergeant* by Eddie Boyd one of a series *Confessions* (1970) the leading part was taken by Donald Pleasence who was a 'method' actor. In one scene he was required to lose his temper and murder another character by bashing his head in with a billiard cue. On the 'take' he went berserk smashing the overhead lamps, tearing the cloth on the billiard table and finally breaking the cue. Dramatically very effective but a little costly.

On the other hand they can sometimes save the day. Time is always precious and an incident which occurred during the filming of *An Aspidistra in Babylon* for *Country Matters* (1972) nearly cost us dearly. There was a beach scene near Dover and the leading lady was meant to appear in a 1920s bathing costume but she refused to come out of her caravan because she was ashamed (wrongly) of her shape. Jeremy Brett, the leading man, offered to help. He entered the caravan and five minutes later she came out smiling and as docile as a lamb. I've often wondered what he did.

The tools of the trade

JOHN FINCH

I needed Granada long before Sidney Bernstein brought it into being. For some years after the war you were told that if you wanted to be a writer London was the only place to be. It wasn't a bad place to be at that time (wild horses couldn't drag me there now) but I wanted to write about the north and I felt that ideally I needed to be close to my material. I have also always felt a need to be involved, not just to hand the script over with one hand and take the cheque with the other. I needed help too from people who knew the medium I was interested in, which was television.

I had most of the other equipment you need to become a writer. My father left us, never to be seen or heard of again, in 1934 when I was nine. By that early age I had been to at least six schools and learned nothing. We lived as a one-parent family with my grandfather, a retired miner, in one of the roughest pit villages in South Yorkshire in the latter years of the depression. When I was eleven my mother could no longer afford to keep me and I was placed for my own good in a charity school in York. In 1941 when I was just sixteen I went to sea and served on a petrol tanker in the North Atlantic at the height of the Battle of The Atlantic. It was all grist to the mill for an embryo writer.

Post-war, after a brief spell as librarian in the Miner's Welfare library in the place where I was brought up, I spent seven years in London, two as secretary to the sculptor Jacob Epstein, the rest in a basement off Baker Street struggling to become a writer. I scratched a bare living working for magazines such as *Illustrated* and *Picture Post*, with the occasional sound radio programme and odd spells washing pots at Joe Lyons, but at an age when others of my generation were emerging from university, after their wartime experiences, I was basically a blank sheet of paper waiting to be written on. In the end it all fell apart and I went back north, married, and got down to the essential task of earning a living in the world of heavy engineering. But despite the fact that I achieved managerial status and was on my way to the boardroom I still had the ambition to earn my living as a writer in television. Night after night, after a hard day's work, I laboured, with a reasonable store of experience but no real grasp of technique.

I had everything but that which I needed most, which was someone to show me in practical terms how to do it and, that achieved, some means of getting in touch with the generation I wanted to write for. In the end they came in one package in the shape of Harry Kershaw, Michael Cox, Denis Forman and Granada Television, and since Granada was the brainchild of

Sidney Bernstein I am deeply indebted to him too.

I was not the only one engaged in the learning process. Practically everyone working in the building in Quay Street in Manchester was operating on a trial and error basis. A few brought outside experience from the BBC or from overseas, but most simply brought their varied talents and a strong desire to use them. The disciplines which carried me through the next thirty or so years were initially learnt under Harry Kershaw on *Coronation Street*, then about to go on air. I became the first writer on trial at the time to stay the course. Other writers as diverse as Jack Rosenthal and Jim Allen have acknowledged their debt to HVK. Those of us who really wanted to write one-off plays, and were slightly embarrassed to be earning a reasonable income from series and serial writing were buoyed up by statements such as that from Derek Granger, who said, 'The battle for higher standards will be fought in the area of mass entertainment.' I wonder does anyone say that now? More particularly, I wonder if anyone knows what it means.

I hope I always made it clear that my wish to leave *Coronation Street* and do my own thing in no way diminished my gratitude to the series as Harry Kershaw uniquely developed it. Without the background it gave me, both as writer, editor and producer, I might never have taken flight. There was a definite technique to television writing which needed to be learned, though some writers snootily turned their backs on it. They didn't like being told that big casts were impossibly expensive, as were exotic locations abroad. They failed to appreciate that if you employed a good actor you had to give him a good part and not two lines, however important, at the end of Act One. (Jack Howarth once stopped me in the foyer and icily said of the script I had written, 'I'm going home to learn my line.') They also had a pronounced antipathy to the concept of drama as teamwork. There is no doubt that in the majority of cases, though not all, the best production of a piece of good dramatic writing takes place in the writer's head as he laboriously puts pen to paper. That said, however convoluted the progression from then on the final creation depends, in various degrees, on many other creative people who, as much as the writer, need to have their contribution acknowledged.

More often than not, however, it is the writer who has to take the stick from the critics, many of whom seem unable to assess where blame lies in a poor production. The best critics, of the calibre of T. C. Worsley or Philip Purser, can be of enormous assistance to a writer, helping him to make an honest analysis of his work. On the other hand they can be depressingly negative. I have often had to try to shrug off descriptions of my work as 'dour' or 'glum' – inevitable I suppose since most of my writing has been about poverty or war. The audiences for series such as *A Family at War* (52 hours), or *Sam* (of which I wrote all 39 hours), either didn't read or ignored the more negative critics, for both series at some point knocked *Coronation Street* and *Morecambe and Wise* from the top of the ratings, were well-received by the more serious critics and sold throughout the world. In some twenty-five years of writing for Granada the company never attempted to censor anything I wrote and never complained that I was 'dour'. At the end of *A Family at War* Denis Forman, then managing director, asked me what I would like to do next. We spent half-an-hour chatting about my early experiences in a mining community, and at the end, without asking for a pilot or even an outline, he simply said, 'Go and do it.' Trust was a major factor in Granada's creative approach to drama.

They had a policy of teaming writers and producers who were happy working with each other. I was fortunate in that Michael Cox was a producer on both *A Family at War* and at my special request on *Sam*. Michael always told me what he liked before he told me what was lacking. A simple question mark on a script could send me back to the typewriter to re-type pages. Such was the rapport. Pride of place among a number of awards is the Guild award as Best Series writer in 1975, the year I completed SAM. We did other series together but, later, promotion took him away from me, and around this time Granada embarked on *Brideshead* and *Jewel in the Crown*; both adaptations. I had always tried to do original work rather than transpose other people's flowers, and country houses and the British Raj (though I once spent half an hour chatting to Nehru) were not my prime interest. My relationship with Granada deteriorated. I had, it seemed, had my day though I was left to draw this conclusion myself; no one actually said they had no further use for me, though it became obvious that this was the case. Around this time, too, a different atmosphere seemed to be permeating the building. Inevitably new faces appeared. It seemed to me, though I may be accused of myopia, that television drama throughout had become obsessed by a tabloid-like triviality and a frenetic obsession with technical trickery and flashy direction. The striving for artistic potential in mass audience drama was replaced by a growing emphasis on accountancy. An era had ended.

It was an era of considerable stress. I can remember Denis Forman saying, with weary humour, that the time might come when a final caption on the screen would read, 'Programmes have been terminated as we have lost the will to go on.' But it was a time, too, of considerable achievement in the face of minuscule budgets. As a producer I used to carry my budget in my pocket on the back of an envelope; I'm told that today teams of accountants rule the roost. The art is in the accountancy.

In his speech accepting the Nobel Prize for Literature in 1962, John Steinbeck said, 'The writer is delegated to declare and to celebrate man's proven capacity for greatness of heart and spirit – for gallantry in defeat – for courage, compassion and love.' This is a tall order for scriptwriters in a medium where so much is dependent on others, but there was, I think, a time when Granada would not have disagreed with this little speech. That era, it would seem, has now ended.

Was there a Golden Age of television? I'm quite sure there was, but mostly for those involved in production. There was the excitement of pioneering in a new medium, of building foundations for the future. There was also, I believe, a greater willingness to experiment and to give programme makers the chance to fail in pursuit of new concepts. That said, there is much that gives grounds for optimism for the future of television. Some very good writing, which is the basic essential of television drama, more generous budgets and a more flexible technology. What will be harvested from these will depend to a great extent on the attitude to, and respect for, the audience of the people in control.

Some lines towards the end of Waugh's *Brideshead Revisited* come to mind. They refer to the unattractive prospect, as Waugh's main character saw it, of a post-war generation represented by a character called Hooper. 'The builders did not know the use to which their work would descend; they made a new house with the stones of the old castle; year by year ... they enriched and extended it; year by year the great harvest of timber in the park grew to ripeness; until, in sudden frost, came the age of Hooper ...'

I can see what you're trying to do

ARTHUR HOPCRAFT

The first play I wrote for Granada, or indeed for anyone at all, was never performed. It was called *Cyril and the Sex Kittens*. It was terrible.

The trouble was that it was written for the stage, which in the late 1960s I didn't know much about, and still don't. What I knew of drama I had learned from listening to BBC radio, going to the pictures and watching television. What happened was that Gordon McDougall asked me to write something for the Stables Theatre, which Granada had set up, if I remember correctly, partly as a feeder of new talent for its screen productions. As a freelance journalist I had been working two or three days a week for *Scene at Six Thirty*. Gordon thought a journalistic/documentary approach might prove interesting.

Hence *Cyril*, which was supposed to be about a power struggle for the heart and soul of a northern workingsmen's club, the central conflict being whether black people should be allowed in as members and/or entertainers. It was also supposed to be a comedy.

Stated baldly like that it sounds not at all a bad idea, given the (amazing!) social attitudes of the time. I just couldn't bring it off. Gordon kindly said something like, 'I can see what you're trying to do, but ...' I forgot about writing plays and got on with my day job.

A year or so later the Stables folded. All the paperwork in the pending tray eventually found its way into Peter Eckersley's office, Peter now being Head of Drama. In due course he came across my play and found the patience to read it. Over a glass or two of alcopop in the Film Exchange he said something like, 'I can see what you were trying to do, but ...' I said something like, 'Let's not worry about that – whose round is it?'

But Peter persisted. If I wanted to write a play why didn't I try writing one for the television screen, which I knew at least a little about? I think I said I wasn't sure I had the time, what with football reporting and such. But Peter persisted.

A few weeks later we had agreed I should write a play about hill walking in the Lake District, because I'd done a lot of that and Peter wanted to get the camera out of doors. He didn't go much for my first suggestion involving a climbing club's annual dinner dance. Forty-five actors sitting round a table? Then forty-five actors spread all over the mountainside? He was much more sympathetic to a tale about four people. So I wrote *The Mosedale Horseshoe*.

I delivered it, I think, around October/November in 1970. The read-through was on 14 January 1971. Filming began up at Wastwater four days later and finished on 5 February. The play was transmitted on the 23 March. It was directed by Michael Apted. The next morning the BBC commissioned a play from me on the phone. Thank you, Peter. Things aren't done that way these days.

Postscript : A couple of years after *The Mosedale Horseshoe* I took the central character from *Cyril and the Sex Kittens*, discarded just about everything else and reworked the whole thing into a BBC *Play for Today* called *Jingle Bells*. Thank you, Gordon.

A fixer in drama

WALTER MARINER

I realised very early on that television was an industry with as much bull as a Spanish fiesta. I had listed on my application form that one of my hobbies was an interest in American literature. The Personnel Officer asked me if I had read Hemingway's *Cannery Row?*

Jack Martin, Manager in Charge of Production, later confessed that he had chosen me from a shortlist of three because I'd served in the Navy. The other two candidates were ex-RAF. Jack himself had been a Lt Commander RNVR. He was a great judge of men and I joined Granada in 1958 as a senior cost clerk.

One of my first jobs was to search the building for one of the drama producers and help him work out his expenses. This was my first meeting with Derek Granger. Derek had been given a return rail ticket from London to Edinburgh to do some work for Granada at the Festival.

During his three days stay in Edinburgh Derek had been using his own money and held receipts to cover the hire of a chauffeur-driven Austin Princess (Derek didn't drive) plus a stack of bills for wining and dining Dame Edith Evans and her fellow thespians. When complete, Derek's expenses totalled something over £350 – this at the time when OB crews were allowed to draw a £30 advance for a week away from base. My weekly wage was £12.50. So at the end of 1960, with Jack Martin's blessing, I applied to be accepted as a trainee floor manager (FM). I started my training soon after my 34th birthday and I must have been the oldest trainee FM in the history of television.

As an FM I was privileged to work with the best: Malcolm Muggeridge, James Cameron, Brian Inglis, Bamber Gascoigne, Gay Byrne and Bill Grundy. I was also present at the introduction of Michael Parkinson to Local Programmes. Never have I encountered anyone so nervous, not even Bamber Gascoigne when he was thrown in at the deep end on the first *University Challenge.* Yet today 'Parky' is one of the most polished performers on the box.

Quite by chance I discovered that Mike had a phobia about maggots. Every year I fished in the TV Championship held in Ireland. I was down to floor manage the live local *Scene at 6.30* on the Friday night before flying to Dublin around 9 p.m. Behind the *Scene* set I stored my weekend case, fishing tackle and bucket of maggots. Between dress rehearsal and transmission I brought my bucket of bait out into the studio lights for inspection, there was a scream and Mike had bolted to the other side of the studio and was trying to claw his way through the wall. The following week I sent him a few wriggling samples through the internal mail in a well-sealed 'Personal' envelope.

The Woody Allen Show in 1965 was probably the biggest let-down of my Floor Managing career. I'd expected a relaxed, quick-talking, intelligent American in the Bob Hope mould. Instead Allen was morose, rude, unprofessional and as charismatic as a wet newspaper. He was accompanied by a road manager/minder/Svengali who told Allen when to go to the toilet and how to sit in a chair. He never left Allen's side during rehearsals and was a constant pain. Transmission was before a specially invited audience that included many of the *Coronation Street* cast. The result was as funny as a broken arm, and what should have been a 60-minute programme was edited down to 45 minutes.

Granada transmitted the British Film Academy Awards twice, in 1966 and 1968. I was Floor Manager on both occasions. At the 1966 Awards I stumbled across an extremely drunk Peter Butterworth sitting at the bottom of the main staircase. I'd worked with Peter on a comedy series called *The Bulldog Breed* and offered to escort him back to his table. First I had to listen to his tale of woe. It seems that some months previously Peter had agreed to do another *Carry On* film, lured by the fact that although the money was the same as the previous film there was the prospect of staying at the Tel Aviv Hilton for four weeks on location. The week previous to the Academy Awards the backers of the film had decided that the *Carry On* films should be made to appeal to a more international audience. That very night at the Academy Awards Peter had been introduced to Phil Silvers, the international star who would play the lead in *Carry On … Follow That Camel*. Phil Silvers's fee meant that the four weeks at the Tel Aviv Hilton was now four days on Redmire Sands the UK. That was the reason Peter had got drunk.

It was at this same ceremony that Taylor and Burton received a special award for their roles in *Who's Afraid of Virginia Woolf.* Mike Scott was doing interviews with all the award winners but had been told that the Burtons never gave interviews so he hadn't done any homework on them. When I brought them into the studio I thought he was going to faint. The result was probably the worst interview in the history of television. There's no record of this in the GTV archives.

During my time as an FM most of the technological advances took place. We already had telerecording in 1961, which meant that programmes could be pre-recorded and stockpiled although still treated as live – no stopping, apart from commercial breaks. This meant that during recording the studio floor still resembled an obstacle course of sets, camera and sound equipment, quick change rooms. The release of a camera and boom from one set to another was similar to the chariot race in *Ben Hur* and the noise of lens changes and cables being dragged was a constant background to the dialogue.

These factors placed severe constraints on script writers. The introduction of videotape with its editing facility changed all this although in the early days there were limitations because of the cost of videotape and the fact that we only had one editing suite. Later on the introduction of colour meant that studio production could compete with film.

It was just after the first colour productions that Denis Forman asked if I would help out Richard Doubleday and Mike Cox who were setting up *A Family at War* – so for an extra £5 a week I became Series Planner on this exciting project. I think it was about this time that Peter Eckersley became Head of Drama.

During the run of *Family* the series acquired an associate producer (Michael Dunlop) plus a trainee producer (Jonathan Powell). The office always seemed full of bodies and not enough chairs to go round. So with more cooks than there were pots on the stove I asked if I could return to floor managing. Once again Denis Forman convinced me that my destiny lay elsewhere and I became Drama Planning Manager to Peter Eckersley (there was no mention of an extra £5 a week). After the completion of *Family*, Mike Cox joined us as Head of Drama Series.

Undoubtedly my most enjoyable time at GTV was the period I spent with Peter as his 'fixer' in Drama. When I look back at this time I marvel at the quality and amount of Drama produced. The annual requirement was for some 52 one-hour series programmes plus 12 to 14 one-off plays. There was always pressure; pressure to meet transmission deadlines, pressure to find scripts and ideas added to the worry of making the yearly budget stretch out. We were always searching for a studio-bound series with a running set – *Village Hall* for example, which I suggested – or one-off plays with limited sets and cast. All were necessary to subsidise the more ambitious projects.

There is a nice story to emphasise that 'some idols have feet of clay'. We had just completed and transmitted the second Catherine Cookson novel *The Mallen Breed* and the viewing figures had been phenomenal. We had our regular meeting with the programme controller, in which he waxed lyrical about the young couple who had played the leads (John Duttine and Juliet Stevenson). 'We must get Cookson to continue the Mallen story,' he said. Somebody had to tell him that his dream couple had drowned, clasped together in death in the clear water of a river. Obviously he hadn't seen the final episode.

Peter was a lapsed Catholic and some of his early indoctrination stuck. He felt uncomfortable with any script which featured the supernatural, the occult or anything that went against Catholic teaching. We had received an

unsolicited play from a new writer, Brian Clark – *Whose Life Is It Anyway?*
The subject was euthanasia, beautifully presented with the arguments for
and against finely balanced. I had made up my mind that this play had to be
made and not just because it had one set and a cast of four. It took me a
couple of weeks to convince Peter, but the clincher was Dick Everitt. It was
Dick's turn to direct a play and Peter had three scripts ready for him to read.
I bet Peter a bottle of wine that if he included *Whose Life* with the other
three, Dick would pick *Whose Life*. The rest is history.

We all knew of Peter's liking for a drink, especially at lunchtime. I always
suspected that the drink really didn't matter, it was more of a prop for the
conversation of his mates Hopcraft, Stevenson, Shipperbottom and others.
Upon his wife's instruction I tried to get him into the Festival Cafe for something to eat before going up to the Film Exchange. I was seldom successful.

After being extremely ill Peter took a break from being Head of Drama
and I was moved to the executive floor to work alongside Bob Williams who
was shortly to retire. My future at Granada was to produce the weekly Blue
Book of programme planning. In 1981, the week before I had arranged to
take my holidays, Peter called to see me. David Plowright had given him the
go-ahead to work on a series of Welsh short stories and Peter was wondering
if I would be interested in working with him again. Naturally I said yes and
we arranged to get together more formally after my holidays. In the meantime he told me that he had to go into hospital for a straightforward operation.

Peter's favourite saying was: 'It'll all end in tears.' It did for me when on
the morning of my return, Joyce Wooller rang to say that Peter was dead.

Behind the cycle sheds

ALAN PLATER

The first time I crossed the threshold of Granada Television in Manchester I
felt really wicked. It was like seeing my first French film (which must have
been *La Ronde*) or sharing a Woodbine behind the cycle sheds at school.

The reason for my guilty frisson (catch Ena Sharples using a word like
frisson) was very simple: the BBC. As a writer, I was discovered and nur-
tured by the Corporation, initially by the great Alfred Bradley, who produced
radio drama in Leeds, and then by Vivian Daniels, who did the same job in
television for the BBC in Manchester. In the early 1960s the BBC North
Region had genuine autonomy, with a budget to match, and grovelled to
nobody.

My first television play, *The Referees*, was rehearsed (hands up – who remembers rehearsals?) and recorded at the old Dickenson Road studios during the Cuban missile crisis of 1962. I remember praying (not to a specific God, since I'm a devout atheist, but probably with a nod towards Kennedy and Khrushchev) that World War Three would be delayed until after the play's transmission, since I hoped to pass into oblivion with at least one television credit. All is vanity, as the preacher said.

The leading character in *The Referees* was played by Donald Churchill, who went on to write, with Julia Jones, a wonderful series called *Moody and Pegg*. Donald always gave the impression that 50 per cent of his psyche was living a parallel life on some other, more congenial, planet and consequently we got along famously since 50 per cent of mine was playing left-back for England and evenings in Duke Ellington's band.

Don mentioned that his next job was a series for Granada – some kind of off-beat comedy, laconic as all-get-out and why didn't I talk to them about contributing? I don't remember a thing about the practicalities, but I vividly remember sneaking out of the gallery during studio rehearsals and finding my way to Deansgate where I met Derek Granger.

He told me, very gently, that the show was already written but would I like to meet Harry Kershaw to discuss writing for the *Street*? I was frankly a bit sniffy about this. I was a young, principled artist, dammit. I wasn't going to sully my sensibilities working on a series. Within a year, I was a fully-fledged member of the *Z Cars* team but if you can't live with compromise, you don't buy the typewriter in the first place.

But the enduring memory, as reported, was the guilty excitement of betrayal. Was I being unfaithful to the BBC? The question-mark made it all the more exciting.

According to the credits list, the first work I did for Granada was a play called *Fred* in 1964. David Langton played the lead and Fred was a large stuffed teddy bear – hence Fred Bear, which was a joke and almost certainly a metaphor but I can't be sure after all these years. I'm pretty sure *Fred* was part of a short anthology series. They were very much in vogue with portmanteau titles like *Seven Deadly Sins* or *Aspects of Love*. The titles were so vague the writers could write the same plays they would have written anyway. What sticks in the mind was that credits on this occasion included not only the writer's name but his picture: a grainy, stylised profile. Only a dedicated trainspotter could confirm this, but aside from the opening credits of vintage *Hancock* shows, which included pictures of Ray Galton and Alan Simpson, I can't recall any other examples of writers' portraits being part of the title sequence.

It was during the production of *Fred* that I made the extraordinary discovery that Granada was a dry company. The actors showed me where the pub was. Some of the *Coronation Street* gang were in that night and I remember the great Anne Reid saying her recurring nightmare was an endless scroll of script reading Ken/Val/Ken/Val/Ken/Val ... One night I met Hugh Leonard and possibly Eddie Boyd but the rest is a blur.

My best friend at Granada was Howard Baker, who produced and/or directed much of my work. He was a quiet, gentle, literate man and I miss him still. He was the first producer to introduce me to the joys and agonies of dramatisation in 1975, with a thirteen-part series from A. J. Cronin's *The Stars Look Down*. Howard shared the directorial duties with Alan Grint and a young guy called Roland Joffe.

Later I wrote a six-part dramatisation of Thomas Hardy's *Tess of the D'Urbervilles* for Howard. Unfortunately Roman Polanski's movie version came along at exactly the right time to derail our project which, purely for the record, would have been better than Polanski's if only because the book needs the six hours that we'd given it. It remains the best of my unproduced work.

Also for the record, it's obvious that the experience gained tangling with Cronin and Hardy was a huge help when taking on series like *Barchester Chronicles*, *Fortunes of War* and *A Very British Coup*.

One of the sweet sequels to all this was the night of the BAFTA Awards in 1983, when *Barchester Chronicles* was nominated as Best Series and we were all beaten a distance by *The Boys from the Black Stuff*. During the break between the meal and the prize-giving I went to the gents where I found myself at an adjacent urinal to Michael Cox, then Granada's Head of Drama. He told me that a long-planned project – a film about the mystery of the Mary Celeste – had come to life again. 'I'll call you,' he said. I returned to my BBC table and caused a stir by saying: 'I've just been for a pee and got a job from Granada.' I got the old frisson again.

The end of that story was I did a damn good screenplay but the American co-producers pulled out when they discovered Mary Celeste was a sailing ship and not, as they had expected, a beautiful woman with an exotic sex life.

My most recent dealings with Granada – aside from a strictly marginal consultative role in Rob Ritchie's splendid *Who Bombed Birmingham?* – were a couple of scripts for the first *Maigret* series.

Frankly, my dears, the show wasn't as good as we'd hoped, partly because Simenon's work, so epoch-making in its time by its focus on the psychology of crime, has been overtaken by the Ruth Rendells of the world. These days every quality whodunnit is a whydunnit. We were also victims of the observable reality that Budapest might be cheaper to shoot in than Paris, but doesn't actually look like it. But the core of the problem was much simpler. John Glenister, a fine director and good friend, telephoned me with a query about my screenplay: not a major point but strictly a nuance.

'We can sort that out in the rehearsal room,' I said.

There was a long, ominous silence.

'No rehearsals?' I said.

'No rehearsals,' he said.

Well, it may be cost-effective, but it doesn't make the drama any better.

Back in the 1980s (remember them?) I was briefly caught up in a wacky project to start a company. It began like a old joke when a writer, an actor, a director and a producer went into a bar. There we met a Man from the City with a briefcase full of promises. All we had to do was develop projects for film and television and ultimately transform the cosmos. The Man from the City would finance everything. A sum of money was mentioned: £6 million to be precise.

I put my question carefully, anxious not to upset him. 'Where will this money come from?'

'You'll be filling the leisure niche in someone's portfolio,' he said.

We never saw the man or his briefcase again and that was the end of the joke.

In my gloomier moments, the Granada story seems a bit like that. What was once an adventure playground, where I felt really naughty simply by walking through the door, is now a leisure niche in someone's portfolio.

Does anyone else remember *The Younger Generation?* This was, in effect, an in-house Granada repertory company of young actors who did plays by new writers. I stayed close to the phone for weeks but the call never came. John Thaw was in the company and I still remember a lovely Tim Aspinall play about a man building an aeroplane in his bedroom.

Each play was introduced by a Salford poet called Johnny McDonald. We later used some of his work in our radio series, *The Northern Drift*. One of the poems, called, I think, *There's a Drunk in the Streets*, contains the couplet:

> If your soul catches fire when you walk these streets
> There is no one to help you at all.

Excellent work still emerges, courtesy Jimmy McGovern, Kay Mellor and the peerless *Coronation Street* writing team; but the price of that is very simple. If they don't deliver the ratings, the game is over and if your soul catches fire on the streets of Salford, tough.

I wrote elsewhere that one of my recurring nightmares is a phone call from my agent, early in the next century, saying: 'Granada would like you to write *Prime Suspect 27.*'

It looks like I'll be too busy with my weekly column for the *Luddites' Gazette*.

Granada drama from 1956

PHILIP PURSER

In the records, Granada's first drama was *Shooting Star*, a football play from the days when footballers wore decent shorts and never kissed. In folklore, always more interesting, the pattern of Granada drama was laid down some 18 months later, in March 1958, when an obscure Irish piece called *The Iron Harp* scored an unexpected success both in the reviews and the ratings. This was mainly due to the performance of a previously unknown actor called Richard Harris, and Sidney Bernstein is supposed to have ruled next day that such should be the aim henceforth – to be popular with the audience, praised by the critics and use no actor costing more than 50 guineas, or £52.50.

In prosaic fact Granada never attached as much importance to the single play as did the other companies or the BBC. I remember being told quite early on, and indeed writing a column about it, that as an outfit which had always studied the American experience assiduously, Granada was already planning to concentrate on series and serials. Of this, more in a moment. Meanwhile, it is important to remind ourselves just how plentiful and how valuable drama was throughout the 1960s and into the 1970s. When I did a rather ponderous survey for the BFI television quarterly *Contrast* in 1961, ITV was on the air some 50 hours a week. Of this total about 12 hours were devoted to live or as-live drama, including three regular single-play slots, and Harold Pinter had just bluffed his way to the very top of the Top Ten with *A Night Out* for ABC.

At first, like everyone else, Granada raided the theatre; then, like everyone else, shipped in scripts from the brief golden age of studio drama in America. Maybe because they had also imported Canadian directors who were more comfortable in the idiom, North American accents seemed to linger on a little more persistently in Granada's output than elsewhere. You would get not only Reginald Rose's powerful *Thunder on Sycamore Street* (written for TV) but also a splendid production of *Death of a Salesman* complete with Alex North's haunting flute score. Albert Dekker, flown over from New York to play Willie Loman, gave me his version of the great American dry Martini joke. Barman: 'Twist of lemon with it ?' Customer: 'If I wanted a goddam lemonade I'd have asked for one.' Both these shows were directed by Silvio Narizzano. The first native television original I remember was J. B. Priestley's *Doomsday for Dyson* (1958), very much a special case, or tract. After a genuinely scary impression of the nuclear unthinkable coming to pass (Silvio again) proceedings settled down to a kind of celestial inquest, in the style of progressive theatre of the 1930s, into who was to blame – answer: everyone, for not campaigning vigorously enough against the H-bomb. But the production attracted much useful attention.

It was Priestley, as it happened, who about this time voiced his boredom with the school of earnest social realism which was springing up – how Bill lost his job or Jack his girl, what to do with old Mum. Granada were late-ish starters in this field, and when they did venture in, it was with something just a little different. *The Liberty Man*, wrought by Leo Lehman from Gillian Freeman's novel about a naval rating who falls for a middle-class school-teacher, displayed some fine social line-drawing and a robust performance from Richard Pasco, who you wouldn't have thought of as a rough matelot but who got it uncannily right, down to the thick fingers fumbling another cigarette from the packet. Clive Exton's dip into the lower depths of life on the road, *No Fixed Abode*, was a dour hit the following year, 1959, along with the wistfully-named *A Bit of Happiness* from Alexander Baron and the same author's *The Blood Fight*, both directed by Herbert Wise.

Levity crept in with Peter Nichols's *Ben Spray* (1961) and *Ben Again* (1963), and in many ways this was how Granada single drama would go on until single drama faded away. There was no pronounced house style, as from *Armchair Theatre* or the *Wednesday Play* under James MacTaggart, but all the going writers (even Dennis Potter) were represented sooner or later, new ones were discovered, light relief was welcome, and individuals were encouraged to pursue individual strains – notably Arthur Hopcraft, who as a newspaper sports writer, played himself in with a sequence of gentle comedies rooted in outdoor pastimes: *The Mosedale Horseshoe* (hill-walking), *The Birthday Run* (cycling) and *The Panel* (bowling). His encourager was Peter Eckersley, who by then would have been Head of Drama, I think, though he produced the Hopcraft sporting yarns himself – I had the impression that Granada always won its best results from molecular clusters of producer, writer, director. In 1976–78, when Peter was indubitably in charge, you would still find Julian Amyes nursing a little clutch of new originals on to the air while Derek Granger masterminded that grand climacteric of traditional television drama, the *Best Play of ... '* season with the Oliviers. Actually, there was an autumnal whiff to both these enterprises. Julian's trio of video plays, which included a tricksy one from me and a nice one by David Nobbs, must have been one of the last of such packages. From now on the few single offerings would be films; otherwise, only series and serials.

In Eckersley's time many of the best of these had been hatched – the monumental if ramshackle *A Family at War*, *Sam*, two lots of *Village Hall*, one of *Red Letter Day*, the splendid *Hard Times*, and what I cherish as the finest literary anthology series ever, *Country Matters*. Still to come were those landmarks of the 1980s, *Brideshead Revisited* and *Jewel in the Crown*. I joined in all the praise for them, as far as my niggardly critical nature would allow. But I still can't help thinking of them as a little too opulent, a little too shepherded, classy package tours through vanished landscapes. Traipsing round Castle Howard for a travel piece, a year or two after *Brideshead*, I heard a cerise-blazered attendant say, 'Though I'm afraid I can't show you it, through this door is the room where Sir Laurence Olivier passed away as Lord Marchmain.'

Let's whizz back, for a moment, to the start of the series and serial preference in the early 1960s, and to one of the producers to whom it fell to implement that policy, Philip Mackie. What he did with the form, doubtless at short notice and on a thrifty budget, was quite phenomenally ingenious. The one-hour format was just coming – or rushing – in. The other companies either extended trusty crime formulae (*No Hiding Place*, out of the half-hour 'Murder Bag') or came up with worthy new series (*Probation Officer*) which were really consecutive helpings of the social realism so disdained by J. B. Priestley – honesty compels me to recall that Granada had one of these too, in *Family Solicitor*. But Mackie reached for a source he liked and understood, the short story, and did something with it that no one had done before. From the tales of Saki, then de Maupassant, finally a diverse bag of magazine authors for the series he called *The Liars*, he constructed, well, dramatic collages, I suppose you might have called them: three, four, maybe six different stories melting into each other, sometimes overlapping, a character stepping from one little plot to the next. And if you say that's all very well, but if it was such a great idea why hasn't it survived to this day, the answer has to be that it failed to offer what was emerging as the essential constituent of popular drama.

That was most clearly to be seen in Granada's more durable innovation of the 1960s, *Coronation Street*. What people liked was familiarity. Series – other than anthology series – featured the same characters and same milieu every time, no need to work out who everyone was. The serial added the powerful attraction of a continuing What Happens Next? Soap opera made it forever. Anthology series forfeited most of these advantages, and with his riffle of stories Philip gambled the lot. Never mind, he went on to apply some of the same flair to a more sustained, if still unconventional, storyline in *The Caesars*, which I bracket with *An Age of Kings* and *The Voyage of Charles Darwin* as the bravest costume serials ever. With *Mr Rose*, which he produced in 1967, Mackie also supplies a cue for the drama genre which cannot be omitted from any survey of television: crime.

Shadow Squad must have been Granada's first effort, fairly forgettable and certainly forgotten by me. Next came *The Verdict is Yours* which I am going to treat in a separate piece, followed by one or two forensic spin-offs and then– ah then! *The Odd Man* (1962–63), written by Edward Boyd, whose work I knew from my days as a reporter in Scotland. He had a line in jaunty radio serials starring the crooners Pearl Carr and Teddy Johnson as husband-and-wife private investigators. *The Odd Man* deployed the same two characters but now played by Sarah Lawson and Edwin Richfield, transposed into an altogether darker key – doomed figures drawn each week into someone else's troubles, unable to tackle their own. 'Can't live with you, can't live without you/What's the answer?' Was it imagination or did the lines scan? A second batch of episodes introduced William Mervyn as the fruity Detective Chief Inspector Rose, and whether or not this was intended, Rose proceeded to take over.

It's Dark Outside (1964–65) still had a distinctive tone but as far as I remember the original hero and heroine had vanished, the focus was on Rose and his sergeant (Keith Barron) and there was certainly a change of producer, from Stuart Latham to Derek Bennett. With *Mr Rose* the takeover was complete, and I have to say that Philip Mackie steered the result firmly towards geniality. In a quite separate strand of crime fiction, however, the reverse was happening. *The Man in Room 17* and its successor *The Fellows*, had set out to be cerebral. Richard Vernon, Michael Aldridge and, later, Denholm Elliott were academic criminologists supposed to solve crimes entirely by logic, without ever leaving their eyrie. The 1968 spin-off called *Spindoe* abandoned such rigour to concentrate on the fortunes of a gang-leader jailed as a result of their deliberations. Now out of prison, he was trying to re-assert his old authority the only way he knew. With Ray MacAnally in the part and Robin Chapman as writer and producer, Granada was back in the *film noir* business – or at least it was until Chapman's next show, *Big Breadwinner Hog* was much reviled for its violence.

All of which I have been rehearsing at undue length, perhaps, because – of course – it brings us handily to more recent times. Apart from good old Coras, which I am sure is being fêted elsewhere, what had Granada in the 1990s to offer? Crime, crime, crime and Jane Austen. The peaks of television drama are yet another *Prime Suspect* or yet another overwrought, over-praised *Cracker*. Dear God, is there no one with the talent and energy to interest the audience in something other than serial murder?

The verdict is yours went against me

PHILIP PURSER

In 1958, after I had written about it a couple of times in the *News Chronicle*, I was commissioned by Granada to do a book about that extraordinary exercise in dramatic extemporisation, *The Verdict is Yours*. Like many of their early shows it had been adapted from an American format, orginally put out by the now-defunct Dumont network under the title *They Stand Accused*. Dumont had been centred on Chicago, and prided itself on its own distinctive school of production, grittier than New York's, let alone Hollywood's. The idea was that real attorneys contested a case before a real judge, and a jury assembled exactly as a real jury would have been assembled. Only the accused and witnesses were actors, and they were given no script, simply a dossier about themselves and the circumstances of the case. They had to ad lib everything they said, and sometimes became so caught up in the make-believe that tears, tantrums and even a fist-fight would break out in the wings – the American experience incidentally, was that method actors made lousy verdict participants, it was the old stock company hams who excelled.

After the demise of Dumont the programme was taken up and retitled by CBS in New York, where Denis Forman chanced to see it and immediately set about acquiring British rights in the format. English legal protocol ruled out employment of a real judge and practising counsel; a few company lawyers were tried out, there was even a proposal to persuade some young barristers to give up the Bar in exchange for long-term contracts, but in the end Forman decided that the safest course would be to entrust these roles, also, to actors. If someone could be found who had a legal background, so much the better. A former Scotland Yard prosecutor, David Ensor, became *The Verdict's* Mr Justice Ensor. At the time he struck me as too scolding in some of the moral judgements he handed out; these days, I guess, his performance would be thought understated.

The programmes were among the first to be pre-recorded as a matter of course. Usually they were in three parts, going out over three evenings. I sat in on one from start to finish, beginning with the writers. Geoffrey Bellman was a sometimes actor who had worked in commercial radio, where he had met and teamed up with the young game-show entrepreneur John Whitney, eventually to be the last Director-General of the Independent Broadcasting Authority. They had written one or two conventional scripts together but *The Verdict* seemed to suit them; this was their fifth commission.

The plot this time came from a doctor friend of Whitney's who was concerned about the rather questionable law under which a person could be temporarily committed to mental hospital on the word of a close relation, providing the latter could produce some reason to believe he or she might otherwise come to harm. With Bellman he hatched a story involving a horsey ex-major down on his luck and his young nephew, who has apparently attempted to take an overdose. The major gets him put away under an Urgency Order. Suspicions are aroused, and the trial will be of the major, charged under the Lunacy Act of 1890 with wilful mis-statement.

They took this scenario to Denis Forman, who ran *The Verdict* as a kind of uncredited executive producer. If the major was up to something under-hand, he wanted to know, what was his motive? Money, they explained. The boy is heir to the family fortune. If he is committed to a mental hospital, even briefly, under the terms of the will he is disinherited. The major would get the money instead ...

'OK,' Forman had said, 'but let's make it his niece rather than his nephew. A girl would be more dramatic. In fact, while we're about it, let's make her a nun.' He hadn't lightly exchanged the safe grazing of an institutional career as Director of the British Film Institute for the jungle of showbiz, but here his instincts turned out to be right. The unworldliness of the young novice, as she became, made the case more plausible. In the production schedules it went down as 'Regina v. Farrell', Farrell being the major's name. Unofficially, it was referred to as 'The Suicidal Nun'.

Bellman and Whitney had to research the law thoroughly, summarise it for the opposing counsel and prescribe a few bits of examination or cross-examination which conveyed essential facts. They had to provide a CV for each witness, down to details of income and hobbies. They had to furnish depositions from all concerned that would never be drawn on directly, because they were to be written not in impersonal police prose but in character, the better to help the actors bring these people to life. What they were not to do at any time was indicate – or even decide between them-selves– whether the major was or was not guilty. The aim was to construct a sequence of events for which there could be both an innocent or a sinister explanation.

On the train to Manchester I fell in with Helena Hughes, the rather beautiful redhead who was to take the part of the niece. She had been in the original Royal Court production of *Look Back in Anger*, poor girl. After that, playing a suicidal nun should be no problem. All that perplexed her, as she thumbed through the blue duplicated pages of her dossier, was what they would actually be doing over the next three days. 'If there's no script,' she said, 'how can we rehearse?' What they did in fact was huddle together in a variety of sessions, usually just two or three people, working out each stage of the trial with the writers, the producer or the director – on this case,

Warren Jenkins and James Ormerod respectively. When everybody eventually did come together for something like a rehearsal, it was customary for counsel to put on their best forensic style but ask frivolous, even naughty, questions: they didn't want to give away too much of their strategy in advance, not take the edge of a witness's spontaneity before he or she went in front of the cameras. I jotted down a sample exchange as Martin Benson pretended to examine Helena, and Helena neatly headed him off.

'You were in a convent. You would know what a nun's habit is?'

'Yes.'

'What were the habits of the Mother Superior?'

'She did a little gardening.'

When the family doctor, played by Monica Grey, took the witness box, the temptations offered by medical matters lowered the tone rapidly. 'It does get a bit near the knuckle sometimes,' Warren Jenkins admitted, 'but it helps the actors to relax. 'Wasn't Martin salacious?' Helena whispered to Monica. Benson, a character actor often cast in powerful, intimidating roles, was a natural choice to play prosecuting counsel, which he did under his own name. Leading for the defence was John Chandos. Like Geoffrey Bellman, he was an writer and occasional actor, but also the spokesman in Britain for the French champagne industry. He said he'd got to know a good deal of civil law, anyway, during the long action they had lately brought in English courts to stop the Spaniards using the term 'Spanish champagne'. Nights on the town with Chandos turned into a crawl round old commercial hotels with brass fittings and engraved glass, at each of which he would order a bottle of champagne, just to see what would be produced. He was delighted this time to turn up a rare Piper Heidsieck. Attached to the production were two further actors who were being auditioned as counsel for future episodes. One was Tony Church, who was soon to be used in the programme. The other was Leo McKern, who seems not to have been called on. Maybe he showed no aptitude for legal roles.

The three parts of Regina v. Farrell were recorded on three successive days, using the Ampex system which had only just been introduced – Granada were the first to have it in Britain. Editing was still impossible and even a break in the recording tricky to handle. Granada were adamant that cast and crew should treat recording as if they were on air. The direct perils of improvisation were eased: it would no longer be irreparable if someone suffered a mental blackout or mere hysteria; but the ordinary tensions of live television remained. On top of those, all the curious confusions of pretend and reality noted by the Americans came crowding in as the trial approached its climax. 'It's absurd,' said Monica Grey, 'but I'm absolutely dreading being cross-examined by Martin.' On the eve of the third recording, when the verdict would be reached, it was noticeable that the actor playing Major Farrell was very depressed, and he was Basil Dignam, a good old trouper who could have stormed through *Macbeth* while working out his tax return.

Of course, he knew something that almost no one else knew. The one person who couldn't share in the elaborate pretence that the guilt or innocence of the defendant was never predetermined was the defendant. Dignam had to know whether he had done it or not. At some stage he and the director, or perhaps the producer, or maybe even God himself, also known as Denis Forman, had quietly decided. It was still only human to hope for the best or fear the worst as the jury, recruited from members of the public and treated very much like any other jury, filed back – one of the few recording breaks allowed was to give them time for their deliberations. I remember Dignam telling me something about the feeling in the pit of his stomach as he waited. After Denis Forman had proposed making the nephew a nun, the fear had lingered with me that the whole approach to this episode was a bit lurid. But it had turned out an oddly gentle, haunting story. *The Verdict is Yours*, I decided, was the quintessence of make-believe television.

My book about it, alas, was never completed. Unwisely, I sent in the first few chapters and the project was scrapped overnight. The letter said it wasn't what they wanted. I assumed at first this was because of the aversion to the cult of personality which Granada maintained as dourly as the Soviet Union. Mr Sidney could be a bit of a character, and Mr Cecil might have liked to be, but for everyone else it was surname and one initial. And there I'd been, allotting star parts to Denis and Warren and Jim. Someone suggested to me later that the impediment was just as likely to have been Granada's eternal aspiration to be high-minded AND make a profit: secretly, they had been hoping for a TV tie-in called *The Case of the Headless Nun* or whatever, which would sell millions in paperback. if only they had told me that earlier, we might all be richer.

Experience of life

JOHN STEVENSON

One day in 1968 I was having a drink in the Film Exchange with Peter Eckersley. He was head of comedy at Granada; I was the *Daily Mail's* northern theatre critic/showbiz reporter. 'Come and have a look at this sitcom pilot we've just recorded', said Peter. It was *Her Majesty's Pleasure*, brainchild of Les Duxbury, then and for a long time after a mainstay of the *Coronation Street* writers' team.

I watched the pilot. 'See if you can think up an episode plot,' said Peter, 'and put a page of dialogue on paper.'

So that night I did, and handed it to Peter the next day, and on the spot he commissioned me to write an episode. My first script. Within three months it was written, rehearsed, recorded and transmitted.

I tell this tale to convey just how confident, optimistic and dynamic things were at Granada then. And to point the contrast with the present condition of ITV where a producer, though supported by squads of script doctors, nurses and consultants, hardly dares to make a move without the approval of higher authority – layers of it.

Back then ITV was still a teenager, the single play was in its heyday, and the Manchester studios buzzed like a beehive. Bees, mind you, with bags of attitude and ego, and no shortage of pretenders to thrones. Every bee his or her own queen. Or, as Peter used to say: 'every egg a bird.'

At that time an intake direct from universities of sharp, ambitious people was getting underway. People like the Mikes, Apted and Newell. It was Mike Newell who directed that first script, mentioned earlier. But most people in television then already had previous lives behind them.

John Finch had been teenage merchant seaman, Jacob Epstein's secretary, a manager in a heavy engineering works. Others, like Eckersley and Mike Parkinson, had been in newspapers. Many had seen war service; from Denis Forman who left a leg in Italy to Harry Kershaw who had a brilliant repertoire of surreal tales set in the sergeants' mess of the Cheshire Regiment. This was a bond between Harry and me, because when I was a soldier (of sorts, only 1950s National Service) I too saw action and suffered wounds (nasty collision with a snooker table) in the Cheshire's sergeants' mess.

This experience of life outside broadcasting had its benefits. Even allowing for a bit of those-were-the-days syndrome, I think most of today's movers and shakers are one dimension short.

I willingly grant that in the 1960s and 1970s it was much easier to be bold and confident. ITV – as the sole commercial channel – still had a licence to print money. The proliferation of channels and the fear, seeping in like damp, of high-cost failure was still in the future. There was still scope to experiment, to gamble; and if the result was a resounding flop it was not automatically death to a career. The response to a flop was – well, OK, that taught us a lesson, on to the next, and let's get it right this time.

In 1968, the year of my first script, I met Bill Podmore. After ten years as a cameraman he was now a novice director working on *Nice Time*, an off-the-wall feel-good sort of entertainment presented by Jonathan Routh,

Kenny Everett and Germaine Greer, for which I supplied the odd idea like choirs of massed ventriloquists' dummies, that kind of thing. Its producer, amazingly, was a chap called John Birt who eventually abandoned the entertainment business and joined the BBC.

There followed twenty years of working with and for Bill Podmore, on sitcoms like *Nearest and Dearest, Last of the Baskets, Brass* and – of course – *Coronation Street*.

In 1976, when Bill was pushed into producing it, the original glories of 'The Street' were faded; it was just an elderly soap, rather droopy and plodding. Bill did two things for the show: he put the comedy back in and, even more importantly, he made it a writer-led programme once again.

Bill liked and valued writers. In the rehearsal room one day on *Last of the Baskets*, Arthur Lowe invented a delicious bit of business. Pleased with himself, and wishing to needle me, he said loudly, 'We don't need writers, do we Bill?' to which Bill replied, 'Of course we don't Arthur. Not once we've got the script.'

He was seldom awe-struck by actors, especially the awkward ones. I heard some innocent ask him one day what was the nicest thing about Violet Carson. Bill thought for a moment, then said, 'Her sister.'

Under Bill 'The Street' re-entered a golden period, which even survived his retirement by a few years. The show was loved and cherished, not just by the people who wrote, acted and produced it – but also by the people who owned it.

'The Street' was cultivated, farmed if you like. Of late it has been more like open-cast mining. Four episodes a week – four and a half counting the 'specials' and hour-long episodes – hacks away both the quality, and the affection of the viewers.

And of course, each time a TV serial is made to up production by one more episode per week – there go 26 hours of something new that now will not get made.

Lost masterpieces perhaps? We'll never know.

The bear hug

KENITH TRODD

My Granada was a strange but truly memorable spell in the early 1970s just after Tony Garnett's and my pre-historic prototype in independent production, Kestrel, ended. The bulk and heart of Kestrel's output was cutting-edge drama by the best of the developing *Wednesday Play* crop – Potter, Loach, Welland, Simon Gray, Alan Clarke and Jim Allen among them. The Jim Allen piece, *The Talking Head*, had John Thaw as an overworked and over-loved soap writer trying to run away from the psychologically lethal bear hug of a paternalistic TV employer, operating on a 'you meet our deadlines, we guarantee you life' basis. In flight from the pressure and finally tracked down to a Hebrides nursing home, our hero comes to the phone to plead to his caring programme controller: 'Please leave me alone to pay for my own nervous breakdown.'

I recognised this as an affectionate if jaundiced tribute to Granada's legendary welfare attitude to its people, but when I was myself asked to come to Manchester (while conveniently and lucratively remaining London 'based'), it was clear, both contractually and emotionally, that a different relationship was on offer. Neither the bear hug nor the nursing home but a cooler assignment in every way. Granada felt they needed for quality reasons – maybe as someone was to say much later to help keep themselves honest – a taste of the brand of contemporary drama, talented and troublesome, in the streets and in your face, which Sidney Newman and James MacTaggart had introduced to the delight and disgust of the nation.

By 1970 Granada Television was gloriously awash in the champagne bathtub of its own success and mythology. *Brideshead* and *Jewel* were still around a few corners but the company had a record in devising cheap programmes that were both gems and good earners (*All our Yesterdays, University Challenge, What the Papers Say*), committed TV journalism in *World in Action*, strong drama and a local identity that was the envy of all other licence holders. Granada's banner wore unique stripes – northern, canny, Jewish, working class and yet able, when inclined, to out high-culture the snooty and constipated boulevards of the south. Everything was in that corporate mental armoury except perhaps the irony to undercut its justified pride. I remember a huge clambake in Studio 2 not long after I arrived to celebrate, was it, the 1000th or 10,000th edition of the *Street*. Sidney Bernstein himself introduced the guest of the night. 'And now I want to present a man to whom this country owes a great deal for his achievements in many fields, his wisdom, his adornment in our national life ...' And I was there in the eager throng thinking – Graham Greene? J. B. Priestley? Spender at the very least – '... My brother Cecil!' It was all very endearing if innocuously deluded and always with an admirable touch of steel.

In Granada I was beginning to feel like an anomalous guest – invited to the wrong party through the best of misunderstandings, still welcome but definitely out of place. I became aware again of that trail from the bear hug to the nursing home. Roy Battersby and I did some filming in Warsaw for my Julia Jones series *Home and Away* about a northern middle-aged woman who left home and family to find a job. Away in Poland, we'd managed to sneak in Tony Imi, a superb freelance cameraman, and now back home, in Granadaland, we wanted him again. Refusal. We were allocated a staff man. Crisis appeals, and eventually the sweetest and firmest of audiences with Denis Forman, then as now an adorable icon and role model. He pointed to the line of the matter and gently laid us on it. 'You two are birds of passage. We love to have you here, but you'll be flying onwards. We have to look after 700 people who are with us for good, nurse them through their good years and their poor ones too.'

I suppose the most typical Granadaland programme I made was Colin Welland's *Roll on Four O'Clock*, an award-winning threnody to scrap-heap modernism in a sad, heroic corner of Manchester. Welland, Battersby who again directed, and I relished making this so much that we then came up with a northern idea on a much bigger scale. This was *Leeds United*, the story of an epic strike by women in the clothing industry, and which we thought would put our collaboration with Granada up several notches. For us the project had everything – northern setting, heart-tearing and pyrrhic struggle by little people against mighty bosses; it was real and very recent, and there was a sharp political tang to our take on the story. But mysteriously the project did not thrive. Yes, they thought it was a great idea but ... Why didn't I offer Colin a 3-play deal and renew my own, with Roy in tow? We asked, couldn't we do *Leeds* first though? We were already on a roll with it. Maybe, but I have to run now and I'll catch up with you later for a jar, OK? (This was a code for oblivious rounds of champagne with brandy chasers in the Film Exchange. No work was ever discussed there.)

This limbo seemed to go on for ever and we kept up our spirits spending a lot of time at the other end of the Pennines, firming up contacts with sweatshops and back-to-backs. Most of Leeds was already making the film with us but in Manchester its future was beginning to look indefinite.

Eventually Colin, Roy and I did a terrible thing. Unable to pin down Peter Eckersley, the lovely but elusive Head of Drama, we bribed his secretary to let us hide under the office table until he returned. Then a fearsome threesome popped into vision like so many grotesque pink elephants, and the poor man could do nothing but come to the point at last. There were real tears.

Through them we learned that though they loved us, they loved *Leeds United* less, though they could not explain why (they never did) and most importantly they were desperate not to fall out. Anything but that.

In the room there were sighs of relief and of great affection and of blessed clarity at last. There was also a sound like wings being flexed. I took

Leeds United straight to the BBC and despite its horrendous scale they took it on as to the manner and mission born. It is still the film I am most proud of and it still feels like a Granada programme, not just because its stars include Lynne Perrie, Liz Dawn and half the future cast of *Coronation Street*. For we probably would never have dreamed it up at all, without going through that warm, sizzling and slightly mesmerising time between the bear hug and the nursing home.

The younger generation

CLAUDE WHATHAM

It was, I think, Denis Forman's idea. We would get young first-time playwrights and a small permanent company of actors and do a series of plays about young people and the issues that concerned them. The idea was way ahead of its time. The 1960s and the emergence of youth culture hadn't happened. The press was frankly puzzled. It was not a critical success.

The idea was revolutionary for television. The actors would be contracted for six months or so. It had to be made worth their while to make that sort of commitment. So they would appear in all the plays and in a variety of characters. They were guaranteed a main leading role, at least one substantial supporting role and play 'as cast' in the remaining plays (which could be quite a good cameo role or virtually a walk-on). Peter Wildeblood became Producer. He was a writer and journalist and had been imprisoned for his involvement in a high-profile homosexual prosecution. His book *Against the Law* about the case was the first sympathetic book about homosexuality to be widely acclaimed. I believe this was his first production.

Gordon Flemyng and I were the two permanent directors. We each did three plays and two other directors directed a play each. Peter found the writers. Most were either unknown or unproduced – and all young. The first play was by Patrick Garland, then still an undergraduate. Another was by the poet Adrian Mitchell, who had never written a play before.

Whilst Peter worked with the writers Gordon and I searched for a cast with Margaret Morris – a casting director with an uncanny ability to find talent (she cast both Michael Caine and Richard Harris in their first leading roles on television in Granada productions). We interviewed hundreds of young actors. We were very lucky with the ten we chose. All gave beautiful performances and most went on to have fine careers – not always in acting. John Thaw gave his first TV performance in the series and became probably the most famous face on television. Ronnie Lacey became the archetypal sinister film villain in the Bond movies. Judy Cornwell has grown in size as Hyacinth's sister in the comedy series *Keeping Up Appearances* – but has also written two novels. Johnnie Briggs is Mike Baldwin in *Coronation Street*.

Bill Douglas left acting and became a film director. He only made four films – including his autobiographical *Trilogy* – but after his recent death he has been recognised as one of the finest film makers Britain has produced. A Centre for Film Studies named after him opened at Exeter University in 1997.

The company brought an ensemble style of playing unusual in TV drama. They were a very close team. And two sets of couples got married! If the plays had been produced even two years later I have little doubt they would have been a sensation. But they were just too early.

The opening play gave me the most excitement I ever had in a studio. And one of the others gave me my worst and most embarrassing moment. I had just finished the dress rehearsal of this delicate heart-rending little tragedy ... I looked round for comments from Peter Wildeblood and the young female playwright ... a silence. Then Peter said, 'There is nothing that I can say that will do any good at this stage.' And he left the control room. It wasn't meant to be a tragedy, you see. It was supposed to be a comedy ...

The hindsight saga

PETER WILDEBLOOD

It was at Banff, 6000 feet up in the rocky mountains, where I finally realised that the Canadian Broadcasting Corporation was never going to be a substitute for Granada. The International Television Festival was ending with a magnificent seafood buffet supper. Behind me in the queue a producer I knew was talking to a high-ranking CBC woman executive. He introduced us, and in a voice as cold as the mountain lobsters and prawns confronting us she remarked, 'Oh yes, I've heard of you.' This after I'd been working for the Corporation for eleven years.

So different from the Granada canteen in 1958, where Sidney Bernstein often stood in line and the menu offered Eccles cakes and black pudding. These did not really go with Sidney's personality, but having been lucky enough to land the Independent Television franchise for Manchester he probably felt some gesture towards provincialism was called for. The Eccles cakes and black pudding, however, harmonised nicely with the way the future Lord Bernstein and his brother habitually referred to each other as 'Mr Sidney' and 'Mr Cecil'.

The company's rather silly name needs a word of explanation. The Bernstein millions had been made in film exhibition, with a chain of cinemas in suburban London. These were famous for the extravagance of their decoration, each being done up in an individual style, from Oriental to Tudor to Medieval Castle. The jewel in the crown of the Bernstein raj was their Arabian Nights picture palace with its fountains and minarets and Moorish washrooms, the Granada Tooting.

All the same, Granada's programme output was anything but suburban. One of the earliest successes was a series of Jacobean plays. This may, of course, have had something to do with the fact that at that time there were only three TV channels, so it was a choice between Mozart, Muffin the Mule and the Duchess of Malfi. If the ratings were not good, Sidney had the answer to that too. 'It is not polite,' he would tell the shareholders, 'to talk to people in a language they cannot understand'.

One of the problems at the beginning was the shortage of experienced TV directors. There were very few in Britain, and the BBC had most of them under contract. Not being able to compete with American salaries, Granada did the next best think and hired half a dozen Canadians, who were as experienced in television drama as anyone in the world. In my fledgling years I learned most of my craft from directors like Silvio Narizzano and Henry Kaplan.

My role model as a producer, and later a writer-producer, was unquestionably Philip Mackie. The coolest of the cool, he appeared to lead a calm civilised life, with a flat in the Adelphi and a Gloucestershire manse which he shared with his wife and four pretty daughters. A gentleman of the Regency, you might have thought; but in fact Philip was a demonic worker who spun off interlocking one-hour stories with the dexterity of a Scheherazade. One typically neat idea was a series called *The Liars*, about a family swapping stories of allegedly true, though improbable, experiences. These tales were all adapted from short stories by such as R. L. Stevenson, Lord Dunsany and Guy de Maupassant.

I could not always match Philip's composure under stress. I remember one day when everything was collapsing around me and disaster threatened on every side, and I fled into Cecil Bernstein's office gibbering and shaking. Looking up from his desk, 'Peter,' he said, 'it's only television'.

Those were the days, of course, when television was truly live: there was no videotaping and the audience saw the performance as it was given, warts and all. If a flustered actor skipped half a page, the rest of the cast had to be given urgent hand signals to get them to talk more slowly.

To make matters still more harrowing, I produced for several years the series of improvised trials called *The Verdict is Yours*. These produced some remarkable performances, but caused great havoc among actors. Thorley Walters was accused of holding an onion in his handkerchief to produce real tears, Geoffrey Hibbert had to have massive vitamin injections. The story goes that Gretchen Franklin, arriving early, followed the signs to the canteen and ordered toast and coffee. Mildly surprised at the number of costumed extras engaged by Granada, and unaware that she had strayed into the new Manchester law courts, she went to the reception desk and asked where her dressing room was. That, she was told, depended on whether she was a witness or a member of the Jury. 'Neither', she replied demurely. 'I'm the murderess.'

Another innovative programme of those years was *The Younger Generation*, which brought together television's first (and perhaps only) repertory company of eight young performers, in original plays by young writers. Among them was the 20-year-old John Thaw. The writers Michael Hastings and Robin Chapman are still going strong after more than forty years.

Where did it come from, the extraordinary combination of zest and taste that was the old Granada? Partly, of course, from Sidney Bernstein but also in large measure from the Controller of Programmes, Denis Forman. Once he had given the green light to a project he backed it with the full force of his energy, influence and charm. He looked pretty good to me then; but now, after working for two other major television companies, I can see that he was unique.

Yes, Granada was a rather silly name. I'd have called it Camelot.

My most exciting years

VICTORIA WOOD OBE

I was first employed by Granada in the mid-1970s. Joan Bakewell was presenting a women's programme called *Pandora's Box* and I wrote and performed the songs for it. It was deadly, but not quite as deadly as *That's Life* and the chips were better.

My first proper job came early in 1979 when Peter Eckersley, Head of Drama, bought my play *Talent* which had just been performed at the Crucible Theatre, Sheffield. He had told the director, Baz Taylor, that he thought there might be a television play in there somewhere.

The few years I had at Granada working with Peter were the most exciting of my professional career. Peter's expertise, his love of words, his innate sense of what would and wouldn't work, his skill as a script editor, and his encouragement were all a real inspiration to me. It was the first time since I had been in television that I was being helped without being patronised. He was also a real laugh, and I treasure the memory of many evenings we spent together in the lounge of the Midland Hotel, though, because I was always drunk, they are not memories I actually remember.

My impression of Granada then was that it was full of very witty, bolshie, hard-drinking men who laughed and shouted a lot, and were absolutely dedicated to television. It was the sort of place where the woman in charge of the mashed potatoes in the canteen was more intimidating than the executives.

I did three plays at Granada with Peter – and the pilot for *Wood and Walters*. We did the series of *Wood and Walters* the month after Peter died, and it was complete chaos. Partly because someone else had to be drafted in at the last minute to produce it, and partly because for some reason the Comedy Department at Granada was much more hopeless than the Drama Department. We seemed always to be finding ourselves in the wrong costumes, on the wrong set, in front of the wrong audience. We would be frantically adjusting our wigs and shouting, 'The next sketch is set in a boutique!' and the audience, who had turned up hoping to see Russell Harty would be banging their hearing aids and quavering 'What's a boutique?'

Peter Eckersley was Granada to me, and I lost heart after he died, and didn't do any more big work there. I filmed there a few years ago for the *South Bank Show*, and was standing outside the front entrance with the film crew. One of those women that hang about Granada hoping to see stars came over to us. 'Is it anybody?' she said. I said no, it wasn't anybody. 'Thought not', she said, and walked away.

THE
ILLUSTRATIONS

1 Sidney Bernstein on the roof of Granada Studios in 1963

2 Cecil Bernstein: the power behind much of Granada's light entertainment and comedy

3 Party time on *The Street*. Clockwise from left: Bill Podmore, Barry Hill, Helen Worth, David Plowright, Adele Rose, Harry Kershaw, Jean Alexander

4 *The Jewel in the Crown* proves successful at the 1985 BAFTAS.
Left to right: Tim Pigott-Smith, Christopher Morahan, Dame Peggy Ashcroft, Jim O'Brien

5 Programme meeting for *What the Papers Say*. The people shown, clockwise round the table from top left:
Paul Vickers (researcher), Eric Harrison (director), Gill Blunk (PA), Roy Hattersley (performer),
Brian Armstrong (producer), Floor manager (unknown), Irene (unknown surname, Autocue operator),
Peter Wheeler (voice), Delia Corrie (voice), David Mahlowe (voice)

6 Eric Harrison,
director, talking to
Fred Friendly and
Denis Forman during
production of
Hypotheticals, c.1980
from Chester

7 Meeting of the *World in Action* team in 1963, possibly at the time of the Profumo affair. Clockwise from the top of the table: Clare Bradley (secretary, standing with teapot), Tim Hewat (producer in charge), Liz Sutherland (PA), Michael Shanks (consultant), Stephen Peet (producer/director), Peter Heinze (chief film editor), Alex Valentine (producer/director), David Floyd (consultant), (man with his back to the camera is possibly Reg Sutton, sound recordist), Clare Ash (researcher), Bill Grundy (producer), Duncan Crowe, Douglas Keay (producer/writer). Not present at the meeting were: Mike Wooller producer/director), Diane Farris (researcher) and Dick Fontaine (researcher)

8 Banff TV Festival 1985, on the Award of Excellence to Granada Television. From left to right: Michael Cox, Gus Macdonald, David Plowright, Leslie Woodhead, Barrie Heads

9 John Finch with the 52 scripts of *A Family at War*, of which he wrote thirty and edited the rest (*c.*1973)

10 *A Family at War* title background ...

Ashton-serien i fjernsynet er forbi.

Skal gammelt venskab rent forgå ...

11 ... affects Scandinavia

12 Johnnie Hamp with 'one of the new groups'

13 JH making sure Bernard Manning keeps his promise to refrain from rude jokes on *The Comedians*

14 JH teaching Burt
Bacharach how to write
hit songs in 1965

15 Jerry Lee Lewis
performing on *Whole Lotta
Shakin' Goin' On* in 1963

16 *The Comedians*, 1972 (*The Comedians*, 1971–85). From top: Mike Reid, Bryn Phillips, Jim Bowen,
Ken Goodwin, Colin Crompton, George Roper, Bernard Manning, Duggie Brown, Johnnie Hamp (producer)

17 A film stars jazz band from *Scene at 6.30*, with among others, Terry Thomas on guitar

18 Eric Harrison's daughters (Jackie and Christina) and Alan Rothwell's sons with Humphry Cushion during filming of *Hickory House*, 1973. The performers on the show were Amanda Barrie and Alan Rothwell; both stalwarts on *Coronation Street* (in the 60s and the 80s respectively)

19 Elaine Grand with 'Charles', the cookery expert and another guest on *Sharp at Four*

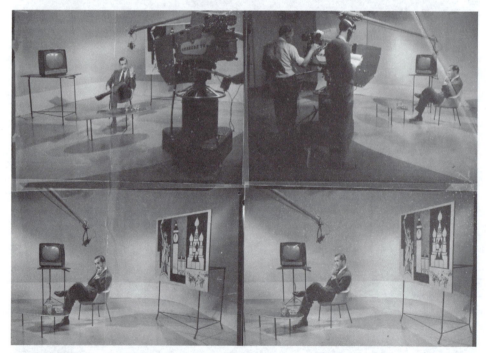

20 Edward R. Murrow giving the second of the Granada Lectures in October 1959. Murrow's subject was 'Television and Politics'. He said: 'The eye of the camera should pursue the politician to the very limits of privacy and decency. When the politicians complain, as they have in several countries, that television turns their proceedings into a circus, it should be made clear that the circus was already there. Television has merely demonstrated that not all the performers are well-trained.'

21 Sir Neville Cardus in the Long Room at Lords cricket ground (1969), rehearsing for a series he presented. With him are Peter Jones (director) and Marjorie Giles (producer)

22 Looking through the door of No. 10 during filming for the *World in Action* broadcast with Harold Wilson. The Home Office changed the picture behind the Prime Minister prior to the broadcast from a Turner to a Lowry to 'make it look more northern'

TECHNICAL REQUIREMENTS

TO *Director* E HARRISON ☐, *Engineering Office* ☐, *Racks* ☐, *Sound* ☐, *Production Office & File* ☐

PROGRAMME TITLE MARATHON LEEDS PROD. NO. JB 353 STUDIO

XM or VTR Date: 22/23/24 & 25 March 1966 Studio Rehearsal Date

A: STANDARD FACILITIES

STUDIOS 2 AND 6		STUDIO 2	STUDIO 6	STUDIO 4	
P.D.3 Mounts	3 Tape Machines	3 Cameras	4 Cameras	3 Cameras	1 Tape Machine
2", 3", 5" and 8" Lenses	Echo	3 C.28 Mics.	3 C.28 Mics.	P.D.3 Mounts	Echo
6 Slung Monitors	Distort	3 D.25 Mics.	5 D.25 Mics.	2", 3", 5" and 8" Lenses	Distort
Cue Dot	Foldback	3 STC 4033 Mics.	5 STC 4033 Mics.	1 21" Monitor	Foldback
2 Standard Booms	Public Address		1 C.12 Mic.	1 14" Monitor	5 C.28 Mics.
1 360° Boom			Second 360° Boom	Cue Dot	1 D.24 Mic.
2 Gram Decks			(Mon. to Wed. only)	2 Gram Decks	3 BK6 Mics.

B: ORDER ADDITIONAL STOCK FACILITIES

VISION		SOUND		VEHICLES	Licence No.
3 Cameras	Pye	10 Mics.	Reslo Ribbon	TE1 Travelling Eyes	XTF 313
2 Lenses	10:1 Zooms	2 Mics.	Neck	M.V.R.—1 cam/2 cam	
Box 1 Lenses	3,5,8 & 12 inch	Mics.		Eagle Towers	
Lenses		Mics.		Links	
Lenses		4 Head Phones		Landrovers	
Vinten Pedestals		1 Deaf Aid	Long Lead	Tenders	
Vinten Pathfinder		2 Tape Rec.—Speeds	10 hours audio tape 7½ IPS	1 15 KVA Gen.	Noisy
M.R. Academy		Miniboom		15 KVA Gen. (Silent)	
M.R. Dolly		Fish Poles		7½ KVA Gen.	
Mitchell		GENERAL	2 x Barron Boxes		
Cinderella		Genlock		OTHER REQUIREMENTS	
Debrie		T/C Insert		3 x 8" Peto Scott Monitors	
Proctors		VTR Insert		1 x Conference Stand	
Moy Men		VTR Editing		1 x Flashing Cue Light	
Tripods		Aldis Slide/+ operator		QX: L Collison, Maint	
Skids		Stand/+ operator			
Long Persistance Monitor		Back/+ operator			
		Cellomatic/+ operator			

C: HIRE, NON-STOCK FACILITIES *(Budget approval required)*;
REMARKS:

3 x Red Arrow ITV/BBC Offair Receivers with standby engineers
1200/1500 daily. Instal Monday 21st am.

23 Planning sheet for *Marathon* in Leeds, during the General Election of 1966. Note that the monitors would be supplied by Red Arrow, the forerunner of Granada Rental

24 Paddy Owen, Transmission Controller, in the Granada Central Control room

25 Brian Armstrong at the desk of *Scene at 6.30*

26a–e   SOME WRITERS

a   Stan Barstow with pipe...

b   Jack Rosenthal of the Granada Football
Team... and occasional writer

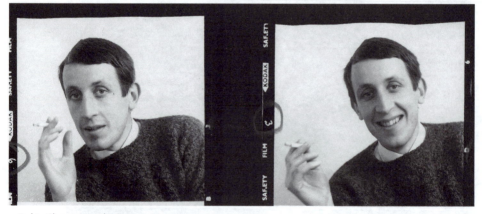

c   Robin Chapman with cigarette..

d Alan Plater with typewriter (*c.*1968)

e Roger Brierley, Julie Walters and Victoria Wood dancing in a studio corridor

27a–d SOME DIRECTORS

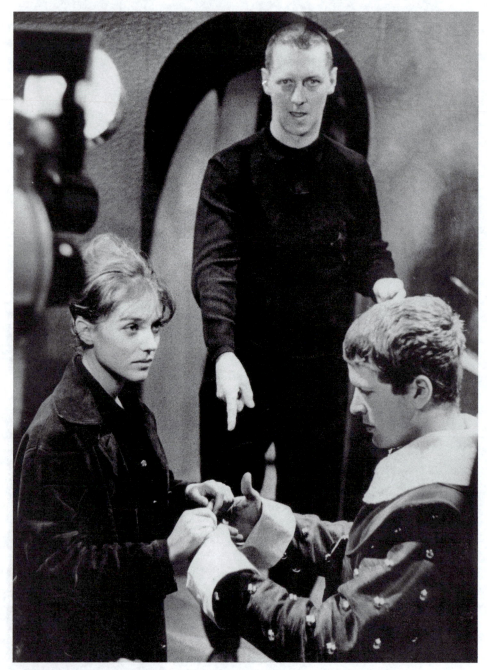

a Derek Bennett directing an unknown piece with some intensity

b Peter Mullings
(after Eisenstein)

c Richard Everitt

d *The Lark* by Jean Anouilh, 1962. Director, Claude Whatham, is *not* being lynched, just standing in for Joan of Arc at the stake

28a–f SOME PRODUCERS

a David Boulton

b Steve Hawes

c Mike Scott

d Mike Wooller (behind Harold Wilson)

e Peter Eckersley

f Philip Mackie

REMEMBERED

Peter Eckersley

Jack Rosenthal CBE

I can think of no one I knew who was more respected and loved than Peter. My own feelings about him are simple: younger than me though he was, I always felt that he was the man I'd like to be when I grew up. Probably because he'd got the whole impossible business of being a man so absolutely, so joyfully right.

Whatever work I did, his approval mattered the most. A pat on the back from Peter meant more than coming first in the ratings. Even when he was critical you felt he'd given you a bag of toffee. Inevitably, whatever work I do is still be governed by the criteria he set. If it's right for Peter, it'll be right.

He was, quite simply, the most knowledgeable man I'd ever met; the most intelligent and, in its true sense, the most educated. But he wasn't just a pretty forehead. Inside it may have been the most massive encyclopaedia I've ever dipped into, but it was also the warmest and the wittiest. And it was made all the wiser because he, himself, took everything with a pinch of Eckersley salt. It was really half encyclopaedia, half Bumper Fun Book. So, naturally, my memories of him are mostly memories that made me laugh.

We used to sit opposite each other across two desks in an office on the fifth floor, producing comedy shows. That was often a comedy show in itself; we were the best audience we ever had. Peter always warned, 'It'll end in tears.' In this case it usually did, with him shaking with laughter, poking a handkerchief under his glasses to dry his eyes. In the Happy Hour around lunchtime, Margaret Ogden used to chance her leg at teaching us Greek dancing. Or, in Peter's case, Greek laughing. It's the only thing he wasn't better at than me, and I was pathetic.

In the early 1960s, Peter was one of a rabble of seven writers called Group North. We used to huddle round a freezing fire in the Pineapple to discuss Life and Art. Or, more often, to tell jokes and moan.

Eventually we decided to disband, and held a meeting to resolve what to do with the £300 of our combined subs still left in the kitty. There were noble suggestions like giving it to an old couple for Christmas or to a young couple just starting out in life, and not-so-noble ones like renting a flat to entertain chorus girls from the Opera House in. Then Peter, of all people, made the most iniquitous proposal of all: that we should set up a Writing School to exploit little old ladies from Newton-le-Willows who wanted to learn to write for television. I couldn't believe it was Peter talking. All six of us bitterly argued against him; but the more heated we got, the more cynical and adamant – and eloquent – he became. At the end of a long night, minutes before closing time, three of us were still violently against him – but he and his silver tongue had swung three in his favour. Peter held the casting vote. He got to his feet, said it was a grotesque idea, that he was appalled it had even been proposed – and voted against it. He then collapsed in laughter, dried his eyes and went home. It was the best night Group North ever had.

Peter's great regret was that we lived in an age and a city that had forgotten the pleasures of café society. But, as the years went by, he established his own. He and the closest of his friends and most kindred of spirit became their own café society. Peter, Arthur Hopcraft, John Stevenson, Mike Murphy, Di Bramwell, Paddy Owen, Roy Shipperbottom and others talked and laughed Life and Art into a cocked hat. Witticism for witticism, I'd bet that their corner of the Film Exchange left the Algonquin Round Table without a leg to stand on.

I once went in and saw Peter and John standing together in silence. I asked Peter what they were doing. 'Ssshh!,' he said, 'We're in a BBC documentary. It's called *The Disappearing World*.'

TV drama was significantly shaped and sharpened by his talents, by his judgement – and by the man himself. So were all of us who worked in it with him. Even his vocabulary rubbed off. Hear any of us talk – and he's in there somewhere. As a writer, I believe he was the best of us all. As a producer, he brought out the best out of us.

I once told him I wanted to write a play. 'All right,' he said, 'What you'll need is a pen.' I told him my mind had gone blank. 'All right,' he said, 'Write about yourself.' My mind went blanker. He then told me to tell him the story of my life, beginning at birth. I got as far as being evacuated as a kid in the war, when he stopped me. 'There's the play,' he said, 'I'll lend you the pen.' The play changed my whole career. Which means he did.

As colossal as his sense of humour, his sense of irony, was his compassion and a unique humanity. One day in 1967, we were working at our desks when news broke of the Arab–Israeli war. On the corridor of the fifth floor, small groups congregated, arguing about who'd started it, who'd finish it, what was happening. Peter stayed in the office, lay down full-length on his desk like Lowry's *Man Lying on a Wall* saying over and over again, 'What's happening is that kids are being killed. Arab kids and Israeli kids. The kids they've gone to war to give a better life to. That's what's happening.'

His courage in being himself and true to himself we saw every day. It was only in later days that we learnt of his physical courage. Days before he died he was once again lying full-length; this time in a hospital bed, desperately ill and in great pain. Sue Jolly told me that when Anne came to visit him she asked was there anything she could get him. He was so ill he could hardly speak. When he did, he said, 'There's a very nice blue handbag in Kendal's.'

As a man of television, he was prodigious. As a man he was a triumph. He always seemed to know when shrugging your shoulders is better than clenching your fists, when toughness is better than tolerance, when people come first or a principle comes first. He knew how to be a man, and always acted like one. To me, this is what lives on after him, above all else; and why he's still the man I want to be when I grow up.

'A prince among men' was Peter's favourite tribute. And that's exactly what he was.

Gerry Hagan

JOHN STRETCH

Although he wore his learning very lightly, what struck me most about Gerry was his erudition. When I arrived at Granada in 1968, full of the smug confidence of youth, I felt that I already knew most of what there was to know, but it soon became apparent that it was difficult to mention a writer, painter, musician (apart from Jazz musicians, about whom he knew rather less that the average person of his generation), choreographer or film or theatre producer about whom he didn't know far more than I did.

He was also a great ideas-man and extremely helpful. It was often difficult to get a word with him as there was a constant stream of producers, directors, researchers and designers visiting his office for advice and encouragement. In fact I used secretly to think of his very small office as 'the confessional'. This was when he was running the Reference Library, but the pattern continued after he moved to the Script Department, with the addition of writers to his clientele.

When eventually I followed Gerry to the Script Department I was at first bewildered by the names he kept firing at me as I desperately tried to remember which writer was represented by which agency. Gerry's memory was so fantastically good that he genuinely couldn't see the difficulty. Matters weren't made any easier by the fact that the names he dropped tended to be first names, and sometimes pretty oblique ones at that. 'Edna' was Edna O'Brien, of course, that was easy, but 'Anna' was probably Alice Thomas Ellis, 'Harry' might well be Jack Higgins, while 'Jack' was more likely to be Hugh Leonard.

I remember one day I put my hand over the telephone mouthpiece and gleefully told him 'There's a man on the telephone who says his name is Jasper Parrott!'. 'Give me that telephone at once', he hissed, 'That's Andre Previn's agent!' and it was.

Although he was never much of a one for jokes as such (i.e. there were these two fellers, etc.), he usually had something funny to relate which had actually happened to him. These were often stories against himself. For example, when he represented Granada at North West Arts there was another committee member called Tom. Gerry was overjoyed when, in the middle of a very serious discussion, someone chipped in with, 'Well, I agree with Tom and Gerry.'

For a long time Gerry travelled to Southport every evening by train to see his mother, who was dying in a hospice. Even in these distressing circumstances he found something to amuse him, finding the overheard remarks of other train passengers and hospice patients and visitors worthy of Alan Bennett. Gerry's mother was sharing a room with another lady, who one evening remarked in a stage whisper, 'She's an R.C., you know.' 'Yes', replied her visitor, 'they get in everywhere, don't they?'

For a long time Gerry worked away in his spare time on a projected book about the Hollywood musical, and actually managed to interview Gene Kelly at his Beverley Hills house. One day, to his horror, he opened 'The Bookseller' to find an announcement that the book, on which he'd barely started, was going to be published in about three months' time. Eventually, pressure of Granada work meant that he had virtually no spare time, so he put off completing his book until after his retirement, and sadly, as far as I know, it was never completed, unless the manuscript is still lying around somewhere among his papers.

Outwardly frivolous, he really took life very seriously, and his religious beliefs, which I couldn't share, were at the heart of his thinking. Even so, we liked and respected each other, and kept in touch after we had both left Granada. He last telephoned me just a few weeks before he died, apparently about nothing in particular. We just gossiped and had a laugh. Perhaps he was saying goodbye, I don't know.

Harry Kershaw

JACK ROSENTHAL CBE

In 1961, two writers changed my life. One was Tony Warren who gave birth to a precociously-bouncing baby christened *Coronation Street*, the other was Harry Kershaw who, if not its midwife, certainly became its post-natal social worker, guardian uncle and guardian angel.

After the opening episodes had been transmitted, I rang Tony to congratulate him. He told me that Granada now thought the serial might (just possibly) run a few more weeks than the six they had originally planned and that they were looking for additional writers; that if I felt this street was up mine, I should call the producer, Harry Kershaw, and ask if I might do a 'test' half-episode. I did and Harry said yes. I passed the test and he commissioned me to write Episode 30. As with so many other writers he'd scouted – among them Jim Allen, Peter Eckersley, Geoff Lancashire, John Finch, Adele Rose – he became my tutor and mentor. He let us play in his Street and taught us the rules of the game before we moved to the big, wide world outside.

As writer, script-editor and producer, Harry K. became synonymous with 'The Street', gradually becoming beloved godfather to an enormous family of actors, directors and fellow-writers. He lived and breathed the show. To him *this* was the big, wide world outside. He loved it and made it impossible for us not to.

The only time he really solicited our help was Friday nights when Stockport County were playing at home. A non-driver, he needed a lift to the ground. And he got it. As all football-lovers secretly know – it's the fans who support the Stockport Counties of this world who are the real football-lovers.

He was unlike any other writer I've ever met. For a start, he wore a suit and tie and a colonel's moustache. As if that wasn't wild enough, he also wore a smiling genial air of calm contagious confidence. Of all things. For unflappability, he made Harold Macmillan look like a panic-stricken Woody Allen. He was our Man-from-the-Pru guru; a gentle man and a gentleman. His unselfish generosity of ideas to all of us should have got him drummed out of the Writers' Guild.

Writers aren't too keen on script editors who want to change lines. But Harry (another unpardonable sin) wanted to change them for the better. The one time I really dug in my heels insisting that the line change he was suggesting was wrong – and even Harry's bonhomie was beginning to fray – his phone rang. It was a director in the rehearsal room running through a script Harry had written. telling him that one of his lines didn't make sense. For a fraction of a second, I though Harry Jekyll might turn into Harry Hyde, like the rest of us. But no. 'What line's that, then?' he asked. 'Page 7, fourth line down.' Harry flicked through his script and said, 'Ah. The typing pool's missed out the question mark. Read it with a question mark at the end.' The director did and, eureka, the line made sense. Harry put the phone down and turned back to me. 'Bloody directors', he muttered. 'Bad as typists.' Then he smiled and added, 'And script-editors. Go on, leave your line as it is. You know best.' Two minutes later we'd changed my line to the one he wanted.

Harry wrote and produced many other quality shows, but *Coronation Street* is his monument. He dug its foundations 42 years ago and built and buttressed it into the longest-running, most successful TV show ever.

Harry K. was a diplomat, an artist, a motivator, an executive and one-of-the-lads, a peace-maker and a pace-maker – all rolled into one.

If he'd have been the player-manager of Stockport County, it's a fair bet they'd have won the First Division Championship, the FA Cup and the European Cup 31 (?) times. Quietly and calmly and without a single yellow card.

Philip Mackie

DEREK BENNETT

Mackie was the ideal producer, urbane, civilised, totally unflappable. He believed in obtaining the best ingredients, writers, actors and directors, mixing them well and leaving them. He would appear, always smiling, to taste the results a little, and if he needed to add seasoning the smile broadened as he did so. He was also a most generous provider of food and drink.

Two memories: we once attended a very much lauded production of *Hamlet* at the Round House. I found it dull and wrongly conceived. Mackie must have thought so earlier than I did and after fifteen minutes or so his head fell on my shoulder and I was certain he was asleep. He remained like this for the rest of the performance – waking up to down a large gin and tonic in the interval – yet as we left the theatre he launched into a detailed criticism of the production that lasted very precisely through getting into the car, driving to Soho, parking and entering a restaurant for supper.

I couldn't fault his review, I know he hadn't seen the production before and I could have sworn he'd been fast asleep for most of the previous three hours.

Mackie produced a series of adaptations of stories by de Maupassant. I directed several of them and one, due towards the end of the group, I thought wrongly chosen. It was too well known and the adaptation was dull and consisted mainly of narration. Mackie, smiling as ever, wouldn't hear of any changes. I kept on moaning but was more or less resigned.

A few days before we should have begun casting and designing for this episode I went into his office and found him scribbling away with several volumes of de Maupassant, in French, in front of him. 'You may be right about *The Pearl* he said. 'Anyway dear boy, can't have you grumbling all over the place.'

I went behind the desk and saw that he was adapting a totally different story, directly from the French, into dialogue form, with stage directions as necessary, and he continued to do so while discussing where he might like to eat that night.

The adaptation was successful and I doubt whether much of that first draft was ever changed.

COMEDY
AND MUSIC

A base occupation

Brian Armstrong

There is nothing so base as trying to make the English laugh.
(Malcolm Muggeridge on stepping down as Editor of *Punch*)

With the advantage of hindsight, I can now see that there were two premonitions that my television career would slide inexorably into comedy.

The first came in 1967. I was busy with *World in Action* when I was asked to help out a younger chap on a programme called *Nice Time* – a light-hearted frolic led by Germaine Greer, Jonathan Routh and Kenny Everitt. This improbable triad presented a macédoine of sketches, one-liners, wannabe stand-up comics, unusual turns, little drolleries and similar harmless joys.

So I found myself auditioning – with the younger chap, a large, beaming lad called John Birt – a line-up of musical head-knockers, whose pastime it was to fashion tunes in a most singular manner. They rapped themselves smartly on the top of their heads while opening their mouths like fishes to make different notes. These deviants – standing in line in a cheerless committee room – thought their tunes to be instantly recognisable, a fallacy enthusiastically shared by the future Director-General of the BBC. I ventured to disagree ... 'I can't make out any tunes at all.' Young JB twitched like the hazel twig of divination. 'You've got to have an ear for music,' he pronounced. You can see why he became a strategic thinker for New Labour.

The second premonition came a little later in my *World in Action* years. I was in Prague for the Russian invasion of Czechoslovakia in 1968. I had thought I might have to appear on Intervision with a live, to-camera report – so I borrowed a little number from Granada's wardrobe department before I left Manchester. It was a hacking jacket in an audacious shade of dark gamboge. Twinned with my solitary Burton's tie, it made me look sincere.

I had been in the middle of mayhem for three days – sullen gunfire on the horizon, the squeal of heavy caterpillar treads on tarmac, tanks outside the hotel window, Kalashnikovs in nervous hands – you know what invasions are like – when the phone rang in my hotel room on my third anxious evening. It was a call from Granada, Manchester, England. How on earth did they get through, I thought, as the line crackled. It was May, Head of Wardrobe.

'Can I have Albert Tatlock's best jacket back immediately?'

'But, May ...' I began. 'No, it's no use you pretending, Brian. I know you've got it. In the storyline he's going to a reunion and he needs it.'

Clearly, the muse of comedy was padding behind me. Did I heed these warnings? I did not. I went on making current affairs and documentaries with their occasional rum upshots. I was manhandled by the IRA on the Lower Falls, tear-gassed in Washington, tracked by the Shah's secret police in Iran, stoned by malcontents in Calcutta, declared *persona non grata* in Eastern Europe – innocent, happy years, five in all.

I made a drama series set in Ireland called *The Sinners*. Then I was offered Comedy – or, at least, subtly drawn into it by way of *Coronation Street*. My elevation coincided with that of John Hamp, who became Head of Light Entertainment. Inevitably, I was dubbed 'Head of Heavy Entertainment'. Unsolicited scripts thudded ponderously on to my desk immediately. Some, I felt sure, were from senior Granada management, writing under noms de plume. They were uniformly dreadful.

I quickly learned another thing about comedy – that it is with some justification seen to be the mine-strewn no man's land of television. The band-width of response was so wide that I rapidly minted a new verb, born of bitter experience and conjugated thus: I am laughing, you are sniggering, he is snorting and they are ringing up to complain.

I also knew that Granada had a long and honourable comic tradition at the end of the pier, and that since we began in 1956 we had made situation comedies clearly as long as they were broad. Our past Stakhanovite endeavours unnerved me, frankly. What enormous self-confidence had we shown, what vitality, what brio! *The Army Game* notched up 153 episodes. *Bootsie and Snudge* – 100, *Mess Mates* – 50, *Nearest and Dearest* – 47. What giants of the past were these, to which I had been asked to bring 'something new'. And the most vexatious conundrum of all – what is comedy?

I began to collect critical gems from the reviewers, those sabre-toothed tigers lurking in the popular prints. I cherished the observation of Nancy Banks-Smith on the last-named series – 'a rich brown frolic of beer, pickles, dentures, shortcomings, breaches of the peace and ripe smells'.

No one seemed to know what was funny, although many opined that 'that'll get a laugh' as they ticked the punchlines in a script. I recall an early IBA seminar – held in Sheffield, on some ironist whim – addressed by Denis Norden, who told us of his association with Frank Muir in this field. They were engaged by the BBC as consultants and advisers on comedy (they were known as 'C & As'). Quite soon, they were despatched to America to see what comic tails were wagging there.

The first problem was Frank's height. Apparently, in America, if you're tall, you're a director. Writers are short people. 'Oh, no, you can't be a writer,' he was continually being told. Anyway, they found themselves at a party with Mel Brooks and introduced themselves as the BBC's consultants and advisers on comedy. A wide-eyed Brooks gazed at them in awe, took them to a corner and whispered, 'You mean ... you know?'

At the same meeting, Denis uttered the sombre statistics which he claimed were unvarying. 'If you set out to make six series a year, one will be OK, one will be the melon of all time and four will be nothing much to write home about.'

I laboured for ten years in comedy, and now wage-free, look back with no regrets. I entertain a slight – a very slight – frisson of melancholy over some shows which never reached the screen, either because they were stillborn, or because I thought the nation wasn't quite ready for them. Among many others, now sleeping peacefully in dusty archives, there was *All the Queen's Men* – a romp about the covert operations of a wholly homosexual unit of the British Army in the Second World War. I can recall only one deathless line: 'What with all these route marches and invasion training I've barely had time to do the ironing!' There was the notion, tentatively floated, about a man who lived in a very large fridge belonging to an argumentative couple, who emerged to solve their weekly domestic fracas with witty remarks. ('This fills me with a dreadful unease,' noted David Plowright in the margin.) There was *Rock*, the working title for a series celebrating the droll pranks of a hermaphrodite living in Blackpool. It would doubtless go down a storm now.

Of the two hundred and more shows which were made in my time at the comic helm, I now remember – like a sundial recording only the sunny hours – those characters and incidents which have been sieved through selective memory. There was that well-read gentleman Bill Fraser, of *Bootsie and Snudge*, who wanted me to undertake the adaptation of his favourite novel, *John MacNab* by John Buchan. 'And don't make it funny,' this very funny man begged dolefully. There was Dinsdale Landon, who invented for his lead role in *Devenish* a snort copied in pubs the length of the land; it sounded like – again quoting Nancy – 'a dead body being pulled from a bog'. There was the splendid Iain Cuthbertson as the beleaguered actor-manager in *Rep*, a series set in the now-vanished world of the travelling repertory company. I can hear his repeated lament now; 'I've seen brighter horizons in Macclesfield.'

There was Harry Kershaw's long-running *Leave It to Charlie*, and Geoffrey Lancashire's wonderfully engaging *Cuckoo Waltz* – over fifty episodes between them, and every one in the Top Ten. There was the much-missed Beryl Reid, magical in *Nanny Knows Best*, which sadly never ran to a series. There was Paul Dawkins, an actor whose green-room hobby roused my curiosity. He was writing out the Bible in big, inch-high letters on rolls of lining paper. I asked him what he was going to do with this magnum opus. 'Paper the hall when I get home,' he said. He meant it. Truly, comedy has some strange by-ways.

I remember also a neat and scrubbed Gregor Fisher alongside Diane Keen in *Foxy Lady*, long before his apotheosis as the string-vested sage Rab C. Nesbit. And Stratford Johns as the ermined trade union baron lording it over *Union Castle*. And most of all I remember the shining and unmatched talent of Victoria Wood in *Woods and Walters*.

In my time, Granada was home to all of these, and many more. And, as I once wrote in a paper to the Programme Committee under Denis Forman (a man of legendary tolerance), home is the place where you hang your hat. And, I added, when it is ruled by that fickle and akimboed minx, comedy, the place where sometimes – just sometimes – you hang your head.

Comedy is a ghastly business.
                              (Peter McKay, on stepping down as editor of *Punch*)

The advantage of being a bus driver

MICHAEL COX

As a novice programme director in the 1960s, one was expected to do everything. This was called being a 'bus driver' – the implication being that some directors could steer the television hardware through a number of simple, straightforward routes but there were only a chosen few who could be entrusted with the Grand Prix cars.

For a bus driver, the initial training ground was local programmes, followed by a transfer to something which allowed more planned preparation such as the newsreel archive programme, *All Our Yesterdays*. Then, if your ambitions were in drama, a stint on *Coronation Street* was the target.

Having negotiated these hurdles, I was offered a splendid opportunity: the chance to make a documentary on videotape for the distinguished producer Denis Mitchell. I failed miserably and the result was so disastrous that it was never transmitted. I was properly grateful for the 'chance to fail' and even more grateful for the fact that my failure was buried without trace. But a bus driver was not left for long without an assignment which earned his keep.

I was summoned by my boss, Julian Amyes, to be given my next job. 'Now, you mustn't think of this as a punishment, Mike,' he said, 'but you are going to direct the next series of *Pardon the Expression*.'

Why should that be considered a punishment? A very successful situation comedy on its first run, with a great star – Arthur Lowe as Leonard

Swindley – the only character to spin out of the *Street* into his own series. The writers were Harry Driver and Vince Powell – a proven team – with the occasional script by a promising newcomer called Jack Rosenthal. But I was terrified because comedy is a tricky form in any medium; particularly so in television. Not only do you have to put the actors in the right place at every moment but you also have to take exactly the right shot – whether it's the pratfall or the reaction – to point up their skill and the skill of the writer. In television you also have to deal with a studio audience who must be able to see most of the action and that limits your options severely.

But I am not complaining. I directed that show for 26 consecutive weeks, a new script and a new supporting cast on day one, followed by three days' rehearsal, a weekend off for the actors to learn their lines and for me to do a camera script, then a day in the studio – live, no re-takes – then it was day one again. I was lucky enough to have a first-rate producer, Derek Granger, ex-drama critic of the *Financial Times* and the man who went on to make *Country Matters* and *Brideshead Revisited*. I once asked him why he was doing situation comedy. 'Because it's an intellectual challenge,' he said. 'How do I get Arthur upside down in a hammock with a toilet seat stuck on his head?'

Derek loved solving those absurd problems and I learned more about directing television in those six months than I ever learned afterwards.

For those interested in statistics, this series reached as many as 7 million viewers and was in the Top Twenty for 18 weeks. In 1967 Granada capitalised on Arthur Lowe's popularity again with a series of hour-long pieces under the title *Turn Out the Lights* in which Arthur and his co-star, Robert Dorning, became ghostbusters and I was one of the directors. This was scripted by Peter Eckersley, Kenneth Cope and John Finch among others but was hardly an artistic success. Nancy Banks-Smith greeted the first episode in the *Guardian* by saying, 'Hallo, it's only January and here's the worst series of the year already.' It was one of Peter's favourite notices.

Light entertainment

JOHNNIE HAMP

'You'll never make more than two thousand a year if you stay working for Granada Theatres,' said Joe Warton, the company secretary. 'Sidney and Cecil want you to have a go at being a television producer – there's a bit more money.'

It was 1960 and I had been with the theatre group for more than ten years first touring the circuit as a variety artiste with the *Bryan Michie Discovery Show*, then as an assistant theatre manager before being promoted to head office in charge of all the cinema publicity and stage shows.

'When do I start?' I replied.

'Right now,' chipped in Cecil. 'We've got a bit of a problem with the producer of *Spot the Tune*. Get down to the studios at Chelsea – you're in charge of tonight's show. Don't look so worried, you know Marion Ryan and you know about music and Phil Casson is directing – it'll run itself!'

And it did. Of course the live quiz show had been pre-planned by the outgoing producer and I felt a bit of a cheat when I saw my credit come up at the end of the show. But not so the next week when I had to do all the planning myself, and not so for the 2000 entertainment shows I was to produce for Granada during the next twenty-five years.

That was the great thing about working in television in the early days – no training courses, no degrees in media studies, you just learned and made it up while you were on the air. Most programmes were transmitted live so there was no way of editing out the mistakes which added to the spontaneity and created an electric atmosphere.

It seems that the best remembered moments are the fluffs and cringe-making events – like the time John Lennon rang me at home to ask if I was 'coming out to play.' John and Paul had arrived in Manchester to start work the next day on my production of *The Music of Lennon and McCartney*. It was well past midnight and Phil Casson and I were half way down a bottle of Scotch. 'I'm in no state to drive into Manchester,' I replied, 'but the best place to go for some action is The Phonograph.' Then I came out with the line which still makes me cringe thirty-five years on. I said to John Lennon, who in 1965 was arguably the most famous man on the planet, 'If you have any trouble getting into the disco – just mention my name.'

During the 1960s I produced the first BAFTA Awards show live from Grosvenor House in London. It was the first time that the big screen had been used so the diners could see the four clips of each nomination in the various categories. When it came to the Best Newcomer we had a technical problem and only the first clip was shown before the screen went black. The clip showed Michael Crawford in *The Knack*. Our cameraman found Michael Crawford at his table, his close-up filled the huge screen and the smaller screens of millions at home. The audience started to applaud and Michael walked up to the stage only to be told by the host James Mason, 'Sorry old chap, it's not you!' I met Michael many times after that but I never had the courage to tell him that I was the producer of the show which, as he's mentioned many times on various chat shows, caused his most embarrassing moment.

I actually went and hid behind a pillar in the airport at Los Angeles when Bernard Manning emerged from the customs hall. We were making a show called *Bernard Manning in Las Vegas* and I'd flown over a few days earlier to set things up. Now I was at the airport to collect him and heard the first words he was to utter, at great volume, on his first visit to the United States. He had spotted a giant of a black porter sweating profusely as he battled with a mountain of baggage. 'Hello, my friend,' bellowed Manning. 'Free at last – Free at last!' I didn't come out from my hiding place until I saw that the porter was enjoying the joke.

Bernard was one of the club comics to make the big time from *The Comedians*, the series which I dreamed up in the early 1970s. Other comics unknown at the time who made their TV debuts on *The Comedians* include Frank Carson, Mike Reid, Jim Bowen, Roy Walker, Tom O'Connor, Charlie Williams, Stan Boardman and many more, some going within a few weeks of their appearance from ten quid a night to five thousand a week. Such was the power of television in those days.'

There were reservations from all quarters as to how successful the show would be – Frank Carson predicted that a show merely comprising ten unknown comedians was doomed, it would 'die on its arse'. Ken Dodd said that within six weeks all the material would be exhausted, and Lew Grade said it couldn't work without top name comics. No one in the south would understand Charlie Williams's broad Yorkshire accent, Bernard Manning was too blue for television, and so on – and that was before anyone had seen it. The series ran on the box for fifteen years and in 2001 the 30th reunion anniversary show at the Blackpool Opera House was a sell-out.

Colin Crompton was the comedian I cast as the ignorant concert chairman of *The Wheeltappers and Shunters Social Club* series. He did a string of gags about the seaside resort of Morecambe. He used lines like 'It's like a cemetery with lights – they don't bury their dead they stand them up in bus shelters – the most exciting thing to do is to go and watch the traffic lights change colour – or the bacon slicer at the Co-op.' A few days after transmission I got a letter headed 'Without Prejudice' from the Morecambe Town Hall which said they were considering legal action regarding the put-down. They must have sent a copy to the press because the papers covered the story the next day. I was a bit concerned until I received a phone call from the Dean of Lancaster University. He said that if it came to a court case he would be happy to let us have a copy of a recent survey undertaken by his students which more or less came to the conclusion that all Colin had said about Morecambe was true! It never went to court.

Michael Parkinson and I worked together a lot, first in 1962 when we launched *Scene at 6.30* when Mike was responsible for the current affairs items and I for the Light Entertainment, and later we did *Cinema* together. On *Scene* our boss was Barrie Heads and he strongly objected to a group of long-haired scruffy youths in filthy T-shirts whom I had booked into the show. Barrie wanted them out of the studio, but gave into my objections reluctantly – thus allowing the TV debut of The Rolling Stones.

For two film buffs like Parky and me making *Cinema* was not like working at all. We interviewed all the movie greats Hitchcock, Kazan, Gene Kelly, Olivier, Danny Kaye, Rod Steiger, David Niven, Lee Marvin and others. We used to have fun with the censor who would come in to view the clips we intended to use in the programme. When we had what we thought might be a dodgy clip, dodgy for those days – maybe a bit of passionate lovemaking – we would slip in a clip from a really hard porn film. He would laugh and throw it out, but we usually got away with the questionable clip which was of course tame by comparison.

I always had the impression that to travel abroad in the early days was considered a treat rather than work, although I must admit that my first visit to New York was a treat from Sidney. In 1960 along with David Plowright and Jeremy Isaacs I joined Sidney to get my first taste of the Big Apple. We were each given a $1000 expenses before we left London. What I didn't realise was that at that time there was some sort of restriction on how much cash businessmen could take out of the country, and that when we left New York we were expected to hand over all the dollars we had left to Sidney who was on a long visit, for his own use. No one had told me about this arrangement. All he got from me was $16.

So many of my early productions are repeated these days, mostly on Channel 4 or satellite, that it's almost impossible not to be reminded of some particular incidents: My guests who appeared on *This Is Your Life* when I was presented with the big red book. For instance Liz Dawn – Vera Duckworth in another life – was barmaid at *The Wheeltappers* and throughout rehearsals supplied the crew with so much beer that there was none left for the studio audience. And the occasion when I told Andrew Lloyd Webber that I didn't think that a musical about Argentinean politics stood a ghost of a chance. Mick Jagger saying in 1964 that he thought The Stones might be around for another two years – skinny-dipping with Larry Hagman at his home in Dallas – getting smashed with Bill Grundy, Lee Marvin, Trevor Howard, Sam Peckinpah, Mike Parkinson – so many happy days.

The great thing about making programmes in those days was that Sidney and Cecil Bernstein, and later Denis Forman and David Plowright trusted you. I wish now I had kept more memorabilia – like the magnum bottle of Scotch which I got from the Beatles in 1963. What I do have framed on my office wall is one of my expense vouchers from that period which reads, 'To lunch – The Beatles and Brian Epstein – fifteen shillings,' 75p in today's money! And I probably padded that by two bob.

Bloody-mindedness

CHRIS KELLY, PRODUCER/PRESENTER

In 1965 when Michael Parkinson left Granada, they were looking for a new producer/performer. I got the job. During the next five years I produced numerous local programmes, and wrote and presented *Clapperboard, Sixth Form Challenge, Zoo Time* and the last edition of *Cinema*. I was also commentator on *World in Action* for fifteen years.

Joining Granada from a smaller company was like signing for Manchester United from Plymouth Argyll. Everyone working for it knew it was the best. When Lindsay Anderson turned up at a morning meeting for the local programme, no one turned a hair. This confidence did border on arrogance, but I like to think that's because we were young.

We were encouraged to be competitive, ambitious, rigorous, daring, iconoclastic, and to puncture pomposity with humour. But at the same time the company was surprisingly tolerant. When Bill Grundy, the best broadcaster of his generation, succumbed to tiredness and emotion one evening while presenting *Granada in the North* (ominously shortened to *GIN*), and slid mysteriously out of shot in a remote studio, he was simply called before the beak and told to watch it.

I benefited from this spirit of forbearance too when, together with John Birt, who for a brief, heady period was my researcher, I produced a 'happening'. (Curious how some words conjure up an entire era.) In order to test Marjorie Proops's healing powers, we devised a scam whereby a young woman (played by Annette Robertson) with a small child, gets an invitation to appear on a Granada discussion programme. Being fed up with being left at home while her husband (Warren Clarke) goes down to the pub, she accepts, leaving the baby and a note saying where she is. Husband gets home, reads note, goes hairless, and storms into our studio in the middle of the show. After a short, sharp exchange of views, presenter (Brian Trueman) will turn to the Agony Queen and say, 'Well, there you are Marge, sort that lot out.'

That was the theory. However, convincing myself that we'd have a better show if we kept briefing to a minimum, I hardly told anyone anything.

Consequently, when Warren Clarke burst through the fire door half-way through the programme, his aggression was so convincing that, fearing for his 'wife', cameramen left their cameras and started laying into him, helped enthusiastically by other guests. It all turned into an appalling shambles, Marge looked pole-axed, and five national newspapers turned up to get pictures of the abandoned baby.

The following morning the northern editions all bore headlines calling for my blood. I got a message saying that Denis Forman wanted to see me. Mentally readjusting to life at Plymouth Argyll, I took the long, lonely ride to the sixth floor. 'These people want your head,' he said. 'They're not going to get it.' I couldn't believe my luck.

With its talent, its unshakeable sense of identity, its bloody-mindedness, and its creative vigour, Granada in its prime was the benchmark against which you have to measure all other British television companies. In a lifetime as a freelance, I've worked for most of them. I haven't found one that even comes close.

Granada, you had me under your spell

BARRY TOOK

I enjoyed my four years with Granada, 1960–63, more than I can say. I was involved with excellent people and, what is more, I met my wife who was also with the company and who is still putting up with me nearly thirty-five years later.

My first contact was with the producer of *The Army Game*, Peter Eton. He invited me to join the cast as there were to be changes and he very kindly offered me either the part of the young lieutenant or one of the oicks in the barrack room. As I was just out of West End revue and a long stint on TV cracking topical jokes on Associated-Rediffusion's *Late Extra* I wasn't terribly interested in performing and had just started on a reasonable career as a scriptwriter. So Peter said, 'Well, write us a script then.' I told Peter, 'I write a with a chap called Marty Feldman.'

'Never heard of him,' he said. 'We'll make the contract with you and you can pay him what you like. The contract duly arrived, I showed it to Marty and suggested we split the fee 50/50. Of course he agreed and we set to work. I was 31, he was 26. We wrote our first script in a day! After the BBC's 30 minutes, ITV at 24 minutes 30 seconds (thanks to the adverts) seemed a doddle. We edited it, had it typed, sent it in – it was accepted.

In fact we wrote seven scripts for *The Army Game* and learned a lot about Granada in the process – that it was a much more liberal outfit than the other ITV companies, run much on the lines of a family business.

One particular *Army Game* script which Marty and I wrote featured Alfie Bass ('Excused Boots' Bisley, known as Bootsie) and Bill Fraser (Sergeant Major Snudge). They were each writing to an agony aunt, using pen names, complaining bitterly of persecution, unaware that the person they were writing about was their army colleague. Bootsie complained of bullying and Snudge complained about this toerag who was a permanent source of annoyance. Through the magazine they agreed to meet and to their horror, at Waterloo Station at midnight, realised the awful truth.

It was Philip Purser writing in the *Daily Chronicle* who spotted what we had unconsciously written: that psychologically Bootsie and Snudge were linked in a love/hate relationship, each one half of a whole personality, the two making a whole person. Granada sniffed a new series and Marty and I were asked to write a pilot show starring Alfie Bass and Bill Fraser.

The situation that existed in the army with its tight hierarchical rule of law where behaviour was governed by army regulations did not apply in civvy street. Getting them out of the army was easy – but what then? Eton, Feldman and I discussed many ideas and we wrote a couple of scripts neither of which really worked. Eventually light dawned. A Pall Mall club would be just the place where the hierarchy was the same as the army. The club secretary was the officer, the major-domo the NCO, and the Boots or dogsbody the scruffy private. Bingo! We'd invented *Bootsie and Snudge*. A couple of visits to a club which shall be nameless gave us the general feeling of a typical, slightly run down London club; the rest followed naturally.

The series was to be 39 episodes long with Marty and me providing 26 programmes and John Antrobus writing the balance. It didn't work out like that. John only wrote 3 and Marty and I, with outside help from several writers, did the rest. The first episode showed our heroes leaving the army and winding up, as it were, by accident in the same place, and the situation was established. The other main characters were Robert Dorning as the Hon. Sec. and Clive Dunn in one of his old man roles as the waiter, Johnson.

The series was popular getting a regularly high audience percentage and, in fact, lasted through four series (100 programmes) until everyone connected with it was exhausted. During this period Marty developed the hyper-thyroid condition which gave him the goggle-eyed look he used effectively as a performer on TV and in films, and he left *Bootsie and Snudge* well before its end. I soldiered on script-editing the work of a number of writers and when we were in trouble writing episodes on my own. I became, virtually, Peter Eton's assistant and we hunted around for new ideas.

We approached Patrick Campbell hoping to use his stories as the basis of a series. Paddy, as all will remember from his time on *Call My Bluff*, had a clock-stopping stammer and curiously enough in his younger days so had Eton. Over lunch telling each other tales of various embarrassing situations Eton's stammer returned and Paddy became increasingly tongue-tied. I watched, fearing that both would have apoplexy as they struggled to communicate. It didn't come to that but although our relationship with Patrick Campbell remained amicable I could never quite turn his prose into acceptable television dialogue.

Shortly after that I came up with an idea for a vehicle for David Kossoff: an elderly furniture manufacturer and his forward-looking son. I called it *Heart of Gold* (Gold being the fictional Kossoff's family name). Peter Eton liked it, as did Kossoff, and Jack Pulman was engaged to write the series which became *A Little Big Business*.

I left the company when they shut down the Chelsea studio. I was offered a job in Manchester but regretfully declined and went back to the BBC. To misuse a well-known phrase – You can take a man out of Granada but you can't take Granada out of the man. Granada, I love you still.

Early Beatles

LESLIE WOODHEAD OBE

'It must be dead glamorous being in TV,' said the man in the pub. The setting was mundane enough, a Liverpool drinking den near to closing time, a winter's night in 1962. My drinking companion was a jaunty young man with the eyes of a spaniel, implacably confident of its charm. He was keen to hear about television, I was more interested in what he did. His name, I gathered, was Paul McCartney.

I'd been working at Granada for just a few months, and as a very raw researcher on *People and Places*, I felt scantily equipped with evidence of the TV glamour I was being asked to supply. It struck me that the startling performance by Paul and his chums I'd witnessed that evening in a nearby cellar was easily the most exotic thing I'd encountered in my brief and unspectacular showbiz career. But I fancied any admission along those lines wouldn't exactly burnish my image as a gilded TV type with these four unknown hopefuls. Anyway, I was still feeling a bit stunned by the banquet of noise they'd served up in that cellar, and I was aware that the sharp one called John would probably have a withering response to any version I might offer of myself as a media fast tracker. I mumbled something humble in reply to Paul's wide-eyed speculation about my glamorous life and bought the embryonic Fab 4 some more beers.

A few days later, we shot the first film with the Beatles – a primitive black and white montage like something smuggled out of Eastern Europe. I can still recall snapshots of that sweaty lunchtime beneath the Liverpool pavements: fighting our way on to the tiny stage to shoot wobbly close-ups with a clockwork camera; John Lennon wringing out his sweat-sodden shirt into a bucket after the shoot; being marooned below ground for an hour with the lads while alarming-looking minders took care of disgruntled fans who were waiting to set upon the new drummer Ringo Starr, the upstart replacement for their hearthrob Pete Best. On the way back to Granada, still dizzied by the raw energy and impact of it all, I had to stop my Mini on the East Lancashire road to be sick in a ditch.

And then my problems began. We discovered we couldn't transmit our Beatles film. It had been intended to make half of a 5-minute feature about northern musical contrasts: the Brighouse and Rastric Brass Band cross-cut with clamorous young rockers. The four Beatles had cost us a total of £58 12 shillings, a heavy burden, but sustainable. The Musicians' Union fees for the stalwart men of brass would have bankrupted *People and Places* for a whole week. So the Beatles went on the shelf.

But I'd become hooked. Struggling against my previous loyalties to modern jazz, I pursued the aspiring Beatles through seedy Manchester nightclubs and even seedier concert dates. It all came to a crisis at the Tower Ballroom, New Brighton. This gloomy fun palace, as cavernous as a railway station, slouched alongside the mudbanks just across the river from Liverpool. On a foggy October evening, I found my way to the Tower for a concert where the Beatles would be supporting the outrageous Little Richard. As the frantic star screamed his stuff, Brian Epstein pinned me in a dusty corner. He demanded to know when the boys were coming on TV, and I didn't think he'd be sympathetic to our problems with a brass band. It seemed the time had come to do something.

With a colleague who had put me on to the Beatles in the first place, the persuasive and trend-sensitive Dick Fontaine, I lobbied the sceptical producer of *People and Places*. This was a uniquely unpredictable man called David Baker. To this day, I've never been able to decide if I was fortunate or cursed to have Baker as my first producer. A gangling Australian with wild eyes and the face of an outback Karl Malden, he remains one of the most genuinely eccentric people I've ever known. He lived in a suburban house which he had carpeted with straw and furnished with old tea chests, ripping out all the doors so that his untrammelled toddlers could wander where the mood took them. Baker's vision for *People and Places* had the same flourish. On his first morning, he arrived in the office murmuring, 'Coins, kiddo!' and 'Tulips, kiddo!' These mysterious messages were to be transmuted, we understood, into items for that evening's programme. He commissioned films on 'Waiting' and 'Rain', accompanied by soundtracks of aimless whistling. He found a regular spot for a shoal of underwater fish puppets which gurgled satirical sketches in an aquarium. If the production team were bemused, I struggled to imagine how all this was being received over the egg and chips across the North of England.

Baker's finest excess, I thought, was the mounting of a competition to discover 'Miss Big Toe 1962' for which viewers were invited to submit photographs of their feet. Scores of very strange images arrived in the office, and we spent days sifting through the candidates. I considered the comparative merits of toes nestling on red silk, toes circled by tiny sashes. The finals were held in the studio; contestants parading behind a screen which revealed one bare foot and one Wellington boot while a trio played 'Lovely Lady'. Bill Grundy and our resident Gardening expert deliberated the lucky winner. Watching this spectacle on the office TV, I became aware of banging from Baker's office. I peered round the door and saw our producer beating his head against the wall while asking: 'Mary, mother of God, what have I done?'

For all his uncommon demands on his production team, Baker was not an unkindly man, and he wearily agreed to let those bloody Beatles do a couple of numbers on the show. They arrived for their first TV appearance attired in little waistcoats like tacky Spanish waiters to sing 'A taste of honey'. Paul had told me he was fed up that nobody would allow them to sing any of their own songs, so we allowed them a second number, a thing he'd written with John called 'Love me do'. They said they'd done it on a record that was due to be released. As they were leaving, Ringo sought me out to say, 'Thanks for the gig.'

My little footnote in Beatle history had a curious and saddening coda. Two decades later, I woke up in a New York hotel bedroom to find that primitive little film we shot in the Cavern on breakfast TV. Reasonably convinced I must be still asleep and dreaming of times long past, I scrambled for the remote control and yanked up the sound. They were saying that just around the corner from my hotel, John Lennon had been shot dead.

FACTUAL
PROGRAMMES

Early days at Granada

BRIAN BLAKE

It all began in the summer of 1966 and in typical Granada fashion. An advert appeared in the *New Statesman*, 'Wanted: northern graduate to join television company.' Note the wording – northern graduate – no decadent southerners wanted at Granada. However, I faced a problem, I wasn't a northern graduate. I read history at Bristol University. But I did come from the north, a mining village in County Durham. So I applied and got an interview, not of course in Manchester but Granada's London offices in Golden Square. On the panel were Denis Forman and Mike Wooller, in typical Granada dress code, no jackets, shirt sleeves rolled up, braces on display and gin and tonics at the ready. It was a relaxed interview leading to the inevitable trick question, 'How do you feel about leaving London and going to live in Manchester?'

What I didn't realise at the time of that interview in 1966 was Sidney Bernstein's commitment to Manchester. He believed that the cultural roots of northerners were much stronger than those of the soft south of England. Granada prided itself on a blunt North Country style. London was just a city of displaced people while Manchester was a first-class centre from which to watch the world. With no television experience I was thrust into the *World in Action* team.

The programme then was four years old. The whole original concept of *WIA* was to be different, to bring current affairs to a mass audience. Out went the on-screen reporter, the anchorman figure like Richard Dimbleby, and the studio discussion. In came, hopefully, dramatic film and a punchy commentary. The pace was designed to be frantic and aggressive. The new programme was transformed by the introduction of 16 mm cameras, rather than the old and cumbersome 35 mm variety. It was now much easier to get at the heart of the action. The end product could be dramatic. This is how *TV Times* introduced a new series in 1969:

> A recruiting centre for Biafran mercenaries. WIA is there.
> A Green Beret accused of murder in Vietnam. WIA got the first interview.
> They have been beaten up in Africa (fractured pelvis, broken ribs, battered faces, abdominal injuries).
> Shot at in Jordan (one cameraman wounded in a fleshy part of the body).
> Punched in Korea (same cameraman, one black eye).
> And stoned in India (!)
> The WIA team are the Green Berets of journalism, the hairy chested Hemingways of current affairs, the hard men and women of television.

They don't write copy like that any more!

Jeremy Paxman, writing in the 1980s believed that, '*WIA* is the one proramme every television journalist worth his salt wishes he had worked on.' My favourite description of those early *WIA* days comes from a younger producer and later feature-film director, Paul Greengrass. 'I was a child of Watergate. When I left University in 1977 I wanted to be like Woodward and Bernstein. Bring down governments. Wear a flash overcoat with a belt. See bent coppers tremble. Be glamorous. So I went to work on *World In Action*, where programmes were put together in a haze of marijuana. Not surprisingly a whole generation of young men gravitated towards Granada.'

In those early days Granada cast its net wide to recruit for *WIA*. A remarkable collection of talent was assembled. As well as Irish, Welsh and Scottish, there were Americans, Australians, South Africans and even a Czechoslovakian. There was an ex-convent girl and at least two members had been taught by the Christian Brothers. There were grammar school boys and public school boys. Some were products of red brick universities, many came from Oxbridge, even though degrees in engineering and geology seemed unusual for a career in the media. Staff were recruited from Fleet Street (the *Sun*, the *Express*, the *Guardian*, the *Observer* and the *Sunday Times*). Others came from the local press, the *Knowsley Reporter*, the *Scunthorpe Star*, the *Yorkshire Post*, the *Bradford Telegraph and Argus*, the *Slough Observer*, the *Welwyn Times* and the *Crosby Herald*. There was a former nurse, an air hostess and even a military policeman. Gus Macdonald left school at 14 and worked as an apprentice fitter on Clydeside. Others were young graduates from Granada's own production training scheme, working alongside the Second World War veteran and former *Daily Express* Far East correspondent, Russell Spurr. Mike Wall was a former curate and a winner of the MC while serving in the Guards on the Rhine in the closing stages of the Second World War. Two researchers on the team, Jack Straw and Margaret Beckett, became cabinet ministers. Two editors of the programme were later to join the House of Lords, Lord Birt, Director-General of the BBC, and Lord Macdonald, the transport minister in Blair's cabinet. For all these people, Granada was then arguably the most adventurous and the most serious centre of television journalism.

Myths grew up around this strange collection of people. The rest of Granada regarded them with deep suspicion and envy. The *WIA* team worked privately, commando-like, from their office base in London, over-looking (appropriately enough) Carnaby Street. They rarely came to Man-chester, except to edit their programmes – indeed some scornfully referred to Manchester as Toy Town. For the *WIA* team normal office hours counted for nothing. Some would arrive for work as the rest of the building were going home, and would still be there at midnight. A common sight next morning would be socks and pants being washed in handbasins.

The team revelled in their special status. Passports in hand, they jetted in from exotic places like Vietnam and Cambodia. John Shepperd once spent weeks out of touch. He finally contacted the Manchester office with a true sixties-style telex. 'Emerged undergrowth. Stop. Movie Groovy.'

Then a legendary expense claim followed: 'Ten thousand kip to opium party for Lao General.'

Of course it wasn't all like this, especially for some of the new researchers. I did have some exotic trips, to Hong Kong to investigate police corruption, or to Italy examining the pollution of the Mediterranean. But many programmes were based on old-fashioned foot slogging or telephone bashing. My first research job was to track down 400 Wolverhampton families who had been rehoused after a slum clearance programme. Later I had to phone 300 GPs to find out their views on prescribing aspirin. Heady stuff! The aspirin programme was two years in the making. The joke was that the skirt lengths of women interviewed in the first weeks of the programme had shortened by 12 inches by the time it was transmitted.

A more rewarding research assignment came in 1971. That year *WIA* spent a month persuading the tiny village of Longnor in Derbyshire to give up cigarettes in a week-long experiment. My enviable job was to sit in the village's three pubs playing darts and dominoes and persuading the hardened drinkers to join in the trial. Expenses proved a major problem. At the end I could only come up with: 'Entertaining the village of Longnor, £169!' Amazingly they were passed by a disbelieving accountant, if a shade reluctantly.

The programme operated on the old Lord Beaverbrook saying, 'Do you want to make mischief?' Not surprisingly the new brash style of *WIA* proved too controversial, especially for the regulating body, the ITC. Trench warfare broke out. There were rows over programmes on the cost of the Olympic Games, waste in defence, Angola, the drugs industry, Idi Amin and the coverage of Vietnam. There were allegations of a permanent left-wing bias, and a certain element of Marxist/Communist and anti-democratic views.

In 1971 the ITA totally banned *South of the Border*, a film on the growth of the IRA in the Republic, because it was 'aiding and abetting the enemy'. To their credit, Granada held firm. It championed the investigators and when they were attacked it defended them. Huge legal fees were spent to protect *WIA*'s right not to reveal their sources in the British Steel case, and again to fend off a libel suit from the Conservative politician, Reginald Maudling. Granada was always willing to back up and pay for serious journalism.

After 1963, *WIA* was on the air almost continuously for more than 30 years, a thousand programmes, 500 hours of archive film, hundreds of miles of celluloid and tape. One of the last programmes I worked on concerned the death of young James Bulger. A special edition of *WIA* was commissioned at the end of the trial. We obtained exclusively audio tapes of the two young boys accused of the murder and the actual interrogation by the Merseyside police, but only after several hours of hard drinking in a run-down Liverpool pub. More than 10 million people watched the programme but the Broadcasting Standards Council weren't impressed. 'Neither the public interest nor the exceptional circumstances could justify the decision to make use of the actual tapes of the interviews with the accused boys.'

WIA received a rap on the knuckles. But I think Sidney Bernstein would have approved. Mischief had once more been made, but mischief to a purpose.

Was there a Golden Age?

DAVID BOULTON

If there was a Golden Age of television, I missed it. I was told I'd missed it when I joined Granada in 1966 and ITV was already a growing lad of ten. The old hands who ended each day with a bottle of claret in 'The New', as the squalid little old pub down a dismal back street where the Manchester law courts now stands was perversely known, went on about the old days when programmes were transmitted from a shed left over from the industrial revolution. Sidney Bernstein called it Studio 4 to give the impression he had three more, and when drama was live and the only way of recording a programme was by filming it off the screen.

Legend has it that *Scene at 6.30* was the brightest and best thing on Granadaland's screens, what with Truman and Scott, and Grundy and Parkinson. But they all left the programme soon after I joined. It must have been something I said. Or perhaps it was because the demolition gangs had pulled down 'The New'. After six months as a researcher, I thought it was time I was made a producer, but wee George Reid, who told everyone he was going to be the first prime minister of an independent Scotland, whispered knowingly that it all depended on what was on my file, so I walked into Personnel, which in those days seemed to consist of one very young lady and a filing cabinet, and with the unique air of authority which marks out a television researcher on the make, demanded to see my file.

Said young lady consulted said cabinet and produced said file, wherein I read the judgement upon me) of Barrie Heads: 'Will make a producer in God's good time.' Armed with this secret knowledge, I went to see Denis Forman to negotiate my elevation, confident that a show of boldness could advance the divine timetable. Wholly ignorant of how he was manipulated by a God in whom, as a closet humanist, he passionately disbelieved, Denis made me Senior Producer of *Scene*.

I lasted a year, in which time I was responsible for some of the most risible programming ever to go out under the sign of the primitive arrow which was Granada's embryonic logo before logos were logged. Like when Bill Grundy, who had carelessly lunched on four instead of his usual three bottles of claret, slowly slipped sideways out of his newsreader's chair, continuing to read in impeccable tones, but out of sight of the viewers because we were using an unmanned, fixed-position camera. Like when we did a live item on the largest and the smallest dog in Granadaland, where the big one yawned and the small one took a closer look and lost its head – literally. Like the Christmas special where I filmed cute little children speaking breathlessly of the shepherds, wise men, stable and star, and brutally intercut them with John Allegro, a Manchester University professor who had just published a book arguing that Christianity was the product of an hallucinogenic drug cult and the baby Jesus was just a magic mushroom. An unknown housewife named Mrs Whitehouse cut her teeth on that one, before she graduated to sex.

But we did have our prouder moments. One week we discovered where the illegal pirate *Radio Caroline* ship was moored in the Irish sea, and made arrangements to put a film crew on board to interview the pirate king the following weekend. Sitting back and congratulating myself on our forthcoming scoop, I took a call from one David Plowright, who had been elevated to the dizzy heights of Executive Producer of *World in Action*. 'Lay off Caroline', ordered Plowright. '*World in Action* is doing them next week'. So I did the only thing I could do in the circumstances. I cancelled the weekend shoot – and brought it forward to Friday. That gave us the weekend to edit, and get the show on the air a couple of hours ahead of *WIA*. Ten seconds after Part One hit the screen, our assistant film editor told me an enraged Mr Plowright was on the line. 'Tell him I can't talk till we've finished splicing Part Two together', I told him. 'It's due on the air in fifteen minutes.' In thirty years I think this was the one and only time I really put one over on DP. He proved remarkably forgiving – perhaps because he would have done the same in my shoes.

As *Scene* (which I had insanely titled *Newscene* – 'new scene', get it?) reached its nadir, Denis Forman took pity on its remaining viewers (a man and wife with 2.4 children in Liverpool 8 and an elderly couple in Accrington, if my memory serves me) and hauled me off to what he insisted was a promotion to Network Programming. So I became the proud producer of *What the Papers Say* (which I tinkered with, and creatively rechristened *Papers*) and *All Our Yesterdays* (which, mercifully, I couldn't mess about because its veteran presenter Brian Inglis was far too wily to let anything out of his own immensely capable hands). Running *Papers* and *Yesterdays* left me with time on my hands, which, in the spirit of the age, I idled away with a little harmless subversion.

Gus Macdonald joined *World in Action*, making his debut with a film unsubtly titled *Give Us The Works!* Ten years earlier or later, this would have marked the end of a short television career, but this was the 1960s, so our hero was quickly promoted. He rang me at home one night to say, 'I've been offered the joint editorship of *World in Action* with John Birt. What do you think?'

'What do you mean, what do I think?'

'Maybe it's their way of neutralising us, buying us in.'

I told him what he wanted to hear: 'Go for it, Gus!'

A few weeks later I too was 'bought in'. My first *WIA* was a community portrait of the Catholic Falls Road in Belfast, paired with a similar look at the Protestant Shankhill. The troops had just gone in to separate them by a walled 'peace line', but the two films revealed almost identical working-class communities living in common deprivation under common exploitation. That was enough to provoke angry accusations of media Marxism but, truth to tell, we only knew and told the half of it. I struggled with Ireland for several years, while Gus and John moved on. I often wonder what became of them.

If any part of my time at Granada was a Golden Age it was probably my brief run as a *WIA* producer, learning to make programmes that excelled both as Films and Journalism. We really did turn the world of TV current affairs upside down, even if the world itself remained stubbornly the right way up. But my run was brief because I soon took over from Birt and Macdonald as programme editor. This was a mistake. The team thought the time had come to elect their own editor, and I was the management's appointment, not theirs. I knew how to make good programmes, but not how to manage good programme makers. After two years I stepped back into the ranks and the team elected one of my most unrelenting critics, Ray Fitzwalter, to succeed me. Lessons were learnt, damaged relationships repaired (Ray became one of the best friends I made in a rough-and-tumble business) and when I again took control of the ship as head of current affairs it seemed we could all look forward to calm seas and a prosperous voyage.

Not quite. Within weeks we hit the British Steel crisis. A 'mole' had supplied us with a full set of internal memos which seemed to give the lie to the claim by both the nationalised steel corporation and the government that there was no government interference whatever in the corporation's conduct of a crippling industrial dispute. We told British Steel we had the papers and invited them to comment on the programme. They did so, then asked for their papers back. We complied, but not until we had snipped off the corners containing tell-tale references which might lead to the identification of the mole. British Steel said they wanted their corners. We refused. They sued, demanding that we named the mole. And they won – only to be defeated when Granada admitted that the company had no idea who the mole was, since the researcher who had been given the papers had refused to divulge the name even to his producer and head of department.

The newspapers (which rallied behind the principle of the protection of sources) speculated that I might go to jail. The *Daily Mail* sent a photographer to follow me on what they clearly expected to be my last heroic journey from Cumbrian homestead to court and cell. There was even speculation that Granada's grandees, Forman, Plowright and Group Chairman Alex Bernstein would all do porridge if they refused to name the researcher or fire him if he refused to betray his mole. Our lawyer, Sir Arnold 'Two Lunches' Goodman, warned that Granada's assets could be sequestrated, bringing the company to bankruptcy. Astonishingly, and heroically, the grandees kept their nerve and refused to put any pressure on the researcher. British Steel retired hurt. Though they had won their legal point in the High Court, Appeal and the Lords, they took a mauling from the press, lost the propaganda war, and never got a name out of Granada.

Maybe that was our Golden Age. How confident can today's investigative reporters (assuming there are some left in today's Granada) feel that their present bosses would put a journalist's integrity before commercial expediency, even to the extent of risking a crippling sequestration? I hope, for the journalists' sake, that the matter is never put to the test.

My university

RICHARD CREASEY

I would like to share three memories of Granada, the place I always considered my university. I was studying survival. The three memories cover the beginning, middle and end: Getting in, getting on, getting out.

Getting In: Autumn 1965 – my sixth interview. I was desperately (the right word) trying to get on to the telly ladder via a trainee assistant floor manager's job. I'd failed my first five interviews, presumably because my grounds for going for the job tottered on such sandy ground. In truth, it was the only job I could think of in that new and intriguing world – about which I knew absolutely nothing – which didn't appear to need a skill. It didn't demand a good eye – which a cameraman would need. It didn't require me to write – which, as a dyslexic with no qualifications, I wasn't too good at. And it was a step up from the trainee assistant stage manager's job that I was coping with at the Salisbury Rep.

Working in the theatre, before the coming of the VHS machine, didn't give me much, if any, chance to watch television. But the night before I had seen an amazing documentary shot in the Australian outback. I was glued to the screen partly because I'd only recently driven on the desert road that ran from Port Augusta to Alice Springs. But more importantly, there was something really special about the film which I couldn't identify. I had no idea who had directed it, but had recognised the Granada logo on the back. That, I told Quinn, was the kind of documentary I wanted to produce!

In fact I had struck lucky. It was directed by Mike Grigsby, a young film maker who had been spotted by Lindsay Anderson and brought to Granada as a star by Denis Forman. Andrew Quinn mistakenly presumed that I had at last done some homework, told me there was ' no chance ever' of my working on that kind of documentary but did give me the job as a trainee assistant floor manager.

I was in telly with the best possible start: 'No way', 'no chance', 'no can do' are challenges that University Granada expected its undergraduates to take on and I quickly learned never to resist them. Two years later I became Grigsby's researcher, the most privileged job any documentary starter ever has had or indeed is ever likely to have.

My 'getting on' memory comes, of course, from researching for Grigsby. Denis Forman had agreed that Grigsby should spend a year making *If the Village Dies*, a one-off documentary special, commissioned to coincide with the centenary of Mahatma Gandhi's birth. My 'impossibly good' job was to work with him from start to finish.

The first challenge had been to find a village that would remind Grigsby and Forman of Satyajit Ray's *Pather Panchali*. And I had done well: the village was called Sarawan, buried in the heart of Uttar Pradesh, 40 miles north of Varanasi and 5 miles from the nearest road. Grigsby didn't want any traffic noise or any of the twentieth century clutter that comes with that mode of modern transport. I had got there on the crossbar of a villager's bicycle. But unfortunately, Sarawan didn't have a railway near by – which had been a key feature in the *Pather Panchali* trilogy – and Grigsby needed some aerial shots.

My search for a similar landscape near a railway line took me 600 miles away to Patna where I found it all – the landscape, a plane and pilot. All I needed was permission to film. But the pilot had told me that that was going to be the really difficult part, mastering India's bureaucratic forests of paper and wooden filing cabinets.

So imagine the scene as I sat in the office of the superintendent of Patna's aerodrome, a rather grand office with a door leading off to a secret inner sanctum. The superintendent was adamant. No one could fly from his aerodrome without form '1,000,001' with three copies. These particular forms were locked in a safe in Delhi and had to be signed by, among others, the Minister of Defence and the Minister of Transport.

It would take months! Full stop. 'But we need to film tomorrow.' The superintendent merely shrugged – to dismiss me.

It crossed my mind that this, at last, was the time to bribe. But Grigsby was very against that kind of thing and I didn't have any money anyway. Meanwhile, the superintendent clearly had something else on his mind – something pretty important – and wanted me out.

Whatever it was had him in polite mood. A silver tray bearing tea and sandwiches was brought on its way to the inner sanctum and he offered me a cup. With no strategy in mind, except my innate curiosity, I decided to make that tea last three, five, eight hours – all day if necessary.

And you guessed it. The Minister of Transport was stuck in the inner sanctum on a once in a life time visit to Patna. He also said 'no way' as he burst through the door. But my Granada training had taught me that just five minutes of 'never take no for an answer' would bring him round. It did.

My third truncated story starts seven years later. I had spent a year as one of *World in Action*'s three chief investigators alongside Ray Fitzwalter and Barry Cox. Three people who weren't producers but were more valuable than senior researchers. Dear Granada.

For a year I became *WIA*'s man in Belfast. Heady days which led me to a heavy interview with *World in Action* Executive Producer – Gus Macdonald. It was time I became a producer – a proper one not an 'investigator'. Gus understandably looked back at my track record, asked me to write some ideas on paper and quickly came to the conclusion that I had no chance of reaching those heady heights.

That 'no way' didn't feel that lucky at the time. But Gus Macdonald's decision led me to say yes to a job at ATV and three years later I was Head of Documentaries – not a great surprise to those at Granada who thought of ATV as the station with the worst reputation for documentary programmes.

Four years later, I put all I'd learned at Granada into practice, fusing luck with persistence. Grigsby had come across to work with us, as had Brian Moser. Anthony Thomas, Ken Loach, Stephen Frears and so many others, joined us to work alongside John Pilger and Adrian Cowell.

What University Granada had taught me was to scream YES whenever someone said no way. A lesson I'll never forget.

Beware of imitations

BARRIE HEADS

Outside broadcasts, mainly live from two *Travelling Eye* Units, were at the centre of Granada programmes for the first few years on the air. The vehicles, equipped with up to four cameras and, later, with videotape, produced hundreds of hours from across the region, sports and current affairs, the Rochdale by-election, Marathon programmes at general election times, news stories and features.

Within a month of Granada going on the air in 1956 we reported the rapturous return of Manchester City, that year's FA cup winners, with thousands lining the city streets; within a year a fatal Viscount crash at Ringway airport in 1957, with the units on their way within minutes of the crash. Another fatal crash happened at Winter Hill, close to the ITA transmitter site in north Lancashire. It was impossible to get the heavier vehicles up the icy hill. The outside broadcast crew, engineers, cameramen, programme staff, riggers, carried cameras and other gear up to the crash site.

The heavy use of outside broadcast equipment was partly forced on us because of the lack of film facilities: We had no film unit when we began, even for news coverage. Sidney Bernstein had been in and around the film business for some years but he had little grasp of film techniques.. He did know that filming was the most expensive, indeed extravagant, side of show business.

It was an exhausting process to get him to agree to any film being used in early programmes. Later it became so obvious that film had to be used that he gave up the battle.

A series called, with no originality, *While the City Sleeps*, looked at the parade of events which go on in any large town. We planned it with breathtaking casualness. Almost every programme minute was live.

Any Friday night in a city casualty ward, we convinced ourselves, would be the stuff of drama – sobbing mothers, stabbings, mercy dashes. As it turned out the highlight of an otherwise uneventful evening was a man coming in to have the dressing on his thumb replaced.

At Fleetwood we launched the lifeboat. The floor manager misheard the cue, and signalled the launch with the camera well out of position. Viewers saw a far-off faintly luminescent splash in the darkness.

Manchester fire brigade provided smoke and flame. They started fractionally too early with the blaze in a derelict house. While firemen at the front poured on gallons of water and the commentator talked of bravery, battles with the elements, and men who knew no fear, other firemen at the back poured on gallons of petrol.

Afternoon programmes had another style. One day a visit to Liverpool docks, another a look at the making of Cheshire cheese. With such controversial themes, how could we have gone wrong? Half an hour before we went on the air at Liverpool one of the unions involved, engaged in some dispute with their brothers in another union, refused to take part if their rivals were shown. The rivals countered with a similar ban. This put a programme about the work of the docks under a disadvantage.

Manchester has a long history of Whitsuntide religious walks — processions of churches and Sunday schools through the streets. They were covered on television for the first time. Catholic processions featured banners of a topical/religious nature, linking events of the day to some church thought – a series of mobile wayside pulpits. Granada was permanently in the news: the banner read :

> G od
> R eigns
> A lways
> N ight
> A nd
> D ay
> A like

Politicians have always tried to fetter broadcasting – with rules ostensibly to ensure impartiality but in fact to ensure there could be little comment on politicians' doings.

The BBC was in a monopoly position until 1955 but did little to fight. Whatever BBC supporters may say, and many of them have always been self-interested BBC staff, it was never much of an innovator. In politics it was always deferential.

When commercial television began, the 'Fourteen-Day' rule had been in place for many years. This laid down that no matter could be discussed on television if it were to be raised in Parliament within two weeks. The BBC had, seemingly, never thought to question the absurdity. At Granada we believed it to be nonsense and said so. After some debate in Parliament the rule was dropped.

Any broadcast about a by-election, with the exception of the announcement of poll and result, was thought to be impossible. The authorities' view was that the *Representation of the People Act* (1954) made coverage illegal. The Independent Television Authority (ITA) seemed to share this view. The BBC had never tested the theory.

Early in 1958 a by-election fell in Rochdale, a few miles north of Manchester. At this time no by-election had ever been covered on TV, a piece of insanity on which we consulted constitutional lawyers — and then spent many hours arguing with the political parties and with the ITA. Eventually the politicians and the TV regulators were won over. We made a series of outside broadcast programmes about the election, none of them especially interesting but it was a historic series paving the way to modern by-election and political party conference coverage.

Before 1959 the annual conferences had not been covered on TV apart from news reporting and occasional comment programmes. There was even an implication, again because of the *Representation of the People Act*, that coverage would be illegal.

Jeremy Isaacs, later general administrator of the Royal Opera House, was a Granada producer, the most assertive in pressing for conference coverage. He, David Plowright (later Granada TV chairman), and I were assigned as producers. The TUC was the first of the organisations with a conference falling soon after we had made the decision to go ahead with live coverage.

We covered the conferences fairly and were never accused of bias. It was sometimes hard to maintain a balance — more because of the long periods of impenetrable boredom than because of political fireworks.

Television audiences were small — as we had anticipated. It was mainly daytime TV, when most people were at work, many of the debates were complex and technical, some speakers were inexperienced and dull. But there were substantial audiences in terms of total numbers: I once calculated that more people watched at least part of the week than had attended all the TUC conferences in their hundred-year history.

The political parties were quickly in tune with the TV possibilities although it took them some time to establish the wider humiliations of modern conferences, including the artificially induced and artificially-prolonged standing ovations.

Live conference coverage continued annually over several years, was copied after a couple of years by the BBC, who had initially been guarded about coverage. Eventually they joined in. 'Beware of Imitations', said our snide poster.

All new at the New Theatre

TIM HEWAT

Think Tanks as far as my experience ran, had been the upstairs bar of the Hotel Australia (while a cadet reporter on *The Age* in Melbourne), The Red Lion in Poppins Court (while a reporter and sub-editor on the *Daily Express*), the Prince Edward in Toronto (while a rewrite man on the *Globe and Mail*), Yates's Wine Lodge and The Land of Cakes in Great Ancoats Street (while Northern Editor of the *Express* in Manchester) and El Vino in Fleet Street (while Managing Editor of the *Express*).

Then, on my twenty-ninth birthday and my first day with Granada, 4 May 1957, Harry Elton walked me a couple of hundred yards up from the converted warehouse which was the office block and into the New Theatre pub to launch into the first of what became a thousand explorations of how to make exciting television.

I served my apprenticeship, fascinated by the potential of what was to me a totally new medium, as I assisted with such established series as *What the Papers Say* (whose best performers were Brian Inglis of the *Spectator* and Alastair Dunnett of the *Scotsman*) and *Youth Wants to Know* (in which teenagers interrogated a celebrity under the prompting of the enchanting Elaine Grand).

I was also one of the team with Denis Forman and Barrie Heads who pioneered grass-roots political coverage in Britain by broadcasting a show about a by-election in Rochdale. The memory that lingers is of the stupidity of the Liberal candidate, Ludovic Kennedy, who did not wish to appear because it would clash with a meeting at Tottington. Even though he was a newsreader on ITN, he failed to realise that five or six voters might go to his school meeting whereas the whole electorate could see him on television.

For many an evening the Think Tank was in session at the New Theatre and a whole procession of programme possibilities were passed before the purifying Scotch. Two observations must be made: first, everyone was aware of breaking new ground, and secondly, all options were open in both programme content and production technique. Although it was some twenty years since the BBC first transmitted pictures and sound, the whole thing was still virtually brand new.

In due course I was called upon to come up with some of the investigative stuff I had been hired to produce. I was able to secure Mike Wooller as director and, with his steadfast PA Liz Sutherland, we launched a team which won a heap of awards over time and some notoriety if not fame. We had a list of exposés, headed by one on the preparation and sale of dirty food for which SLB yearned. We repaired to the Think Tank to find a style which would project the element of *J'accuse* which was central to our plans.

Remember we were pre-colour, pre-videotape and pre-ENG cameras. Location film was shot in black and white on 35 mm and for the studio portion we plumped for limbo – all the action in front of black drapes, producing the starkest effect. *Searchlight* was our title and the dramatic opening shot of a bursting bright light was secured by rolling film backwards of a headlight going from full-screen to pinpoint and then reversing it.

We chose as our presenter Kenneth Allsop, author and *Daily Mail* columnist who, probably as a result of losing a leg through polio as a child, had a lived-in face which we shot in bold close-up.

The degree to which we were all novices was demonstrated by that first dirty food programme. We were due to film an appalling back-street abattoir on the morrow when SLB suddenly wanted to see the script. His experience was as a producer of such remarkable Alfred Hitchcock thrillers as *Rope* and *Under Capricorn* in which the brilliant director had reduced every line of fiction to a detailed storyboard before setting foot in the studio. Sidney expected us to do the same – not realising that in current affairs you cannot write a script until you know what realities you have been able to capture on film. So I fudged a nonsense script which he recognised but refrained from unmasking!

The early *Searchlights* on topics such as cruelty to children, neglect of the old, road accidents, suicide and so on had terrific impact on the public, and after each show went out live we unwound long and hard at the New Theatre.

I'm delighted to recall that *Searchlight* constantly breached Sub-section 1 of the *Television Act* (1954) which demanded 'proper balance' and 'due impartiality'. Indeed our regulators (then called the Independent Television Authority, ITA) objected from the very first. When we denounced drunk drivers, ITA Director-General Sir Robert Fraser – another Australian but dulled by long association with British bureaucracy – assembled our team and complained that every episode had offended, adding that we should have included a couple of drunks who claimed they were safe on the road!

Eventually the ITA insisted that for every programme exposing a wrong we must do one extolling a right. For these we reversed our style, doing the shows against backgrounds of purest white, and covering things like the Concorde supersonic aircraft and wonderful new antibiotics. But our hearts were not in it, and *Searchlight* was allowed to go out.

For the next couple of years I produced a range of programmes which only a company with the creative eccentricity of Granada would have sanctioned. Several of these were planned in a minor Think Tank, a tiny pub on the Salford side called The Pineapple, which was Denis Forman's escape from interruptions – the only bother was that he insisted on scaling an 8-foot gate to get back to the studios, hard enough for me but impossible, one thought, for a man with only one leg.

While *The Divided Union* (a special on apartheid shot in South Africa immediately after police murdered fifty-six blacks in Sharpeville, directed by Mike Wooller), and *Mighty and Mystical* (a four-parter about India, directed by Clive Donner), and *The Pill* (a special on new contraceptive blessings for women, directed by Pauline Shaw) were in my normal parish, other programmes were definitely not.

Here's Humph was a jolly jazz series screened only in the North, with trumpeter Humphrey Lyttleton and his band and a studio full of teenagers (director Dave Warwick); *One Man's Music* was the superlative Cleo Laine's first solo series, singing the songs of thirteen different composers, backed by husband John Dankworth and his orchestra (director Mark Stuart); and the last four of Granada's flagship *Chelsea at Nine* concerts (director Gordon Flemyng) with stars such as Jonathan Winters, Zero Mostel, Tony Martin, Shirley Bassey, Henri Salvador and *The Army Game* gang.

In this middle period, as Picasso might say, Mike Wooller and I made not only a television first but a show which rendered the next day's papers superfluous. From the day, at the height of the cold war, that a Soviet agent passing as Gordon Lonsdale and four others were arrested for collecting and passing on the secrets of the Navy's Underwater Warfare Establishment at Portland, Dorset, we started reconstructing their activities on film and editing their background so that, on the night they were sent to Wormwood Scrubs, we were able to put the whole story to air. Apart from anything else, this showed how willing Granada was prepared to gamble on a good idea – if the jury had not found them guilty, the show would have had to be scrapped on legal grounds.

Our new series was the big one: *World in Action*. For those who know film history, the shape of our reports harked back to *The March of Time* of the 1930s but was absolutely new to television: no in-vision presenters, no interviews, statements by participants straight to camera and always in English no matter where the film was shot (we prepared idiot-boards in phonetics so that foreigners could be rehearsed into speaking English).

World in Action worked – for more than a generation. Over the years many people contributed to its success, but my core team included Mike Wooller, Bill Grundy, Alex Valentine, Peter Heinze, David Samuelson, Jenny (Izzard) Barraclough, Liz Sutherland, Claire Bradley, Gerald Valvona and the distinctive voice-overs of Wilfred Thomas and Derek Cooper.

Many other shows and specials were generated in the *World in Action* Think Tank, the cosy pub we used behind Golden Square. James Hill, who won an Oscar with his beautiful cameo film *Guiseppina*, directed three of them: *Cuba Si*, a four-parter about Castro's island which was fraught to shoot and then infuriated the former head of the Foreign Office, Sir Ivone Kirkpatrick, who, as chairman of the ITA, summoned SLB for yet another dressing-down about bias; *Sunday in September*, which used twelve crews to contrast the rituals of Battle of Britain Sunday in Westminster Abbey and the mass sit-down by the Campaign for Nuclear Disarmament in Trafalgar Square, and *Paris: The Cancer Within*, another fraught investigation into how the French police murdered many Muslim activists from Algeria.

But the best of all was directed with rare patience by Paul Almond, an apparently dreary Canadian who went on to make several feature films in Hollywood. I had long been fascinated by the Jesuit claim: 'Give us the child until he is seven and we will give you the man.' How much, I wondered, did the class structure in Britain shape the likely lives of its children? The result was *Seven Up*, a fascinating and devastating revelation.

Now the children were selected by a raw researcher named Michael Apted. Seven years later, when he had become a director, he revisited them in *Fourteen Up* and then again in *Twenty-One Up*, *Twenty-Eight up* and so on. This remarkable unfolding of several lives is quite likely to be acknowledged as the truly ground-breaking series of television's first century. For this reason, if no other, I am delighted that young Apted developed my best Think Tank idea.

Tim Hewat adds: 'after ten terrific years with Granada I was on the brink of television burn-out and returned to writing; returned in time to Australia, too, and now we live in the bush by a lazy river ... doing a couple of books a year, drinking the local red wine and watching our ponies grow'.

The story – no excuses

Vanya Kewley

The sun glinted harshly on the barrel. Ten AK 47s were trained on the prisoner sitting on the ground, dishevelled, bleeding.

'It would make a great 360° pan,' I thought distractedly, daring to raise my eyes to the circle of black soldiers. A vicious boot kicked me in the kidneys for my impertinence. An old Africa hand later told me that 'they' usually beat you up – not to the point of unconsciousness – but just enough to 'soften you up'.

'But I'm not a mercenary,' I protested wearily. 'I'm a television producer. Director. *World in Action*. Granada. British.' I certainly didn't even look like a mercenary – 5 foot nothing, 90 pounds, torn jeans, dirty T-shirt, tattered straw hat ... brandishing nothing more threatening than my British passport ... A rifle butt smashed into my pelvis. 'Clever bastards, hitting you where it doesn't show,' mocked the twin track droning inside my head. One track kept telling me to run. If I had, I would undoubtedly have been at the receiving end of a hail of bullets. The twin track, fuelled by my sense of the ridiculous and intense curiosity of people's reaction under duress, prevailed and, not for the first time, saved my life. 'I'm supposed to be making a documentary film on the genocide inside the South Sudan, not taking part in a bloody B-feature movie,' I thought miserably.

The ring of soldiers released their safety catches menacingly. It is an unmistakably chilling sound – even if you were like me, a very young, inexperienced producer who barely knew one end of a gun from another. What made it worse was it was my first assignment abroad as a producer/director. I had sweated blood to persuade Jeremy Wallington and Leslie Woodhead to let me do the story. I remember Jerry laconically sitting back in his chair, insisting that I write the history of the Sudan from the fifteenth century to the present day. 'Just to see if you really know what you are talking about!' he mocked. With Vietnam at its height, who had ever heard of – let alone cared about – an obscure guerrilla war in an area that no one could even locate on a map?

But I did and, having collected the evidence and finished my film inside the South Sudan, I was captured with my interpreter on my way out looking for our transport that had failed to rendezvous. And to make matters worse, I was being accused of being a white mercenary.

To compound the torment, not only was the wonderful Tom Gill (Production Manager of *WIA*) nowhere in sight to fish me out of my predicament but I was caught in the middle of the jungle in No Man's Land having left my crew – and my precious film – inside the South Sudan. For twelve hours I had thought of every permutation of escape as they made me walk barefooted in the jungle with a rifle in my back to 'find the other white mercenaries' (the crew). To the West were the badlands of eastern Zaire. Gruesome stories of what the Simba did to whites in the Congo kept swimming into my head. There was no escape there. To the south, Uganda, whose territory we had secretly left – without permits or permission – six weeks before. To return unceremoniously certified a long spell in jail. And incarceration in an African jail was not exactly my idea of an ideal location. Behind me the war-torn Sudan.

But what concerned me more than the certain death facing me were the words of David Plowright, my executive producer when I was a junior researcher on *Scene at 6.30*, 'Remember, I don't want excuses. You either deliver or you're out.' Delivered, of course with David's usual laconic charm. Which was scant comfort to me in the middle of Africa without my crew and my film. To return without the film or the story was totally unthinkable. On *World in Action* you just didn't return without your story. Hence many of us were labelled 'The Death-Wish Brigade' because of the – justifiable – risks we took to deliver the story. And, yes, I did deliver the story – at the cost of one cameraman's busted eardrum, one sound recordist's broken rib when the Ugandan army found them and they, like me, suffered a 'softening up'.

In those days there were two cardinal rules for the *World in Action* team. The story – and no excuses. As Plowright said: 'If there's no story, end of story! I don't care how much you've spent. If there's no story, you don't make it stand up. You come home.'

Although we were a highly individualistic, competitive and at times a cantankerous team, what no one in the industry could ever doubt was the integrity that Granada had branded into what some called 'The Wild Bunch' of *World in Action*. It didn't make us the most comfortable of bed-fellows in other teams where we later found ourselves. Often (as I was, subsequently) we were told by other editors to make the story stand up. We didn't and couldn't. So if that made us 'difficult, individualistic and opinionated' – for refusing to compromise the story – then so be it. And often there was a considerable price to be paid.

But what no one could ever doubt, what Granada instilled into our very protoplasm, was the integrity by which we signed our reputations – and sometimes our lives – on every frame that we put on the screen. We have been called Communists or Fascists, dependent on which regime we upset by our investigative films, but what no one could ever doubt was the truth which we put on the screen.

Another thing few of us fully realised at the time was the freedom that Granada gave us. Freedom to follow a dream. Freedom to pursue an injustice however unfashionable, however 'minority viewing' it might be. And there could be few causes more obscure than the South Sudan in 1969. Plowright and Barrie Heads once said to me: 'If there's one person who watches the programme or 10 million, it's immaterial. What matters is that if the story is important enough, we transmit it. However unpalatable, however obscure, whatever the viewing figures.'

Today, with the 'bums on the seats' mantra imprinted into the programme-making ethos, producing programmes about forgotten causes in unpronounceable places is now, sadly, the chimera of television legend.

Having now worked all over the industry for more years than I care to remember, I am sure I speak for every one of the *WIA* team, when I remember with affection that Granada was, and is, a hard act to follow.

Under fire

KURT LEWENHAK

Forty odd years ago a weekly 'live' two-way television programme between London and Manchester began transmission on the ITV network. *Under Fire* was a programme where popular entertainment merged with wider movements for participatory democracy and some of the topics tackled because of their headline immediacy had some political impact. On the night of the first Anglo-French troop landings in Egypt, *Under Fire – Suez* asked, 'What the hell are we doing there?' Certainly the series aggressively attracted public attention and the suspicions and ire of the Establishment who in the end closed it down. The opposition the programme generated, if nothing else, justifies its inclusion in the social and political history of the period, and more problematically, because it may carry some lessons for today.

In its first operational summer, with a rather rocky commercial start, Granada TV developed a shadowy complex relationship with Associated-Rediffusion – for a hefty slice of future profits the London contractor gave financial and other aid. Initial motivation for the programme seems to have stemmed from a desire by the two companies to mount a joint discussion forum. The first record I have of any involvement in the project is the admirably lucid minute by our Chief Engineer, Reg Hammans, of a meeting held at Granada Manchester on 8 August 1956 and which Caryl Doncaster, Rediffusion's Executive Producer of Documentaries attended. He writes: 'In essence the programme provides a Discussion Forum, an Audience participating in Manchester and an Expert Panel "under fire" who will be in an A-R Studio in London.' I made the intended confrontation clearer. 'The people will be in the Manchester studios, the legislators in the London one. Both parties in the debate wil be able to hear and see each other. The chairman, Robin Day, will be in the Manchester studio and will control the discussion. Points made shall be as sharp and searching as possible ... ' And I went on to predict accurately: 'This programme, if it is to succeed, is bound to infuriate some viewers and to start controversy in the press and elsewhere.'

To appreciate the enormity, as it then appeared, of opening up public debate on television to the ordinary citizen, unscripted, unedited and 'live' with no chances of amendment or control, one has to recall that the previous attitude of the BBC to politicians and statesmen was one of the utmost deference. And here we were on live television recreating all the freedoms of a public meeting – the right to put questions to MPs and those responsible, the right to heckle even. They'll be demanding the vote next!

Spontaneity takes a deal of organising

Once the subject for the coming week's programme was decided, John Rhodes the Rediffusion London Studio director would book the two MPs or other policy makers most closely associated with the topic under discussion. Meanwhile we in Manchester would try to find some six to eight people most closely affected by the policy London was supporting or advocating and who felt strongly about the matter. They would tell us the points they wanted to raise. The whole programme lasted under 15 minutes (13 minutes 25 seconds to be precise), so time was of the essence in planning and structuring the discussion and all the participants were warned from the start of the time constraints and of the time allocations.

All these matters would be discussed with the questioners over a meal which they ate together with the director and the programme chairman at the beginning of the transmission evening. Then the mass of the audience would arrive, drawn from organisations whose memberships were interested in and/or affected by the subject under discussion. Studio, chairman and cast would then do a complete run-through local rehearsal. If the hook-up with London was established on schedule and vision and sound lines were functioning in both directions, the opening of the show and a few sample interchanges with London on a dummy subject were also rehearsed. But the linking of the two studios was the most fraught part of the operation, with the network generally in constant operational use for other transmissions and the circuits having to pass through Midland control rooms not directly involved in the show. Often two-way communication was only established during the last half-minute of the commercial break which preceded the live transmission.

Even more remarkable, out of all the hundreds of people I have been involved with on *Under Fire* and similar unscripted mass participation discussion programmes at Tyne Tees, Westward and ATV, no single participant has ever behaved other than completely responsibly, or caused me or anyone else the least embarrassment. Only a couple of 'star' guest speakers got a bit drunk on the very odd occasion, but the members of the audience, never. They were boisterous at times, angry, disrespectful but above all effective when they spoke from personal knowledge or experience and the politicians at the London end didn't like it.

Post mortem

It would be idle to suppose that the production team handled this volatile brew of a programme uniformly well from the start. But we improved rapidly, aided by an institution unique to Granada in my experience among TV organisations – the 'post mortem'. After every show a meeting of the crew was held, with every technical department represented and with producer and director present. The meeting was encouraged collectively and self-critically to analyse the programme which had just been broadcast, examine shortcomings and mistakes and allocate responsibility for them. The meetings were edgy, rancorous and universally disliked. But the main result of these mutual recrimination sessions was that, on pain of being pilloried by one's peers, errors were not repeated and standards shot up.

By the time the country was faced with issues of peace or war over the Suez invasion, we were sufficiently familiar with the format and the various techniques required to be able to respond rapidly to an emergency. Did the Suez programme lead or reflect opposition to a colonial war by public opinion, opposition which put an end to the militarist adventure and the political career of the Prime Minister, Sir Anthony Eden? It probably did both. The audience gathered in the Manchester studio reflected and echoed the wider dismay of people generally. But the airing of these grave doubts on a network TV programme undoubtedly reinforced those views and strengthened the doubters in their resolve to oppose government policy. The follow-up programme, *Change at Downing Street?* although largely informational in character, put into practical and constitutional terms the steps required for a change of leadership which most people intuitively felt was needed.

Widening the debate

Outreach

Routinely we would bring in interested and affected groups from the Greater Manchester area, housewives and pensioners to discuss the price of bread, tenants to deal with rents, parents and teachers on the 11-plus. But occasionally we would vary the formula and bring in a geographically homogenous group from further afield. While shaving one morning I heard on the radio that the crofters of South Uist were protesting about the RAF testing rockets in their locality. A phone call to Denis Forman, one from him to Sidney Bernstein, a query about the cost of hiring an aircraft, a wild guess on my part – 'Oh, £400 or £800' – and the same day an unfortunate Granada PR executive, Jim Phoenix, was winging his Road to the Isles to bring back to the studio that Friday the crofters, priest and piper.

On another occasion, at no notice, a bewildered young Jack Rosenthal, then a researcher, was bundled into a Manchester taxi to rush to Liverpool to intercept a march of demonstrators protesting at Liverpool City Hall against the council's plans to flood their village in North Wales, for a reservoir to ensure the city's future water supplies. Under the noses of the rival press, Rosenthal hijacked the demonstration and fixed for us to meet their leader in Bala, North Wales the next day. She was a timid-seeming little village postmistress, very chapel, and disapproved of Jack smoking. We made all the arrangements with her and her father, a Celtic bard who spoke no English. But he took his harp in the coach which brought a band of irate and articulate villagers to the Manchester studio the following Friday.

Subject matter

However, we were not just widening the debate by extending participation socially and geographically. We stretched the subject matter of public discussion. Up until the accident at Windscale nuclear power station in Cumbria, the dangers of the atomic age, nuclear weapons, nuclear genera-tion, radiation and its genetic consequences, had largely been smothered by an almost total clampdown on the pretext of security. (They even changed the name of Windscale to Sellafield in an attempt to obliterate it from public consciousness.) With its special programme, 'Fallout', *Under Fire* blasted away this reassuring blanket of silence maintained by officialdom. It brought a Cumbrian cow from a farm near Windscale down to the Manchester studio and had it milked on air with a geiger counter handy to check for radiation. When held near the milk pail the counter clicked alarmingly. *Quod erat demonstrandum!*

Round about this period J. B. Priestley was writing a series of very illuminating articles in the *New Statesman*, bringing within the grasp of the average layman the facts about hitherto unknown substances like Strontium 90 and caesium with their half lives of radioactive contamination stret-ching hundreds of years into the future. In his articles, which pre-dated the formation of CND, he seemed to be articulating the national mood of the times, as he had done so perceptively in his broadcast *Postscripts* during the Second World War. I was holding forth at length on this theme to Denis Forman over lunch, and even after the end of the meal, into the toilet at the Savile Club. As we washed our hands, I was conscious of a bulky shape at one of the urinals wearing a rakish black felt sombrero. I felt my host kicking me and half heard a Yorkshire voice muttering, 'Ye overhear some funny things in these places!' As a guest, how was I know that Priestley was a member of the Savile? Happily a little while later Granada commissioned the play *Doomsday for Dyson* from him. The ITA thoroughly disapproved of its anti-Bomb sentiments and would only allow it to be transmitted provided that it was immediately followed by a 'balancing' discussion. In March 1958 Silvio Narizzano produced the play and I directed the discussion chaired by Jo Grimond in which Peter Thorneycroft and Manny Shinwell argued for the Bomb and Barbara Castle and the Revd Donald Soper against.

The Conservative Broadcasting and Communications Committee of MPs complained about the left bias of Granada in general and *Under Fire* in particular. They would, wouldn't they! In June 1958 Lord Hailsham, Chairman of the Conservative Party, finally pressurised Sidney Bernstein into taking it off. But the man and woman in the street having gained the chance of 'talking back' on vital issues on the TV screen, have never again been completely banished back into silence and oblivion.

Gone south

rt. hon. Lord Macdonald of Tradeston cbe

My first contact with Granada brought an offer of a private jet to fly me from Scotland to Manchester. I ended up on the train. While waiting to be interviewed I was parked in a viewing theatre where Chinese diplomats applauded cavalry charging into an atomic explosion waving only Mao's *Little Red Book* as future colleagues wheedled for visas. It all seemed a bit more interesting than financial reporting for *The Scotsman*.

The jet was never mentioned again. It had been a fleeting extravagance to help recruit television's first team of investigative reporters. David Plowright planned to give the populist *World in Action* series a harder edge by emulating on screen the exposés of Insight in the *Sunday Times*. Investigative journalism flourished in Britain in the 1960s long before Watergate gave it an aura of international glamour. *Private Eye* dismissed us as 'Grope Squads', forever groping in the dark for stories that seldom stood up. But the relaunched *World in Action* dug deep enough to get noticed and was seldom out of the Top Ten.

The initial approach from Granada (run by the filmic Forman and journalistic Plowright) was to have a joint editorship of *World in Action* with Jeremy Wallington, an ex-Fleet Street wordsmith, teamed with the cinéastic Leslie

Woodhead. The same principle applied to the twinning of producers on particular programmes and was based on empirical evidence of early ITV suggesting that most journalists have no eyes and most directors no brains. Harnessed together, however, the composite could be surprisingly creative, producing pictures that told their own stories and words that whacked home revelations and accusations.

When my turn came for *World in Action* editorship in 1969 it was explained that my journalistic preoccupation with politics and guilty men, albeit worthy, was also pretty boring. The now traditional twinning would therefore be with a more showbizzy persona who would add a bit of chutzpah. Enter capering, from Light Entertainment, John Birt. 'Anyway,' said Plowright, 'You are nearly 29 and John at 24 will bring welcome youthful vigour.' Ageism, I would have cried, had the word existed. After all, John Birt might have come up with the idea of Mick Jagger being interviewed by the Archbishop of Canterbury but I had recently been appointed by former Granadian Derek Taylor, then running the Beatles' amazing Apple office in Savile Row, to be unpaid, unofficial, very occasional current-affairs adviser to John Lennon. In those strange days I even interviewed Jim Morrison for *The Doors are Opening* documentary which Jo Durden Smith assured me was a political/cultural statement to rank alongside other recent revolutionary breakthroughs in current affairs content like the *Stones in the Park* concert and Johnny Cash yodelling in a US prison. However John and I got on well, shared an impatience with bureaucratic beancounting and sent terse memos to Bill Dickson, the Finance Director warning that impertinent questions about programme budgets would not be tolerated. To everyone's surprise we even won some awards. And to our astonishment we find ourselves in the House of Lords, with Alex Bernstein, and now working together again in the Cabinet Office.

At the first *Sun* Television Awards in 1970 the emerging steeliness of John Birt was apparent. Unbeknown to us, the Prime Minister Harold Wilson planned to use the *Sun* Awards as a platform for the declaration next day of a General Election by singing 'Molly Malone' with Violet Carson from *Coronation Street*. Apparently Wilson was concerned I might engage in some leftist lèse-majesté on stage. *Sun* minions therefore told John Birt he alone must collect the award. John bluntly warned that it was either both of us or a public scene. We got our award, Wilson sang his duet unmolested, and subsequently lost the election.

World in Action went on to be one of the *Sun* readers' favourite factual shows five years running, an achievement shared only with Cliff Richard, Cilla Black and *Blue Peter*.

Stability at the top of Granada with its seemingly eternal triumvirate of

Lord Bernstein, Sir Denis Forman and David Plowright allowed many of us an unusual mix of security and freedom. Uniquely, you could opt to move out of management when boredom threatened. I got to make programmes in disintegrating Pakistan, and with guerrillas along the Zambesi before being put back in harness.

In the mid-1970s came oversight of local programmes in the north-west which, with a franchise in prospect in 1979, got a large budget and an influx of talents – Chris Pye, Jeremy Fox, Anna Ford, Tony Wilson, Russell Harty, John Slater, Charles Sturridge and many more. We pioneered social action programming, deconstructed the local news which was read by a man with a parrot on his shoulder and had fun with Russell Harty while also producing the best music series ever – *So it Goes*.

With the new franchise won in the 1980s I was then allowed to gad about as Head of Features, reviving *Disappearing World*, dabbling in drama, even presenting series on the history of photography and early cinema. All this seemed quite normal in a company where the chairman and managing director were executive producers of *The Jewel in the Crown* and *Brideshead Revisited*.

Those deemed to be 'Granada persons' moved in a magic circle where innovation and improvisation were encouraged. We worked for the only bosses in television capable of transmitting a wild concept into something bigger, more radical and often quite different from the original notion. Indeed there was even the ultimate corporate inversion of us having to say, 'now steady on' or 'you've gone too far now.' The attitude to external interference was robust. On appointment as editor of *World in Action* I asked what to say if the IBA phoned. 'You tell them to fuck off,' was the succinct advice.

It was a privilege to sit at the Programme Committee dinners as the conversation crackled between the likes of Peter Eckersley and Derek Granger in drama, Brian Armstrong and Johnnie Hamp in comedy, Jeremy Wallington and Leslie Woodhead in documentary and current affairs with Sir Denis pouring the drink. The discussion was, in a favourite Granada phrase, 'free and frank', utterly undeferential, and just occasionally alarming when an argumentative glass just missed the managing director who, to his credit, barely blinked and never mentioned the incident again except in jest to torment the tosser.

At the same time Granada had the resolve to be deeply serious if the issue was important enough. *The Granada 500* was developed for the 1974 and all subsequent elections. (In 1997 at Scottish Television I unwisely supplanted the Granada 500 north of the border with a Scottish 500 at twice its length.) But the Roger Graef observational documentaries and the Brian Lapping/Norma Percy reconstructions of recent history were, like the drama docs of inaccessible events behind the Iron Curtain, public service at its most committed for those with the necessary attention span.

After almost two decades with Granada my proudest moment came in June 1985. Plowright led a group of us to the Banff Festival where we got an award for being the Best Commercial Television Company in the World. 'Well deserved,' we said. 'What took you so long?' we asked, ever arrogant. Plowright bought us all a decoy duck and on the plane back suggested I stopped prancing about on camera – at that time I was even allowed a day a week off to front *Right to Reply* for Channel 4 – and get back to heavy lifting as a senior Granada executive. In my pocket was an offer of a job at Scottish Television.

Years later, as managing director of Scottish Television, I celebrated success in the franchise free-for-all of the early 1990s over lunch with Sir Denis Forman in Edinburgh. We talked of the golden days of ITV. 'Of course you know it's all over,' said Denis. I do now.

To change the world

CLAUDIA MILNE

I started at Granada on 1 January 1969 aged 21, as a researcher. I earned £23 a week and it seemed like a fortune. I worked on a light entertainment programme called *Nice Time* which was presented by Kenny Everett and Germaine Greer. The producer was John Birt. Every Thursday night, after the studio we would all go off to the Brown Bull in Salford and get completely rat-arsed – probably to blank out just how bad the programme was.

I moved to *World in Action* in 1970. Aspirin overdose was then the favourite suicide method and Dennis Woolf was making a programme about the dangers of it being sold over the counter without a prescription. Dennis wanted to film a clearly distraught young woman going into a dozen or so Edinburgh chemist shops and asking for two bottles of aspirin. There were no women working on *WIA* in Manchester at the time and I was plucked from the obscurity of Local Programmes and despatched to Scotland and stardom.

But I'm no actress and I couldn't raise a tear. So Dennis bought a large Spanish onion, cut it in half and stuck it under my nose telling me to breathe deeply. That did the trick, there were floods of tears, but only for a little while. It's a little known fact that eyes quickly become immune to onions and after about half an hour and three or four chemist shops, my eyes were completely dry. Dennis tried insulting me to make me cry. That didn't work. He tried to make me laugh. That didn't work. So we bought a bar of soap and I scraped off little bits with my fingernails, popped them in my eyes and was blubbing in a jiffy. All the chemist shops sold me two bottles of aspirin, but despite my enormous sacrifice, my contribution ended up on the cutting-room floor.

Once during an all-night edit, I was looking for some staples (in those days we used scissors and staplers to cut up transcripts into a rough script). I wandered into the editor's office and opened his secretary's desk drawer. Inside was a pile of personal reports on WIA staff. They were just like school reports: attendance, attitude to work, time keeping for instance. My own was fine, Tom Gill's was wonderful and most were pretty fair. There was a blank form at the bottom so I wrote one on the editor, suggesting he should spend more time in the office and less time in the pub. I left it along with the others, hoping it would get sent up to personnel along with the others. Whether it did or not I never found out.

There weren't many women about in production grades in those days. And there were very few women producers or directors. There was no such thing as maternity leave, and hardly any women went back to work after having a baby. When I became pregnant in 1974, I asked the union (ACTT) to negotiate maternity leave on my behalf. The London shop refused – they felt it was a marginal issue. So I negotiated it myself with Julian Amyes. He was incredibly sweet and offered me six months' leave, three months on full pay, three months on half pay. He also guaranteed that I could go back on to *World in Action*.

Even though there were only two or three women on WIA when I was on the programme, I didn't feel that I was ever discriminated against. I was sent to Northern Ireland and worked on difficult and dangerous stories. Nor do I remember ever being particularly upset by what is now called sexual harassment, although it did go on. If a man made an unwelcome advance, I simply told him to fuck off! I was certainly never offered any promotion in exchange for a quick roll in the hay.

Like most Granada refugees I look back on those days with a mixture of nostalgia and irritation. It was extremely paternalistic and Daddy always knew best. It seemed to me that the management liked you to answer back, but only to a certain extent. You could defy authority, as long as you did not defy them. They liked malleable mavericks who they could ultimately control. But having said that there was an atmosphere that permeated the entire company. We laughed a lot, we drank a lot, we argued a lot and we cared passionately about what we did. We all wanted to change the world. It's an ethos we have tried to emulate at Twenty Twenty Television.

The first documentary

Patricia Owtram

I was working as a journalist with the *Daily Mail* in Manchester when I was introduced to Barrie Heads in the Victoria pub as a possible writer, and he asked me to write Granada's first documentary, which was *An Hour in Manchester Municipal Greenhouses.*

My only experience of British TV was seeing the Oxford crew sink in a boat race, but a friend lent me some Morecambe and Wise radio scripts and after walking round the greenhouses with the director (Claude Whatham), I hesitantly produced a script. To my amazement, some sentences of it were actually included in the programme.

Only one shot was possible as the greenhouses were E-shaped – probably the longest developing shot ever on TV and if so perhaps eligible for the Guinness Book of Records. The camera started at the far end and tracked interminably backwards as the presenter interviewed gardeners about their succulents, pot plants, and so on. Eventually it emerged backwards from the door, and the presenter did a further interview on the grass outside about park lawns, to allow a posse of ladies to rush from their hiding places inside and put a display of flower arrangements suitable for municipal entertainments in position, ready for a final interview and the closing credits. Claire Horridge, who did the budget, sent me a cheque for £13: I thought this rather unusual writer's fee must represent what was left over when everything else had been paid for.

Another outside broadcast we did was given the unattractive title, *Beauty Becomes You.* Three local ladies, one young, one middle-aged and one elderly, were transformed by Kendal Milne's beauty department in the course of the programme. In monochrome television the difference was not apparent. An embarrassing production for which I was paid £12.

The third programme I was involved with was to be behind the scenes at the Library Theatre, directed by Herbie Wise. We visited the theatre and then spent several weekends driving round Cheshire in my Morris Minor working out the content, which was how Herbie liked to work; stopping at Cheshire pubs for a drink and a sandwich. This was the most ambitious of the programmes; but it never got made, as the library unwisely insisted that everyone on its staff must be paid whether or not they appeared on TV and Granada – for all its socialist principles – could not afford such a large bill.

Granada then started its own northern news and I was offered a full-time contract as a reporter. About ten days after I joined, we got a flash at lunchtime that a passenger plane had crashed at Ringway Airport. I was sent to find out the strength of the story, and headed for Wythenshawe, not sure of the location – but as I passed Withington Hospital a long line of ambulances was filing out, and I tagged on. The aircraft had slewed off the runway during landing and crashed into the middle of a row of council houses in Shadow Moss Road. The middle ones were reduced to a huge dusty heap of rubble with parts of the plane mixed into it. I located a phone line in one of the houses, and had to wait while a man who must have been in great shock, the owner of a demolished house in which had been, I think, his wife and youngest child, phoned his elder child's school to ask them to keep the child there. I rang Barrie Heads and said, 'Send everything.' They were already assembling the OB unit (which had been de-rigged into the studio to do a show, so short were we of equipment, and had to be rigged again), and Granada's coverage of the disaster – which included using the lights as it got dark to help Manchester Fire Brigade's rescue operation – made TV history.

The atmosphere of those early days was extraordinary. Everything was live – if a programme went out at 10 p.m., you were in the studio until it finished. You often knew you were doing something for the first time. And you were living in the middle of the audience, so you overheard people on buses discussing your last night's show – an enormous advantage.

As a journalist, I hadn't realised how much news coverage would gain from television. You could interview survivors and witnesses on the scene of a disaster, and know that viewers really were seeing it as it happened.

There was also more cheerful news. The Jodrell Bank radio telescope opened, and I went out to interview Sir Bernard Lovell. Obviously the only spot was at the centre of the huge dish. We went up in a lift, and crossed to the dish by way of an openwork iron walkway through which you could see the Cheshire countryside 60 feet below. Walking out was bad. After the interview I became certain that I had no head for heights, and announced that I really did not think I could walk back. 'Don't worry,' said Sir Bernard, 'I'll go first and you follow and don't look at anything except the small of my back.' And it was perfectly all right.

Not all roses

ARTHUR TAYLOR

The first series I ever produced was a folk music show from a Salford pub in 1969. We called it *Songs from the Two Brewers* and I was especially pleased because one of the artists involved was Ralph McTell – it was his first television appearance and the first television performance of 'Streets of London'. There were a lot of promising people who didn't get into the series, but whom I got to hear during research trips and mentally marked up for future programmes.

Ralph McTell and I became personal friends: I looked him up whenever I had time to spare in London and if he had an evening free we would fall over together in pubs in Putney. He got invited to perform at a folk festival in San Sebastian and asked if I'd like to go. I said thanks, but no thanks – I couldn't afford it.

A few days later I happened to mention this casually to a friend who worked on *World in Action*. He suddenly became very conspiratorial, as *World in Action* producers were wont to do. Did I speak French? – Yes. And Spanish? – Enough to get by. What was the occupation on my passport? It was still 'teacher', because I hadn't bothered to change it when I joined Granada.

If I went to San Sebastian, and *World in Action* paid all my expenses, would I be prepared to run a little errand for him across the border into France? All I had to do was to find the priest's house in a small village: the aforesaid priest would then give me some names and telephone numbers. I was to go to a public phone box in a larger town and send the information to the *World in Action* office. They were researching ETA, the Basque separatist movement, and this information would help. I had to make sure I wasn't followed. Yes, I said, hand me the pesetas and francs.

Ralph and I picked up a hire car in Spain and drove across the border. The village seemed totally deserted, but we were sure that curtains were twitching as we searched for the house opposite the church. We rang the bell, but no one answered. Suddenly the door was wrenched open and we found ourselves face to face with a double-barrelled shotgun: behind the shotgun was a burly man in beard and boiler suit who didn't seem pleased to see us. They searched us, inspected our papers, and questioned us. After a while, they relaxed and hustled us into another room to meet the priest. To cut a long story short, after a long cloak-and-dagger rigmarole, involving more meetings with passwords in bars and post offices, we got the information back to Granada, then hurried gratefully back to the festival in Spain.

Several months afterwards, my *World in Action* colleague said we had had a lucky escape. ETA was holding a hostage in the house we'd visited. We had arrived in a car with Madrid number plates and they thought we were Spanish secret police. Naturally, they were upset.

Cecil Bernstein was a very nice man. One of the programmes he really cherished was *Cinema*. I took over as producer when Mike Parkinson left and introduced Clive James as the new presenter – it was Clive's first television series. We had a wonderful time but were not especially popular with the film publicity people in London, partly because Clive was never afraid to call a turkey a turkey. Cecil, who had lots of friends among the film people, took a lot of complaints, but always backed us up.

He called me up to his office in Golden Square one day and started talking about the Royal Command Performance – how many years it had been going, all the films that had been shown, and so on. Had I ever thought of making a programme on the subject? I was totally entranced by film and had used *Cinema*, whenever possible, as a vehicle for personal dreams – we'd done interviews with many of my heroes, like Robert Altman, Bob Mitchum, Burt Lancaster. I was trying, and failing, to get hold of Stanley Kubrick.

I had not the faintest clue about politics and wheeling and dealing in British cinema. The trouble with the films selected for the Royal Performance, I said, was that they were almost all so safe and dull and boring. Who on earth selected them? It took Cecil a long time to answer that that one, partly because he stammered quite badly and partly because he was so angry, in his quiet, polite way. He's been on the selection committee for several years and this particular year he was chairman. I asked him if it was all right to jump out of the office window. We didn't make the programme, I wasn't sacked, and Clive and I did our own thing with *Cinema* for another six months or so, until he decided to move on. Cecil never mentioned the subject again. He was a very nice man.

We'd been filming in Tuscany – a pretty and hugely entertaining shoot about Grimethorpe Colliery Brass Band's appearance at a music festival in Montepulciano. The filming was fine, although it was always a worry in those days that you we were never quite sure what you had got until you saw the rushes back at base – only the cameraman had seen the pictures, through his lens.

The long journey back to Rome airport was a nightmare. The heat was ferocious, we were running short of fuel and the petrol stations were all on strike. And we were all savagely hung-over from the end-of-shoot celebrations the night before. Cars were expiring in clouds of steam from overheated radiators all around us on the autostrada. One of our crew was able to siphon petrol from one car to the other two, using a plastic tube and mouth power. At one stage he actually drank some petrol by mistake. I don't think he noticed.

When we got to the airport, fuel gauges of all three cars on zero, there was good news and bad news – our flight had been delayed, so there was still time to get it, but all the baggage handlers were on strike and customs officers were thinking of joining in. There was total chaos all over the airport. Somehow or other, we made it, the plane took off, we changed at

Amsterdam and eventually arrived in the early hours of the morning in Manchester.

We watched the luggage carousel at Ringway for an hour or so, but none of our baggage, equipment – or film – appeared. There was nothing for it but to go home and collapse, then start to chase things up the next morning. When I got back to the office, still bleary-eyed and befuddled after only two or three hours' sleep, I spent an hour or so in film ops – long enough to find out that all our gear had been sent back to Rome. That day, the whole of Granada went on strike.

That particular dispute kept us on strike/locked out for three or four months in 1979, so for all that time, besides going steadily broke, I was running the film through my head and wondering if it was there at all. It was – we called it *Arriverderci Grimethorpe*.

We were at the Royal Horticultural Society's garden at Wisley, setting up the very first shot for the first programme in a series, *Gardeners' Calendar* that was eventually to run on Channel 4 for several years. Sid Love, the floral superintendent, was about to demonstrate the art of rose pruning. The director explained to him that we would shoot his initial remarks in medium close-up, then, when the time came to snip the stem, we would stop and move the camera in tight to the twig for the action. The first sequence came to a successful conclusion, and the director shouted, 'cut' in a loud confident voice. Snip went secateurs and down fell the twig. Our fault, of course – we should have explained that 'cut' meant stop the camera.

It was clear that things were changing in the late 1980s. Up until then, when you had a budget meeting for a new programme or series, all the key people were there and one by one would tell you what their part of the budget would be. There was a cost clerk as well – he would tot up everything on a calculator and give you the final breakdown and total cost. Then you would conspire privately with him to inflate the budget by 10 per cent, because, as a producer, you knew that your executive producer would have to justify his existence by cutting the budget by 10 per cent before approving it. The whole point of the game was that you had to have a reasonable budget to make a decent programme – and everybody knew that.

Came the day when the cost clerk arrived, not as a cost clerk, but as a financial manager. Acting on orders from above, he told us all what the programme budget was right at the beginning and there was no arguing with his figures. We had to learn to cut corners. The budgets got smaller every year and gradually the programmes began to look shoddier.

There was a party to honour Denis Forman's retirement. At the end, he leapt up on to his retirement present, a crate of claret, to make a final speech. He was in Forman working gear – jacketless and wearing the famous red racing braces. He finished by saying in ringing tones: 'Remember, the only function of management is to facilitate production!' We all applauded wildly, because it was already apparent to most of us that the only function of management was to make money.

SPIRIT OF GRANADA

Archives

LESLEY BEAMES

I worked in the Reference Library for four and a half years, combining it with running the Archives Department and it was here that I met the late Lord Bernstein for the one and only time. The archives had been moved to a building that stood on its own, isolated from Granada and separated from it by a busy main road. Apart from two or three other people working in the building, whom I could not see from my desk, I was on my own. Lord Bernstein walked down a long aisle towards me and said, 'I expect you feel rather isolated working here. Why don't you write down your thoughts about working for Granada when you have a spare moment.' I was speechless which is not something that can often be said about me. Needless to say I didn't want him to think I had any spare moments and until now have never thought to write about the happiest working days of my life.

I suppose like many people I look back upon those years through rose-tinted spectacles. I'm sure that there were times when I hated the work but I never recall looking for another job. I considered myself lucky to be working for a company which appeared to care for its employees.

In 1979 I applied for the post of drama researcher and attended a board comprised of Gerry Hagan, David Boulton, Peter Heinze, Steve Morrison and, I think, Brian Armstrong. Can you imagine in these days being interviewed by people of such a high calibre for a researcher's job? But in those days it was the people who made the programmes who did the interviewing not the managers who have never made or been involved in the making of a programme in their lives!

I got the job and within a few months was working on *Brideshead Revisited* and later *The Jewel in the Crown*. I met my first 'real' writer in the form of John Finch who, as I recall, was writing *The Spoils of War* and began to spend large parts of my life on Inter-City trains between Manchester and London. I got to know Colindale library and its staff very well, and I knew the inside of the White House Hotel almost as intimately as my own house; and I latterly became a member of the London Library, something to which I had always aspired. My opening line in almost all conversations was, 'I work for Granada Television, I wonder if you could help me by giving me the benefit of your advice?' It usually worked, everybody knew Granada – the name was respected.

I remember that Granada produced *King Lear*, for some unknown reason, set in AD 800. One of the scenes we recorded was of Laurence Olivier sitting by a stream eating what was purported to be a rabbit – it was a rabbit but stuffed with something edible – caviar, I think. It was a very good production, all done in Studio 12 and was transmitted on Easter Sunday. The following day I opened the *Guardian* to see what Nancy Banks-Smith had to say about it and to my horror, not being able to find anything poor to say about the standard of acting, the design, the costumes or anything else, she pointed out that rabbits did not enter this country until the Norman conquest of 1066. I frantically searched through my own reference books at home to see if I could disprove what she had written but I couldn't and so, because it was a Bank Holiday, I had to sweat it out until the following morning when I checked with the Library at Granada only to find she was correct. This, I have to say, was the only time that any mistake I made was reported in the press.

I loved the work, the people I worked with and the people I met during the course of the research I was doing and was very sad when Granada decided that they no longer needed a Drama Research Department, or for that matter a Reference Library or an Archives Department. I find it particularly sad that the enormous quantity of written archival material is no longer looked after or kept up to date. Granada is the oldest ITV company and I am convinced that if Lord Bernstein were still alive he would be appalled at the thought of all that history just lying in a darkened room somewhere and no longer available to those staff who found it so useful in the making of their current programmes.

Never more alive

ANNA FORD

Granada was an oasis. There were pictures of real beauty and interest on the walls. The canteen had decent food and was egalitarian. Women were liked and often taken seriously. I'm not saying there wasn't the odd bed-head notcher ... but everyone knew them and you made your choice. Eccentric ideas and fun were just as important as meetings. Praise was liberally handed out for good work and commiseration for trying, but failing. You could watch the cast of *Coronation Street* rehearsing what was then a live show, or Laurence Olivier not giving his all in rehearsal (just to surprise them on the take). I met most of my oldest and best worn friends at work. If you had a good idea you were told to get on with it. Granada was robust in its defiance of authority. The film editors were superb, and from time to time you'd catch the man himself, Sidney Bernstein running his finger along the rail in the lift and sending for the cleaner if it wasn't up to scratch. Sometimes it was frightening because brilliant people expected a lot of you: there were punch-ups in the cutting room, but they were heady days, with a touch of glamour, and I've never felt more alive.

Out of the blue

NORMAN FRISBY

Norman Frisby was Press Officer, Manchester TV Centre 1959–88

I always wanted to work for Granada Television. Most journalists in the 1950s did.

In 1959, out of the blue, I was offered the Press Officer's job. I was working then for the *TV Times* and in the course of my work had given Granada some aggravation. I suppose that indicated how forgiving an organisation Granada was. That somebody who had caused so much aggravation should be invited to join the organisation. I soon saw what it was like from the other side of the fence dividing Granada and *TV Times*.

When the Drama Department came up with a series based on the legendary *Saki* short stories by H. H. Munro, the Granada billing described them as *Saki – The Improper Stories of H. H. Munro*, actually the literary title. *TV Times* hit the roof. 'You can't say that,' bleated the billings sub. 'It'll make them sound like dirty stories.'

'We insist,' I insisted. 'I'll have to speak to Sidney Bernstein,' I said. SLB agreed with my stand and sent me away to tell the editor of the *TV Times* that we would sue him if he changed it. The editor, Gerry Scheff, came on the canteen corridor phone – it must have been about 7.30 by now. 'Sidney says he'll sue you,' I reported.

'Tell him I'll see him in court,' laughed Gerry. And *TV Times* cut the line. But only for the first week or two. Honour seemed to be satisfied.

Sidney was often in court. In spirit, if not in person.

My phone rang one afternoon. A senior PR person from the Ford Motor Company said he had wonderful news for me. But I had to keep it to myself. It was absolutely secret. We were not to tell a soul. Ford were launching a new up-market luxury car and had decided to call it Granada. He was sure we would be delighted. He had reckoned without Sidney Bernstein. I knew how jealously Sidney guarded his precious Granada, so I decided to break my oath of secrecy to Ford, and tell him. Granada's legal department was alerted at once, and told to set in train the legal mechanics to stop Ford calling their top-of-the range car the Granada.

Using Granada's revered name in this cheap way on their nasty car was, Sidney alleged 'passing off'. In vain did I urgently hint that there was already a car called an Anglia and a van called Thames. Even a city called Granada. It made for a fascinating day or two in court. We lost, and law students have been tackling the case as a project ever since.

But he did not always lose. The week I joined Granada one of my ex-*Express* colleagues wrote a front-page piece alleging that Granada had sacked a whole raft of senior executives. Certainly a bunch of middle-management people were going, but the story was over the top. Sidney sued Beaverbrook Newspapers. And won. It ruined my holiday with my family in Cornwall, with Sidney on the phone day and night. The triumphant Sidney made the *Express* give the damages to the Duke of Edinburgh's favourite charity – knowing how much Beaverbrook detested Prince Philip.

Sidney loved to latch on to journalistic slang. When I told him one day that a story he was interested in was in the 'box' of the *Evening Standard*, he said: 'Box? What's the box?'

'Sorry,' I said. 'It's what newspapermen call the Stop Press.'

Next day Sidney came up with an idea for a publicity story. 'Get them to put it in the Box,' he advised.

He always took an irritatingly close interest in the weekly staff newsletter, a duplicated foolscap sheet of short paragraphs ranging from news of future programme plans to the personal doings of the staff. Sidney's penny-pinching save-the-paperclips, re-use-the-old-envelopes edicts infuriated the staff. I used to tell the Press Office secretaries who moaned at what they saw as this time-wasting obsession: 'He's a millionaire. We might learn by listening to his helpful advice.' Sadly none of us finished up a millionaire. Sidney used to protest that he was certainly not a millionaire. I managed to scrounge the proof of a Sunday-paper profile of him so he could have a look at it in advance. I knew it was going to be flattering, and he would have nothing to fear.

But it did – as usual with those things – describe him as 'a Socialist millionaire.' 'I'm not a millionaire, Norman,' he sighed. 'I owe Barclays Bank millions ...' I nodded sympathetically.

Granada certainly had a reputation for meanness. It was claimed that the switchboard was programmed to answer every call with 'Your cheque is in the post.' At one retirement party, a long-serving leaver who dated back to Granada Theatres days is alleged to have said, 'Granada is setting up a scheme where every year of your service you take a 5 per cent cut in pay, and when you retire you present the Chairman with a gold watch.'

Sidney was a hard taskmaster, a ruthless operator, a miserly accountant. But he had a compassionate streak too. A lot of us saw it revealed. I was with him in his office one morning when his secretary burst in. 'There's an urgent call for you, Mr Sidney,' she said. I got up to tiptoe out, but he waved me to stay. It was the news that one of our senior executives had died suddenly in the night. Sidney's eyes filled with tears. I backed quietly out of the office.

Towards the end of the Second World War, Sidney – in the army, making training and propaganda films – was with the first British troops to enter the Belsen concentration camp. His unit filmed what they saw. A horror story. On one of the anniversaries of the occasion, he was in Manchester and Piccadilly Radio asked if he would go into their studio to do an interview about it. He was dubious, but I assured him I knew the interviewer and he had nothing to fear. I watched the interview through the producer's glass panel, and when Sidney was asked to describe the scene he found, he just broke down. The interviewer covered up for him. Listeners would not have realised what was happening. But it revealed a different side of Sidney Bernstein. I was sorry I had persuaded him to do it. We had a silent taxi ride back to Granada.

Granada was an exciting place to be in those pioneering days. It probably looks better in retrospect. But there were wonderful stories ...

Before he had found the site for his Television Centre, Sidney was allegedly being driven into Manchester from Liverpool when he saw a site on the corner of Quay Street. A shabby plot of old warehouses, tumbledown sheds, even a terrace of *Coronation Street*-type houses. A 'For Sale' sign had the phone number of the City Council's Estates Department.

Sidney made a note of the number – the story goes – and got somebody to ring the Town Hall to see if the site was available. 'It's earmarked for educational use,' the Granada messenger was sniffily told. The minion reported back to SLB. 'Tell them a television station IS educational use,' replied Sidney. And he got his site.

It could be apocryphal, like the story he did nothing to dispel that when he was considering applying for an ITV contract he looked at two maps of Britain: the map of population density and the map of rainfall. Where most folk lived and it rained most, that was the place to have a TV station.

Sidney had an absolute fetish for tidiness. Noticeboards were not to be defaced with staff holiday postcards. Desk tops were to be left scrupulously neat.

We were at Blackpool for a Labour Party Conference one autumn in the early 1960s. The outside broadcast crew had moved into the Winter Gardens complex, the glass-sided temporary studio erected in one of the wide con-courses.

Sidney decided on his Sunday-afternoon pre-conference tour of inspection of his team. They were alerted he was on his way, so everything would be

Granada-standard when he arrived. As we strode purposefully from balcony camera position to studio, to OB vans in the car park, Sidney spotted what he considered untidy cabling.

A Granada rigger was passing. 'Come, come,' chided Sidney. 'That's not the Granada way. Tidy those cables up, please.' The rigger did as he was bid and muttered as SLB marched on, 'I don't mind, but it's the bloody BBC's cables.'

Some of our publicity stunts were pure poetry ... .

When *The Army Game* was at its peak of popularity in 1960 – a comedy series about a National Service unit – the CO of a Pontefract barracks banned his troops from watching it on their sixpence-in-the-slot TV sets. The adventures of Sergeant Major Claude Snudge and his unit, led by the scrounging Private 'Excused-Boots' Bisley, presented an offensive picture of our gallant soldiery in peacetime action.

The *Yorkshire Evening News* rang me for a comment. I reported to the gallant and distinguished ex-Colonel Denis Forman, on the Sixth Floor, and a splendid scheme was hatched. If the Army were trying to pin down *The Army Game* then we would go on the offensive.

That weekend we rounded up the cast from their London homes, dressed them in their studio uniforms and flew them up to Leeds. Props department got us a camouflaged Army jeep with the right divisional markings. We hired a Yorkshire colliery brass band, and gave the conductor the piano score of the *Army Game* theme so he could transcribe it for brass players overnight.

Saturday afternoon, led by the band, we marched through the crowded pre-Christmas shopping streets of Pontefract and up to the gates of the barracks – which amazingly swung open to let us in. The CO marched on to the parade ground and invited us into the Mess for lunch. He would rescind the order, he announced. The actors handed out bags of sixpences for the TV slot machines. And the *Yorkshire Post* on Monday described the scenes in the town centre: 'Pontefract has seen nothing like it since Mafeking was relieved.'

I missed the launch of *Coronation Street* at 7 p.m. the previous night, Friday, 9 December. I was fogbound in Yorkshire looking for my brass band conductor.

Many of my memories have to be about *Coronation Street*. Good ones like the unforgettable 1966 personal-appearance tour of Australia by three of the cast: Pat Phoenix, Doris Speed and Arthur Leslie. We were used to calling out the mounted police to control the crowds when a *Coronation Street* star opened a bingo hall in Salford. But when the same happened at a supermarket in Adelaide, then that was really something. But there are bad memories too. Like the Crown Court trial of Peter Adamson on child-molesting charges, though it did end with his acquittal. And like the behaviour of the more reptilian of the tabloid newspapers. Photographers fighting among the graves to get close-ups of distraught children at their father's funeral, because he had once been in *Coronation Street.*

Some of the early Granada shows were not exactly the triumphs we had trumpeted in advance. Though we had blown no trumpets for *Coronation Street.* Cecil Bernstein, Sidney's brother who ran the Light Entertainment side of programming, had reservations about its viability. Early try-outs of Episode One – 'dry-runs' – shown to staff on the TV Centre's internal closed-circuit system, had produced a coolish reception.

Some of our London and Commonwealth colleagues were dismayed by the broad north country accents of the unknown actors, and even by some of the nuances of Tony Warren's Lancashire dialect dialogue. It was decreed it should creep on the air, virtually unannounced. No boasting of our confidence in this possible series of a dozen or so half-hours. It was not even sold to the network at first. It was to be May 1961 before the rest of the country met up in the snug of the Rovers with Ena, Minnie and Martha.

The newspaper critics did not unanimously hail it as an overnight success. The *Daily Mirror* famously said: 'It is doomed from the outset with its dreary signature tune and grim scenes of terraced houses and smoking chimneys.' Doomed indeed. The *Guardian* was more perceptive. 'It could run for ever,' wrote their critic, Mary Crozier.

Coronation Street was soon the nation's favourite and the unknown actors soon stars. Patricia Phoenix, 'Elsie Tanner', was pin-up girl of a north country infantry battalion. They were posted to Malaya, and invited her to their last-night send-off party in the NAAFI. Good idea, we thought, and off we went, Pat dressed up, as ever, like the star she surely was. She got what I suppose you would call a rousing reception. She chatted to the boys, signed autographs, was photographed kissing them goodbye. To thunderous applause, she leapt up on a table to make a tearful farewell speech, wishing them a safe journey out and a speedy return to their loved ones. She looked round the crowded hall – 1000 men or more – flung out her arms and yelled: 'Boys. The drinks are on me ...'

Luckily we got pages of splendid pictures all over the weekend papers and I made sure CGB got the glossiest copies of them on his desk the day before the bill arrived.

He was very proud of *Coronation Street* by now ...

Weren't we all?

Once upon a time

BILL GILMOUR

Once upon a time all television drama was live. The one-hour television play was a whole new art form. Directors rehearsed their cast for two or three weeks, while they also worked up a camera script that described the cast's moves and the shots the director wanted. In the studio and over two days, the cast and crew 'staggered' through a rehearsal – run through – then dress-rehearsed the play and finally transmitted it; art, drama, excitements and faults – all live.

Every three or four years companies built new studios that doubled in size.

About 1959, Granada bought a number of the new Ampex videotape recorders. Most 'live' plays became recorded plays but the constraints and much of the excitement of the live play continued. Ampex recommended that these recorders should be used in tandem. Everything should be taped on two machines. Some broadcasters still do that, but quite quickly Granada decided that it was not necessary as the machines and tape were reliable enough to record on only one machine. Granada had spare machines, what should they do with them?

In 1960, the only way to edit tape was to cut it and glue the two bits together. At best, the joins caused the picture to lose sync and roll. The joins often came apart spewing yards of tape out and leaving millions of blank screens. Very messy. I never met anyone who even claimed to have made a good join. No one liked to do it.

At Granada some of the engineers, Don Raw and Les Heyes among them, looked at the spare machines and thought it might be possible to use two machines to edit tape electronically. Les and Don went shopping for transistors and things that glowed or flashed and looked to me like little sweets, soldered them together and had an editing machine before Ampex or anybody else.

I once asked Les what the problems were. To record without wiping the control track was the first puzzle. The control track (CT) was on the bottom quarter inch of the tape. They shimmed the erase head so that as the machine went into record, the picture area was wiped but the CT was left intact. As in any normal use of a video recorder, the machines needed about fifteen seconds to stabilise. The editor found the in-cue and rolled back fifteen seconds. The play and record machines rolled together, during the fifteen seconds their switcher pulled the machines into sync with each other, counted them down to the cue and switched the record machine from play to record. The synching and the counting down were the hard bits to put together. Les Heyes and another pioneer, Ron Swain, were the heroes of the editing suite.

Over the years the hardware became solid state and digitally controlled until the mid-1990s when computers took over. Today tape and film are transferred to hard discs with massive memories and cut and pasted. From that point on, if a production stopped, an actor dried, a camera was soft or a microphone dropped into shot, the show could be picked up and the problem edited out.

Previously, in live drama, as a scene ended cameras that had been on close-ups were peeled off to go to the next scene. That was necessary but the trouble was that as a scene comes to the end, it usually gets more exciting and that usually means more cuts, more close-ups and so more cameras. Directors saw that instead of editing to cover faults they could now plan to use all their cameras at the climax of a scene.

There was, of course, opposition to these changes. People claimed that all these stops must take more time than continuous recording. Some gave the impression that they thought television was about live transmission and anything else was somehow wrong.

But soon we made every show discontinuously. Instead of moving from set to set in story order, we could do all the scenes in one set and so save the time it took to travel repeatedly from set to set. We saw that instead of rehearsing, running and recording the whole play, we could rehearse and record short sections while they were still fresh in our minds. We could design into the running order time for actors to change their make-up and wardrobe better and more often. Designers saw that they could fill a studio, shoot on Day One, strike and reset overnight and shoot again on Day Two. Discontinuous recording became non-sequential recording. Videotape editing allowed hugely expensive studios to be doubled in size.

The directors who first saw this way new of making television in 1967 were David Cunliffe on *Rogues Gallery* and Derek Bennett on *The Caesars*.

Deciding why and when we should stop and the sequence in which we shot became a part of planning the show. Should we go into one set and shoot all the scenes in that set or should we go as far as a make-up or wardrobe change, release the cast for that and go on to another set? We asked ourselves, what sequence was the most economical? When during the shoot, should we record key scenes? The building industry used the term 'critical path analysis'. By deciding why and when we should stop and the sequence in which we shot, we were doing just that. Editing became a tool to be used to make more polished shows using the same amount of time.

Comedies, game shows and others picked up these techniques but by the 1970s another revolution blew in. Writers, producers and directors, frustrated by the limitations of studio drama, pushed and pulled the television industry towards location filming. For the series *City 68*, John Finch and Jack Rosenthal each wrote an episode which was an all film production. Those were Granada's first films – 68 gives the date.

Peter Eckersley followed with a large number of single plays on film, and half the episodes of *The Sinners*. Peter's first film was *The Mosedale Horseshoe*. *Country Matters* continued the trend with over two thirds being film. It won a BAFTA award for best drama series and led Sidney Bernstein in 1972, to ask, 'Is Studio 12 a white elephant?' By the late summer of 1972 we had made around eighteen films. Those involved had worked out what to film and how to do it and crew it. But before Sidney no one above the level of departmental managers, that is above Peter Eckersley of the Drama Department and Bill Loyd who was head of the Film Department had been positively involved in the change from studio video to film production.

We all fell in love with the great outdoors and there is no doubt that film offers more subtlety and fluidity but the standard fifteen-day shooting schedule for the ITV hour drama presented a different set of problems compared with that neat, economical studio experience.

Usually we thought, 'Do Scenes 3, 9 and 24 on Monday, that is $3^{1}/_{2}$ minutes, do $3^{1}/_{2}$ minutes for fifteen days and that is your 52-minute film done.' But in order to do that, you have to load the bus, drive out to the location, rehearse each scene, have a tea break, shoot it – how long does all that take? How long do we spend drinking tea, travelling to and from lunch, before the camera actually turns over? Well these are easy: two 15-minute tea breaks twice a day for fifteen days, makes $7^{1}/_{2}$ half hours, the same count works for travelling to and from lunch. At that time we shot at a ratio of 8 to 1 which meant we shot eight times the film's running time or 8×52 minutes which is 6 hours and 56 minutes. So in fifteen days the camera is whirring for only one day, you drink tea for most of a day, travel to and from lunch for a day. How much time we spent on the road between locations, rehearsing or writhing as Boeings flew by was less definite. After thinking about all the films I had directed or managed, talking to friends and doing a lot of averages, I wrote a new kind of schedule.

Day 1	Monday	Travel to, from and between locations
Day 2	Tuesday	As Monday
Day 3	Wednesday	As Tuesday
Day 4	Thursday	Travel to and from lunch
Day 5	Friday	Drink tea
Day 6	Monday	a.m. Listen to Boeing aircraft booing by

		p.m. Listen to diesel engines knocking by
Day 7	Tuesday	a.m. Listen to men digging up streets
		p.m. Listen to babies cry and their mums saying 'Soosh'
Day 8	Wednesday	a.m. The lads get the gear out of the boxes
		(We're now halfway through the schedule)
		p.m. Rehearse the cast
Day 9	Thursday	a.m. Rehearse the cast
		p.m. The Cost Clerk arrives and hands out expenses
Day 10	Friday	Rehearse the cast
Day 11	Monday	Rehearse the camera
Day 12	Tuesday	Light
Day 13	Wednesday	Turn over – SHOOT THE PICTURE
Day 14	Thursday	And it's a good job you finished because the light's no good today
Day 15	Friday	... and now it's pissing down.

My schedule was a joke but you may notice that the time taken to rehearse cast and cameras, light and shoot, is remarkably similar to the time taken in a studio production.

Making history

ERIC HARRISON

JFK was dead.

A Tannoy announcement urged a director and crew to come immediately to Studio 6. The ITV network was closed, solemn music was being broadcast and we were to transmit one live 15-minute programme about the late President every hour through the rest of the night's transmission.

As frontman Bill Grundy sought reactions and opinions from various sources, I remembered the only footage we had of Kennedy was in the tape library but the librarian had gone home ... with the key. So, armed with a large screwdriver, I broke open the door and freed the tape showing JFK at a press conference and used that as the basis for the broadcasts to the nation.

That was 22 November 1963, I was the director and Meg Farrell who later became my wife was the vision mixer on that historic broadcast.

Granada aimed to be first with the news and often we were so busy reporting the events that there was no time to register the enormity of them. I remember covering the collapse of a Bolton street into a mine shaft, the Winter Hill air crash where we carried our equipment to the transmitter in the midst of a snowstorm to report on the disaster and the Shadow Moss

Road air crash at Ringway. I cried while working as a cameraman on this event because as I panned the site I saw a little teddy bear among the wreckage, a poignant reminder of the tragedy. As I zoomed into the picture, I was aware of tears falling down my cheeks.

In February 1958 our crew was assigned to the first televised by-election from Rochdale. For me, this was the start of nearly thirty years' involvement in political coverage either as a cameraman or director.

Prior to being allowed to televise the party conferences live Granada set up a temporary studio at the Imperial Hotel, Blackpool to interview delegates. A new reporter from ITN called Robin Day came to do their inserts! The BBC followed swiftly the next year.

Many stories come to mind from the 'conference era' especially those involving the rivalry with the BBC, but one fondly remembered was at the time when I had just been made the youngest ever trainee director and was eager for a smooth running event.

The BBC had agreed with the Blackpool Corporation to have all the illuminated trams at a point outside the Imperial Hotel and, at an agreed signal, to have them driven by in procession at the start of the BBC transmission. We, of course, did not know this. However, we were due on the air a couple of minutes before the BBC and our opening shot was to be of the promenade and the Tower. Our camera outside was next to the BBC camera. Just before we went on air the cameraman on the outside camera, Doug Ryan, was having trouble with the red cue lights on the top of his camera. To help Doug see if his lights were working I clicked his lights on and off from the control room vision mixer. Doug said his lights seemed to be working OK, and we went on air almost immediately. Doug's opening shot was magnificent; he had the Tower in shot and a beautiful long procession of illuminated trams.

It transpired that the BBC had agreed that one of their floor managers would flash a red torch at the assembled trams when he wanted them to start, as he could not speak to them by radio. The lead tram driver had seen a red light flashing at approximately the right time and place, he didn't know it was Doug's cue light, and happily led off the procession. We got the spectacular shot, the BBC got an empty promenade. Happily, the BBC director accepted our offer of a large drink in compensation!

For the last fifteen years of my time on the conferences I was the sole director for ITV. We had only one OB unit for colour and so all the output had to come from that one unit. I became very adept at doing my own vision-mixing on a mixer that the engineers had adapted for me. By pressing the right buttons it was possible *simultaneously* to transmit the conference live to the ITV network, do a three-camera discussion in the studio in any language plus captions, give ITN a special feed of the conference that was different from the ITV feed and also feed the monitors which were scattered around the hall – for visitors to see – with conference that did not include anything that was not taking place in the Conference Hall. This meant also that I had to have a special pair of headphones that had conference sound in one ear and a switchable sound source in the other.

There was intense competition between the BBC and Granada but it was always a friendly rivalry. Many times we helped each other – for example, we loaned our mobile generators to the BBC for their early transmissions of the Grand National when they did not have the silent type that we had. And we jokingly said, when people pointed out the BBC painted on equipment they loaned us, that BBC stood for Bernstein's Broadcasting Company!

In the early days, TV equipment was not very reliable and it was a norm that a piece of equipment would break during a transmission. We even rehearsed potential breakdowns in the studio by having the engineers remove a camera picture, at any time and any camera, during the dress rehearsal of an ad-lib programme such as *University Challenge* or *Scene at 6.30* so that the Director could practise alternative ways of doing the programme. The programmes were live and we did not have the present-day luxury of reliable equipment and tape editing.

In the 1960s Granada engineers made one of the first mobile tape recording units in the world. Constructed in the back of a large van, called a tender, which was normally used to carry camera and sound cables, the unit was used for a variety of programmes such as *Zoo Time* with Desmond Morris. However inspirational, it could be hazardous to use. The director and production assistant sat on hard-back chairs at a wooden trestle table at the back of the tender with all the rest of the equipment in front of them. The only way into the unit was via the roll-up door at the back against which the director and PA often leaned! Later the equipment was re-installed into a modified *Travelling Eye* vehicle – oh the luxury of proper seats and air-conditioning!

This unit was also equipped to record at all TV Standards – 405 or 625 European Standard or the 525 American Standard. Because of this the American CBS Network hired me and a small Granada crew to record items in the American 525 line standard, on the death of Winston Churchill. We used a makeshift studio in the basement of Granada's London offices to conduct interviews with key players in Churchill's life and record readings from Churchill's memoirs by Rex Harrison. The unit then went on to Heathrow but was linked to central London to record the funeral procession and service in Westminster Abbey for the entire CBS network in America. In those days there was no satellite in synchronous orbit, so we had to send the tape on the first available flight to America.

We positioned ourselves at the end of the runway at Heathrow with a hole in the fence through which a despatch rider could drive with the bag of tapes. This meant we could record up to the last few seconds before the plane took off, cut the tape with ordinary scissors, hand the take-up reel to the despatch rider who drove to a waiting plane and tossed the bag in through an open door before the plane taxied on to the main runway.

On landing at an American east coast airport, the procedure was reversed – the tape was thrown out of the plane into the arms of a despatch rider who took it to a mobile videotape machine positioned at the end of that runway and from there fed immediately into the CBS network. By doing this CBS was able to be some 15 minutes ahead of its rival ABC.

In May 1979 I was asked to direct a series of *Hypotheticals* from Painters Hall in London. This was and still is, as it has now gone to the BBC, a programme that discusses problems of moral and political difficulties using techniques pioneered at the Harvard Law School. The problem, for the director, was that it was a discussion in which the participants would be sitting in a horseshoe shape and that the chairman, or moderator as the Americans call him, would be walking about and talking to them the whole time. I was asked to come up with a shooting plan that involved cameras being able to see who was talking at any time while at the same time obsuring the cameras themselves. In addition, the pictures should not have 'reverse angles' – that is the pictures should be shot in such a way that if a picture has some one looking right then the picture of whom they are talking to should have them looking left – otherwise the illusion is that they are not talking to one another! Also the sound from each person had to be clear because we were to record for up to three hours and edit it down to one or one and a half hours. I said I thought we could do this and we went ahead.

The first series was called *The Bounds of Freedom* and we were nominated for an Emmy. We went on to do many more programmes using this technique. I have a photograph which was signed by Fred Friendly, Ed Murrow's old producer, who had developed the technique in America for the Ford Foundation to use in conferences, in which he compliments me on the use of this technique on TV.

I remember just as vividly directing the Beatles' last performance on Granada with my wife as vision mixer. At the time she asked the group to sign her boots, all four did so … and then she threw the boots away when they no longer fitted!

I still return to Granada to do the occasional programme. I know it is usual to say 'it was better in my day' – but it was. The spirit of adventure was everywhere. We were pioneers in many TV techniques that are now taken for granted. With heavy equipment which kept working by the grace of God and dedicated engineers.

I can still see SLB – 'Uncle Sidney', in my mind – walking down the corridor and addressing everyone by name. And also running his fingers above the door frames and other surfaces to look for dust and saying, 'Mr Pook this is dirty, get it cleaned.' A happy family, and we probably will not see its like again.

The French adventure

STEVE HAWES

It was really a European adventure, but it began and ended in France, and France was where most of it happened.

Our tour guide was David Highet. Highet was our PR master, the perfect MC, a man who had learned to master panic through a thousand near-misses, our grace-under-pressure man. For most of us, the beginning was Manchester Airport on a chilly winter morning. David Plowright was leading twenty or so Granada programme makers to Paris for a 'conference' with French producers and broadcasters. Though half of us lived in London, we were all flying together from Manchester. There was, of course, a point to this. For all our new-found continentalism, we remained provincial and proud of it. We didn't want anyone in Paris to confuse us with smug South Bankers or Euston Roadwalkers. So the Londoners among us had to catch the train to Manchester the night before in order to arrive in Paris from the right place. As he ushered us through passport control into the duty free zone, Highet advised us to stock up on chocolate. 'Always useful abroad,' he said, with barely concealed lasciviousness.

In truth we were on our way more to a first date than to a conference. We were going to make relationships. 'Don't rush it,' counselled Highet, as we jostled to get on the plane. 'What's called for is a little *délicatesse*.' He kissed his fingertips with Gallic flourish. 'Dellyca– what?' jeered a voice. Highet looked up reprovingly. 'It's French for "tits first", Raymond.'

Once we were airborne, he leaned across the aisle, all sotto voce, *'Entre nous*, Hawes, you've been to France before, haven't you?' he said, checking for eavesdroppers. 'Chairman'll need to know the French for "reversing the flow".' He touched his nose. 'Give it some thought, la'.'

'Reversing the flow', the chairman's own coinage, had become our catchphrase and mission statement. The idea was to make alliances in

Europe, to open our channels to each other, *mi casa – su casa*, to pre-buy, pre-sell, co-finance, co-write, co-produce. 'Co – anything you like,' summarised Highet, a sapper in the minefield of continental sensibilities, 'except ... ' – he looked over his shoulder and nodded appeasingly at the Air France steward, before articulating a confidence *à la* Hilda Baker '... except "collaborate". They don't like to be reminded.'

It was 1986. The idea was not only to resist the flow of cheap program-mes from North America and Australia which, under the deregulation the government were bent on, we feared might wipe us out, but to strike back as well. We thought we could make inroads into the US networks. The Euro-pean market would, we ventured, provide enough finance for us to make programmes first and then sell them to the USA – thus denying American executives the editorial voice which they assumed they could buy through co-finance and which, we sensed, would steer us into debilitating com-promise. We felt we – Granada – were uniquely suited to the job of rallying Europe's cultural fightback. As programme makers from the House of *Brideshead, Jewel, The Dustbinmen* and *The Wheeltappers*, we saw ourselves uniquely mixing the mandarin and the demotic. Who better to fend off North America's worthy sentimentalism and instead to reverse the flow? 'Le reflux,' I suggested as we crossed passport control into French territory.

'Re-what?'

'Flux.'

'Christ, don't tell him that! Think of something else, la'.'

In a way, as we contemplated the future and our place in it, we were collectively a little prim and maidenly. We had been hanging on to our purity. In broadcasting terms this was a kind of cultural Platonism: for other's sake, as well as ours and our ambitions. Might there have been one or two, sitting in the airbus as it flew above the Channel, who were thinking of offering our virtue – and with it the *bonum publicum* – across another sea? *Passons!* There and then, knowing that we had to lose it, we had decided to surrender in a series of arranged marriages – consensually and consentingly, with partners who 'respected' us. The marriage broker was the alluring head of our Paris office, Sara de Saint Hubert.

The word *délicatesse* seemed to have been invented for Sara. As she intro-duced the French partners she had chosen for us, at the reception of the Relais Christine behind the Quai Voltaire, she seemed to be whispering gently in our ears that there was no going back, but that it would all be all right – that we would probably learn to enjoy it. She knew them and she knew us. And she was sure we would find 'a certain *affinité*'. This became our next catchphrase, and we all learned to pronounce it as Sara did – with wicked fricative insistence.

One or two of our prospective partners were sceptical. They were not quite as welcoming as we had expected. Could they be playing hard to get? It seemed a little early to offer chocolate. They had, someone explained in an early exchange, already had experience of the co-pro, and it had not been a happy process. Dealmakers had tried to tie them into output agreements which had all come to grief before the first programme had been made. 'Co-production is the last resort of the desperate producer,' said another. '*Les Anglo-Saxons* in particular failed to understand what the French viewer wanted,' added the man from Antenne 2. 'You think it makes us happy to see France on French television? Albert Finney in the Eiffel Tower. Albert Finney for you, the Eiffel Tower for us. *C'est ça, la co-pro à l'anglo-saxonne.*' But the chairman's team were not deal makers or accountants, we were producers. 'In fact,' he was heard to mutter, 'very few of them are capable of simple arithmetic.' So we began, slowly, *délicatement*, to explore what could be done. And that, we ended up agreeing, at least for the moment, meant sharing the creative, then making the deal. Simple. Anyone could deal. The hard part was the ideas, the flair. What it needed was people of similar taste, creative people prepared to share, *le savoir français, le phlegme britannique, la mutualite, le bon goût* ... Taste. In the end, or rather at the end of the day, it was about taste.

Dinner was followed by speeches. Increasingly optimistic, not to say euphoric speeches. Glass clinked against glass. Eventually, it was time to go to bed. Someone raised a glass and proposed a final toast along the lines of 'the sum of our parts being greater than ... ' Highet sensed danger. 'Don't rush it,' he said, as we rose to brave the night.

Though we didn't know it at the time, the adventure had begun much earlier. Granada were part of a consortium bidding for the main French commercial channel, what became TFI. In fact, that very day, the announcement was made that someone else had got it. Not us. Everyone in the know knew this was a turning point. It turned out to be the turning point. I suspect that David Plowright knew it there and then, and spared us his disappointment.

French television was so dreary at the time – Christine Okrent, a few Balzac adaptations and the Canal + movies apart – that anything was going to be an improvement. Whoever got TFI was going to win. Within weeks, it turned out to be a goldmine, stole all the ratings – and ran away with the prize. And we weren't part of the deal. Better dealmakers had done for us. Bastards. Three years later Granada's Paris office closed. In between times we had boosted European sales a bit, made a couple of good TV movies with NDR in Hamburg and – in Manchester and Bordeaux rather than in Paris and London – had 'shared the creative' on *A Tale of Two Cities*, written by an Englishman, directed by a Frenchman, and with a French and English cast.

There felt to be a lot riding on *The Tale* when it we first broadcast it, two hundred years to the day – give or take an anachronism or two – after the storming of the Bastille. The truth was that we had miscalculated. It was not to the English taste, at least not if the critics were to be believed, although I have several aunts who think they were wrong – and, almost without exception, I'm told, their neighbours agree with them. It did fine in France and – here's an irony – even better in the USA, Simon Schama, no less, fêted it in the *New York Times*, and the *Hollywood Reporter* voted it the second or third in 1989's top five television programmes. But the thumbs went down in England – and Sidney Carton was not the only one to lose his head.

Still, while it lasted, it was the best of times.

I wanted to come home

Peter Mullings MBE

In 1952, after six years in the theatre, I broke into BBC TV as a stage manager, on show-by-show contracts. Three years later commercial TV came into being and I applied, both to Granada and the Kemsley-Winnick Consortium who had been appointed to run the weekday and weekend TV in the north. I was a Mancunian and I wanted to come home. Encouraging letters came from Granada and I had an interview. By now I was working at Associated-Rediffusion TV as a stage manager, on the daily soap opera *Sixpenny Corner* live every morning at 11 a.m. from the Viking Studios in Kensington – the studios which had been booked by Granada for their training course.

I was asked to go to Golden Square. To my surprise I walked into a conference on Granada's training school, which was to open in December 1955. All the top GTV brass were there including Sidney and Cecil Bernstein, Victor Peers and Joe Warton. I was able to give information about Viking. I was puzzled as to why I had been invited to attend. I asked Denis Forman why. He said I should have been told that they wanted me to teach floor managing at the school. I said that I claimed to be an FM but that I had only actually floor managed two shows and that I would not tell others how to do the job with so little experience under my own belt. Forman said he understood and that they would contact me later. They did not – someone had torn up my file!

While I was still with A-R my agent sent me up to Manchester to do a camera test for station announcer. I was asked back for a second audition, this time with all the top brass assembled in the control room to watch (no recording or even monitor distribution system was yet available). The producer came to the floor and thanked everyone, asking three of us to stay behind. I had a job at Granada TV. Not the floor manager's job that I wanted, but a job. I bumped into Guy Nottingham who said, 'Oh, good, here you are. We wanted a floor manager.' I told him I was engaged as an announcer but 20 minutes later I was a floor manager. I gave my notice at Associated-Rediffusion and floor managed the first show to be transmitted by Granada two weeks later.

It has been well documented that only liberal doses of strong black coffee administered to Quentin Reynolds, the famous Canadian Radio and TV commentator who was presenting Granada's first show, sobered him up enough (just!) for the show to open. What is not as well known is that I was the one who saved the camera that was to take the impressive wide-angle shot of the main studio from burning out. I passed the camera on my way to get a last cup of coffee (white!) while the hour long line-up was being completed and saw smoke billowing from the top. In the days before transistors, all equipment was filled with thermionic valves which generated a great deal of heat and the cooling fan had broken down. On my alarm vision engineers hurried to the studio and managed to shut down the channel before any permanent damage was done. A new fan was installed and at 7.30 p.m. on 3 May 1956 Granada Television went On Air.

A few months later when I was floor managing *What the Papers Say* when it transmitted live at about 10.30 p.m., I was having a coffee, in the canteen, during line-up. Denis Forman, who was producing, had taken the presenter for a drink at a local pub (Granada was a dry station in those days) when there was a Tannoy for anyone from *WTPS*. I took the call and it was SLB. He asked me if I had the script: a quick dash to the table and I was back at the phone. He asked me to read the script. I did: twenty minutes long in those early days. At the end he said, 'Very good, there are just two points I would like you to make to Denis.' And he proceed to make two very good observations, one legal and one a matter of better English. As we were ringing off I said that I had thought he was in America. He said he was. At that time it was one of the longest transatlantic calls that I had been involved in – later I discovered that SLB was staying with Alfred Hitchcock who presumably picked up the bill!

When Carl Robert, the Assistant Production Manager, went on a four-week honeymoon in 1957 I was detailed to take over his job. This entailed scheduling all the studios, production assistants and camera crews. One day during the Asian flu epidemic, Jack Martin (the figurehead Production Manager) called out and asked me if we could mount a live commercial for

Aspro at 7 p.m. which was in about an hour and a quarter. A quick look at the schedules showed that we could. Production Office assistants (Graham Wild and Bill Leather) were sent out with schedule alterations. They reported back at about 6.15 p.m. that it was all go and everyone had signed for and accepted the alteration.

Around 6.30 p.m. I called across to Jack saying that the one piece of information I had not got from him was who was directing the commercial. 'Oh,' said he, 'Didn't I tell you? You are!'

'Who is the actor presenting it?' I asked.

'You have to get an actor,' he replied. There was now 30 minutes to transmission!

Happily, the casting office was still open. They contacted my mother who was an agent who supplied six of the original cast of *Coronation Street*. (She is probably the reason why I never directed any drama, although I had been the Senior Drama FM: it would have been inappropriate for me to be involved in casting.) She rang the station master at London Road station (later to become Piccadilly). A Tannoy went out for Tom Gowling, who was on his way home after a previous Granada show. He jumped into a taxi and arrived with about eight minutes to spare.

Dave Warwick (one of Granada's most prolific directors) was ending a rehearsal in Studio 3 – and overrunning. With five minutes to go I chucked him out of the seat and Don Leaver, the floor manager had a few words with Tom Gowling and we had a quick rehearsal. It fell to pieces. I rushed down to the studio floor and had some quick words, rushed back to the control room had another run-through. Again hopeless. More words, back to the control room. Ursula Coburn, the PA, was counting down and had reached 25 seconds to On Air. I had to decide whether to take a chance or tell Master Control that we could not make it and to fill. I decided to go ahead – at 10 seconds. It went perfectly. When transmission was over I shook like a leaf. I went down to the floor to thank everybody and found Don Leaver with an arm round Tom Gowling's shoulder, saying, 'Now, Tom, when we come to do it I'll stand a little more to the left.'

I said, 'When? That was it!'

The two of them then shook as violently as I had done. That was the first time I ever directed anything – and I am still surprised that I wanted to do more.

One assignment I will never forget was when I was sent to the OB of the Royal Lancashire Show as Assistant Director – which meant doing the vision mixing. I had never done this, nor had any training and found it daunting. Having managed to get through the complicated opening sequence of super-imposition of opening credits I breathed a sigh of relief and then realised that Fred Verlander, the commentator, was speaking and not in vision. The shot on air was of a sow with a brood of piglets. Verlander was saying, 'This great fat sow weighs ...' and I panicked pushing the button to transmit Camera 4 (whose monitor was not in line with the rest). As those words came out I had put on transmission a shot of Pat Smythe – the leading showjumper of the day – waiting to be interviewed.

Later I was told that Pat Smythe seemed destined to suffer such errors. Dave Warwick directing and mixing himself, the previous year's show had mispunched to a shot of Pat Smythe waiting for interview whilst the Grand Parade of cattle was taking place. The shot of her came on air as Verlander said, 'This is the prize cow of the show...' Poor lady.

Directing the Writers' Guild Awards from the Grosvenor Hotel in London I lost my voice. During rehearsals the FM, John Oakins, came to the scanner and complained to the sound crew that his radio cans were on the blink. 'What's the matter, John?' I croaked out in a hardly audible manner. 'Sorry, sound,' said John. 'Nothing.'

I directed precisely 750 editions of *What the Papers Say*, the last of which was on the actual day I retired in 1987. In earlier days we taped the show but were not allowed any editing; if anything went wrong it meant starting all over again. We had managed to get a perfect take on one very complicated show and were breathing a sigh of relief as the closing card caption sequence started. This entailed quick changes from the stage hands and as the penultimate caption on Camera 1 was whipped off to reveal the Granada station ident the vacuum effect took it off as well. At that moment the vision mixer mixed to the now missing caption, revealing the blackboard beneath with the words 'Gone to tea – Back in 10 minutes'. We had to do the complete show again.

Our viewers have been deprived of many moments of hilarity because of the now almost universal use of pre-recording. Moments like the occasion when Peter Wheeler took over the presentation of *Junior Criss Cross Quiz*. He was seen wandering the corridors of Granada muttering to himself, 'Junior Criss Cross Quiz. Junior Criss Cross Quiz,' almost convinced that he would get his tongue-tied up around it. Came the recording and he sailed through the title, then added, 'I'm the new boy – my name is Wheeter Peeler.' Take 2 ensued.

President Kennedy's visit to Ireland in 1963 will live long in my mind. Granada had been designated the Eurovision originating centre (why I never discovered) for the Radio Telefis Eireann pictures and I was the Eurovision originating director. Brian Inglis was the commentator, based in Dublin. With two minutes to transmission to the whole of Europe there were no pictures on the line from RTE. I grabbed the control line and asked Dublin what was wrong. I got the reply, 'Oh, well, the President is running late so we'll be having nothing to show you.' I said that we had to have pictures, had they not cameras in the streets of Dublin? Show us shots of Dublin. 'Who'd be wanting to see that?' said the voice at RTE. 'All Europe,' I replied. On the control line to Brian Inglis I explained that he would have to commentate on the views of Dublin that would be coming up. The Eurovision caption and music were transmitted and we cut to the pictures of Dublin and I waited for Inglis to speak. Silence. Back to the control line. Brian – tell us what we are seeing. 'You want me to describe the test card?' said Inglis. Although RTE were sending us pictures they were not transmitting them themselves in Ireland and Inglis only had an off-air monitor. So for about 20 minutes I described the buildings to Brian, over the phone, and he then told Europe what they were seeing. How much we got right between us I do not know.

Those of us who were lucky enough to have worked for Granada when the station started often talk of the spirit that existed among the small staff at the time. Granada went on air with less than 400, including cleaners and canteen staff. One occasion that sums up that spirit for me was when in Studio 3 a live commercial for Jennifer Lee dresses was due. I was the FM. The opening shot called for a camera to dolly into a model of a corridor and as the doors at the end were reached a match mix occurred to full-size doors on the main set. Owing to a problem in another studio we were left without a tracking dolly and all our cameras were mounted on 'skids'. We needed to build tracks to get one to dolly on line. It was 8 p.m. All the chippies had gone home. Carl Robert and I raided the carpenters' shop. Taking lengths of timber and a locked box of tools. We managed to make tracks. The following morning I was in Carl's office when a chippie came in. 'Did it work?' he asked.

'Did what work?' we replied.

'The camera tracks in Studio 3.'

We asked him how he knew. He said that when he had arrived for work that morning he could not find his tools – we had forgotten to return them to the carpentry shop – and that his search had brought him to Studio 3 where he had found them with the lock forced open. He was not concerned about the vandalism to his tools, his only concern was that it had worked. That, to me, sums up in a nutshell the spirit that existed in those early years of Granada Television.

A transmission controller

PADDY OWEN

I joined the Sales Department in October 1958. The offices were in Granada House, now demolished. On the same floor was the Research Department which included Barrie Heads, Jeremy Isaacs, David Plowright and Pat Owtram, a lively bunch who congregated in The Baulking Donkey. It became the first stop for a few jars on the way home, or to other forms of entertainment.

I soon discovered that sales was not my cup of tea, so I had an interview with Norman Price, the Personnel Officer. He spotted that my army experience with the Signals Regiment providing the communications for General Eisenhower's HQ SHAEF during the invasion and subsequently in Versailles, should be more profitably employed. He arranged for me to appear before a Board and I was transferred to the Presentation Department as an assistant controller. The controllers were Jimmy Graham, Keith Evans and Brian Armstrong – a formidable team.

In those days, we were on the air Monday to Friday. The weekends were the responsibility of ABC. Our weekends were devoted to imbibing vast quantities of alcohol, parties and sampling the Manchester club life. I was expected to produce a gourmet Sunday lunch after which Brian Armstrong would conduct various symphonies, particularly Beethoven's 7th, on the record player, baton in one hand and a glass of whisky in the other. Unsurprisingly, during the Monday coffee break in the canteen, people would come up to us to see what state the controllers were in! We worked hard and played hard.

We had to preview all the day's commercials and films for transmission that day. There was then a mad rush to telecine – the first one got a reel of *Wagon Train* to preview so he could nod off for a bit. The assistant controller got the commercials and had to concentrate. We were also responsible for compiling the daily transmission schedule for the duty controllers and the departments involved in feeding the transmitters and the network.

I think the engineers thought the controllers were enjoying themselves too much, and they devised a diabolical automatic panel to be inserted in the transmission desk. This was before computers or any other form of modern technology was envisaged. We were instructed to transmit programmes both locally and to the network, plus commercials. The horrendous machine transmitted VTR clocks, standard leaders, in fact anything but what was scheduled. The machine chewed up the tapes just as the American machine I had experienced did at SHAEF. I tried to explain to the engineers but it fell on deaf ears. It was a nightmare.

I well remember one night being on duty with a colleague and we couldn't close down – the station clock kept reappearing, no matter what we did! In the end my colleague threw his pencils and stopwatch at the monitors and we walked out. During this period the controllers who weren't on duty congregated in my flat with vast quantities of whisky to watch transmission until the duty team arrived – when more Scotch was consumed and we calmed down. Eventually Denis Forman rang down and told us to return to the normal system. We told him that it was impossible to do so. He blew his top and the automatic panel was removed. Normality was restored. The company must have lost hundreds of thousands of pounds in revenue. Granada was not popular with the network and the controllers were nervous wrecks. I was eventually promoted to controller.

Over the years, we went on strike several times, and on one occasion I met David Plowright in the lift and he turned to me and said, 'Not you pulling down those bloody faders again, Paddy?' In fact it became a joke with the management that it was always me on duty when we went on strike.

Dramas in the early days were live from Studio 6. Once such play was *The Lark*. The leading actress was very nervous and being sick all over the studio during rehearsals. Jimmy Graham and I were on duty. Just before transmission, the director, Claude Whatham came into the control room to warn us. He said she had to get through Act 1, but he had been able to get Act 2 and 3 on tape (unedited) and would we run the tape behind the studio performance, so that we could cut to it if the worst happened. Thankfully all went well, and the network never knew how close we were to disaster.

During the period that the American Space Programme was in its infancy, ITN was feeding live pictures of the launches and the astronauts return to Earth. This was very exciting, but caused headaches as programmes and commercial breaks had to be rescheduled at short notice. Very often these occurred on Friday evenings, when the top brass had departed for London and the south.

The early days were the 'Golden Era'. Once middle-management guys were installed, a brick wall was established and contact between the shop floor and the Sixth Floor became impossible. It caused a breakdown in communication and, sadly, disillusionment. The great spirit on the shop floor continued to flourish, albeit somewhat less.

When I retired from Granada, I was given a fantastic farewell party, together with a book containing kind thoughts and messages from so many people, from Sir Denis Forman down. It was a sad day when I left, but I went out on a 'high' and not when I was 'over the hill'.

Before *Coronation Street*

DENIS PARKIN

In early 1960, before the advent of *Coronation Street*, Granada decided to produce a drama series based on the *Biggles* books of Captain W. E. Johns. Each story was to be in three parts of thirty minutes each, and transmitted twice a week at 7 p.m. on the network. I was asked to design the sets for the series. They were to be produced in fortnightly periods, the three episodes for each script being recorded over two days with all the sets for each story being fitted into the studio at the same time.

Video recording in those days, which was of course all in black-and-white, was primitive to say the least. There were no facilities for filming locations which, considering the fact that the stories involved aircraft and were set in distant parts of the globe, stretched the imaginations of writer and designer to the limit. There were also no facilities for editing; any mistakes meant going back either to the beginning or to the commercial break, and starting again. A costly process frowned on from on high. As a consequence of this ruling (which is what it amounted to) mistakes which did happen were left in, often with hilarious results.

To simulate the flying sequences, I purchased the body of an Auster light aircraft, without wings, and this was positioned in the studio against a pale blue backing on to which were projected clouds through a cloud disc. This was an electrically driven circle of perspex placed in front of a 2 kW lamp, the image of clouds around the disc edge having been made by smeared thumb prints in lamp black. So long as we didn't show that the plane had no wings it all worked rather well. Air-to-air shots were made using balsa-wood models. These were pre-filmed and fed into the programme at the appropriate points while the studio portions of the script were being recorded, and this all required split second timing.

The programme was well received and new writers were brought in, none of whom knew anything about aircraft. One was Tony Warren who has himself admitted that he once wrote, 'Biggles pulls the thing which lands the plane.'

The whole design budget for three episodes was around £500, a low budget even at a time of low budgets. Demands for special effects came with every script, and there was no thought of using a specialist, so I was responsible for all the effects used. Granada had in its library just one book about effects used in films, most of which dated back to the silent film days when the movie camera, to produce the illusion, had to be bolted down to be exactly in register between the model and the live action.

To attempt this with a TV camera on a dolly was quite daring, but ignorance and enthusiasm carried us through. None of the programmes survive, which is probably just as well. I have often compared the early days of television with the film industry of thirty years earlier. Everyone was young, enthusiastic and happy to be part of the growth of a new and exciting medium. I loved the challenge of set design, being able to decide the environment of scripted characters. If the set wasn't noticed to any great extent I reckoned it to be right for the particular scene.

Comic mishaps were more frequent on *Biggles* than on any other programme I was involved in – even the comedies! *Biggles Down Under*, for example was partly set on the bridge of a destroyer, and the commander had a line, 'I think the fog is closing in, Number One', at which a stagehand let off the fog gun and the actors were enveloped in a grey cloud.

In another episode there was a scene in a general's office, and through the window was a projection shot of soldiers on a parade ground. Unfortunately the film ran out before the end of the scene, but the actor, with great presence of mind, closed the curtains.

The problem of an erupting volcano in another episode was solved after much experimentation by using hot porridge mixed with red paint and lumps of dry ice to simulate the steaming molten lava, uprooting toy trees as it flowed down the side of my model mountain.

The decision was eventually taken to end the production, which all the crew had realised was inevitable, but new ideas had been tried, some of which worked! My next production was a new serial by Tony Warren called *Coronation Street*, on which I was designer with the original production team, but that's another story.

Shooting the messenger

DAVID ROBINSON

One of the perks of working in Public Relations is that you get to meet your gods. For most, this would mean talking to the stars of *Coronation Street* or some renowned Shakespearean actor. But I always worshipped the pop/ rock giants and I still have my Jagger T-shirt.

The most memorable occasion was when I met the magical Tina Turner after her Manchester concert, filmed for a series called *On the Road*. I watched her show then waited, awestruck, afterwards for 'a quick chat' (sounds better than 'an interview'). As I stood trembling outside her dressing room in the small hours of the morning I thought, 'There won't be any interview. She'll ignore me or plead tiredness.' (It happens frequently with lesser stars.) Eventually, as I was about to fall asleep on my feet, a dresser announced 'She'll see you now.' W-what? WHO'LL see me now? Panicking slightly – I lie, panicking a lot – I sat in the hallowed room awaiting the arrival of the great American legend. She glided in, wearing a long glittering gown and said, 'Hi, I'm Tina. Who are you?' Good question. Who the hell was I? I had genuinely *forgotten my own name*! I mumbled something (to this day, I don't recall whose name it was) and the 'quick chat' turned into an hour-long interview.

On the Road was a great success but it has to be said that Granada has also produced some unbelievably awful entertainment and quiz shows over the years, and many of these were given to me, alas, to write press releases for and promote to the indifferent press. Not an easy task. How on earth do you persuade a national newspaper to run a feature on a quiz that goes out in the early morning with an unknown host? Even bribing journalists with wine and fine food in London restaurants didn't always wash (although it did beat the Granada canteen into a cocked hat). When these bribes were ineffective, it would rouse the fury of some egomaniac producer who couldn't believe that his or her game show wasn't worthy of the front page of the *Sun*. And if it didn't win that dubious honour, a memo would sometimes go to my boss complaining that I hadn't done my job properly. The tales of backstabbing that I'd heard before I joined Granada all too often proved true.

One long-running, peak-time quiz show had been fully exploited in publicity terms. I had sent innumerable biographies of contestants to their local papers over the years. But now I was called upon to hold a national press conference to launch its tenth series. Having rung a few friendly journalists to gauge the interest factor (zero), I flailed around desperately for a gimmick. Then it dawned on me that the press conference would be held on Beaujolais nouveau day. So – hey presto – a Beaujolais breakfast with the star and the team. And a full house of journalists.

In the late 1980s Granada was transformed. It dispensed with hundreds of its workers. As a shop steward, I watched the ghastly process being played out, but I like to think I was sacked in a more interesting way than most. I was told that my job was being 're-defined' and advertised externally. Yes, of course, I could apply for my own job (jolly good of them) and I'd have an excellent chance of getting through the first interview and possibly the second. Perhaps even the third, but if I didn't succeed I'd have to take 'voluntary' redundancy. In the meantime I was advised to take 'soundings' among friends, Since I'd already made up my mind that 'moving the goalposts' like this meant the sack, I took a series of three-hour lunches with journalists, all on handsome expenses. Then I took Granada's gold and went freelance.

Ironically, an early assignment was for Granada – publicising the first series of *You've Been Framed* – The Head of Light Entertainment, David Liddiment, then Head of ITV, told me that he had great hopes for the programme and wanted to see it beating even *Coronation Street* in the ratings ('gulp!') So we hired a swanky gallery in London, laid on Buck's Fizz and arranged to play a compilation tape. 'No expense spared' was the rule, but would it be worth it? Thankfully, it was a roaring success – the place was bursting with photographers and reporters. Massive publicity and yes – it hit Number One in the ratings, thanks in great part to the first host, Jeremy Beadle. He comes in for a lot of stick but I found him courteous, co-operative and a complete professional.

The producer sent champagne to my office to thank me for my efforts, but any kind of thank you was the exception rather than the rule during the sad, bad days at Granada in the late 1980s. It was always easier to blame the messenger rather than the increasingly feeble message about the boring programmes that I'd been called upon to promote to the yawning world.

The Film Exchange

Roy Shipperbottom

The Film Exchange was as necessary to Granada as a saloon is to a Western film, there being nowhere else to meet easily, informally, free from the hierarchy. It was necessary to get away from 'The Building' or what Jim Allen called 'The wireworks'.

The first Granada pub was the New Theatre, famous for serving massive wedges of cheese, but it was due for demolition and the Film Exchange was found. Up the hill from Granada Studios in Quay Street, between the Skin Hospital and the post Office Social Club was a hidden windowless club. It was convenient, being almost opposite the Opera House and there were no signs. The discovery of this anonymous club is usually attributed to John Finch and Jim Allen who raised the hopes of the owners by immediately enrolling over one thousand members of the Writers' Guild. We somehow became lifetime members, free.

It was used by producers, directors, sound and lighting, cameramen, vision mixers, presenters, editors, musicians, actors, actresses, a credit list which would roll for ages. It was a particular oasis for lonely writers. The managers were Spanish, the most durable being called Patrick. Maureen Byrne and Terry were the long-serving, long-suffering Irish barmaids.

Maureen either liked you or didn't and it was soon apparent which mood she was in. Even the eminent did not escape. Laurence Olivier who was extremely familiar with the soliloquy as a dramatic device must have been astounded to hear the use of a loud, sustained, very audible mutter from one of the barmaids whose thoughts were a constant soliloquy. If he asked for a lager: 'Oh a drink is it?' soliloquised Maureen. 'Oh, Sir Laurence, or is it Lord, he wants a drink does he? Comes in here and I'm supposed to drop everything and get him a lager ... nothing else will do.'

The club kept pub hours and although there were those who heroically fought against closing time there was no chance of late drinking. Their problem of getting back to Granada after lunch remained. Some favoured the direct approach straight down Quay Street others, feeling guilty or vulnerable, and wishing to escape being observed from the upper floors by senior management went out of the back door, down a back street across a small park, a dash secured by the protective cover of the old St John's school, and then a swift walk across the street and they were in the building; it was known as the Ho Chi Minh trail.

There were young directors, Mike Apted, fresh from the explosion scene in *Coronation Street*, or Mike Newell who then wore a curious knee-length knitted garment like a collapsed cardigan would both, separately, put forward the need to produce some drama entirely on film. Mike Newell seemed to be about to win this race with John Finch's *Them Down There* which was made first, but Mike Apted with Jack Rosenthal's *Dustbinmen* was the first transmitted.

Drama producers included Derek Granger, who triumphed with *Country Matters* and whose *Brideshead* was interrupted by the strike that thinned out attendances in the club. Michael Cox's high production values were firmly based on talent and research. I remember his early discussions about the nature of Sherlock Holmes and Dr Watson and, later, telling the latest episode in the mystery of who owned the copyright of some versions of Sherlock Holmes. Richard Everitt entertained the family whose Cheshire home they borrowed as a location for Arthur Hopcraft's *The Birthday Run*, by telling them about his schoolmaster, Arthur Marshall. The new producers included Jonathan Powell, later to become Controller of BBC 1,

The producers of *Coronation Street* were handling a highly regarded treasure. Some were writers turned producers like Harry Kershaw, Peter Eckersley and John Finch.

Gus (now Lord) Macdonald, in charge of *World in Action* seemed to know everything. I had seen an advance copy of a paper on the reappearance of rickets in Britain and mentioned it to Gus. The location of the disease was secret but Gus knew about it, revealed where it had occurred and high-lighted the problems of using the information.

Brian Inglis was always shouting about doing *All Our Yesterdays*, a pro-gramme that ran forever and of which it was said that the last programme would be transmitted twenty-five years after the end of the world.

The gents' toilet was tiny and had traces of partially removed graffiti, a drawing of two cubes, captioned Picasso's Balls, and, in small capitals: Bill Grundy is ... (the rest was erased). I met Bill in his pre-television days when he was reviewing a play in York; he was perceptive, highly intellectual, bright, fluent, and became a great professional, combative, irascible, incisive but flawed when he had too much drink and his volcanic spirit erupted and increased in frequency.

World in Action reporters and documentary film makers came fresh from the airport with tales of tribesmen and terrorists. Mike Murphy and Brian Armstrong told of infiltrating Czechoslovakia as the Russians were invading, driving along lonely roads through pine forests and being trapped by Russian tanks.

Peter Eckersley, former *Guardian* reporter turned TV reporter, who wrote plays and scripts and (at one time) produced *Coronation Street* became Head of Drama and who fought for hour-long one-off plays was one of the centrepieces of the club. He seldom stopped working, longed for a café society, was witty, loved anagrams and word puzzles and was sometimes very vulnerable.

The conversations were often intense, there were those who in lighter moments, over a dry sherry, would discuss Hegel, but there were jokes, a few new ones, some very witty comments topical and transitory. There were more jokes about when John Hamp produced *The Comedians*. He came in one evening in a state of near ecstasy – he had taken a chance phone call from a potential performer who had told jokes brilliantly, non-stop for an hour and he had booked a winner and his name was Mike Reid.

The Film Exchange became so popular that it was expanded and the day came when we entered an enlarged club and gazed into dim landscape of small barrels with stone slab tops – these were meant to be tables and overhead more barrels suspended by chains; there had been an attempt at design. The bar was now a flat-based U-shape and the other side was sometimes occupied by barristers, who tended to behave themselves, and their clerks, who did not. Here were also journalists hoping for stories about *Coronation Street*; their persistence and ingenuity knew no limits.

Then it all ended. Entrepreneurs sensing that here was a moneyspinner of a place where crowds would come to see the stars, spent too much money on alterations, glossy finishes and polished floors, and it was too much. The Variety Club was started and Granada started its own club in the Old School and eventually the building that housed The Film Exchange was demolished. Many of the regulars had left Manchester to establish themselves in London; there were retirements and advancements and some deaths; Peter Eckersley, Mike Murphy and Bill Podmore died and I still miss them and the times when it seemed we had all the joy in the world.

Francis Head

Mark Shivas

'There's a job going in the Story Department at Granada,' said Philip Oakes to me at a movie press show late in 1963. 'If you can stand to work for the woman who runs it,' he added darkly.

I tiptoed along to Golden Square one afternoon for the interview. Tiny, behind a wide desk, leaning her considerable corsage on small, white folded arms was Bette Davis. No it was Francis Head, a lookalike. A dazzling smile extinguished immediately into a pouting gash of red. What books did I like? 'Well ... Scott Fitzgerald, for instance.' 'Everybody's read him,' she snapped back. 'Nothing more original than that?' I wasn't then used to the insult interview technique but I fought back and landed the job – Assistant to the Head of the Story Department. £1000 a year, a lot more than I'd earned hitherto.

Nothing has been as difficult since as working for Fanny Head. Ernest Hemingway could have named a book after the experience because around her department it was truly 'Death in the Afternoon'. Pint-size she may have been, indeed supposedly the Pocket Venus of 1935 in New York, but she was drunk four afternoons out of five and we were only spared the fifth because she visited the hairdresser and ate sandwiches in the office. The other four she went to a dank Spanish restaurant in Beak Street named the Barcelona and demolished Rioja by the yard.

One memorable day, dragging her mink along the carpet behind her, she returned at six and couldn't understand why her staff were packing up to go home. On another, she and a rather bulkier and taller lady producer tottered the hundred yards back to Granada's front door, propping each other up for support. As the producer lurched up the steps to No. 36, it dawned on her that she was holding nothing but an empty mink; Fanny had dropped out of the bottom.

Most people knew better than to phone or visit after lunch. If they did, they'd be abused or insulted. We, her staff (two secretaries and two assistants) had no choice but to be there. She had an unerring eye for weaknesses. My defence was not to rise to the bait, which was always tempting. My face was a mask – still is, perhaps. The other assistant, Ray, was less able to dissemble. She would rile him mercilessly and he would often emerge from her office white with fury.

But she taught me a hell of a lot – to be fussy about detail, never sloppy, to absorb information about the theatre, write reports on some of it. I went to an early performance of Joe Orton's *Entertaining Mr Sloane* at the Arts Theatre. I had to know what was on television, though there were only two channels. I had to read and report on unsolicited scripts that came in – Fay Weldon, then working for the Egg Marketing Board, sent a rather good one, I remember, and shortly afterwards was commissioned by Dick Everitt. I was supposed to follow what was going on in entertainment in New York and Los Angeles. I soon learned to stop talking about the movies even though I went to them. Concentrate on the theatre and television, she said. I'd had some old-fashioned idea that my evenings were my own but she invaded them telephonically rather too often and couldn't remember calling the following morning. She didn't seem to have a private life and didn't expect those who worked for her to have one either.

I helped to draft some of the deals for Granada's writers and producers (I possessed an indifferent legal degree, one of the reasons for my hiring) and not just in drama but right through the *World in Action* and documentary areas. Many of these people would walk or lurch into Fanny's office from time to time and a lot of them would ignore us, her staff, completely. It seemed to me there was a macho cult of rudeness and arrogance at Granada, fostered by the journalists, which overflowed into most areas of the company, with the exception of Julian Amyes and Gerald Savory. There were others who tried to get me to go drinking round the other corner of Golden Square to the unsuitably named 'Coffee Pot' or to the awful basement club of drunken drama queens called Gerry's. Usually I avoided going.

Two years of this seemed more than enough. Francis had given me my first job in television, but I'd put in enough work for her. I said I'd leave the company if I couldn't get into production proper, and so I became a researcher on *Scene at 6.30* in Manchester, followed by directing *All Our Yesterdays*, producing and then fronting *Cinema*, all in the space of two years. That sort of speedy progress was quite common then.

I stayed in touch with Francis, particularly after we'd both left Granada. We got on better. She liked to think, and she could have been right, that what she'd taught me had been partly responsible for my later success at the BBC. We even had lunches from time to time. They were fun and we didn't drink too much. But I didn't risk dinner.

Educational production

JACK SMITH

Granada's schools television broadcasting did not have the best beginnings. Sidney Bernstein was persuaded by friends and advisers (several of them distinguished scientists) that science in the sixth forms of our secondary schools presented the area where help from television might be of the greatest value. Accordingly, the first schools series was intended for the sixth form elite studying the sciences for what were then the A level examinations which controlled university entrance. (Later, sixth-form arts programmes were also produced.) As a characteristic gesture, Sidney presented TV sets on free loan, and with free servicing, to all the secondary schools with sixth forms in the Granada area.

But the problem was that schools simply were not geared up to using television programmes during school hours, whatever their relevance or quality, and never would be until it was possible to record the broadcasts and store them for future use when they fitted into the timetable and teaching schemes. And it has to be said that these early programmes were not relevant in the real worlds of school classrooms and laboratories.

At my first interview with Sidney (and I didn't get that first job) he told me that he intended *Television* for schools, not what he called an apeing of the instructional films made by a number of commercial firms and by one of the educational foundations, which schools could hire and project when it suited them, and which many teachers admired and made use of. But in fact the provision of a much greater number of such films, screened on the school TV set, was exactly what teachers wanted and needed (granted the timetabling difficulties which were to limit all school TV usage until the 'home video recorder' became available.) What Sidney thought best (encouraged by advisers who were far distanced from schools) was to invite distinguished scientists into the studio to give half-hour talks on their current research interests. In an ideal world, perhaps, an ideal choice. But teachers and their pupils did not want a succession of talking heads; they expected television to bring into school pictures of the world outside, chosen to make relevant educational points. Even the interpolation, in these *Discovery* programmes, of 'visual aids' in the form of ingenious animated captions, utilising much cardboard and mixing between studio cameras, with the occasional minuscule film sequence (sometimes library footage, sometimes film specially shot for the programme), did not provide the visual excitement that could be captured by an all-movie presentation.

At the same time, distinguished scientists were not necessarily distinguished TV performers – and they had to do their stuff, straight to camera in the unfamiliar atmosphere of the studio, after one stagger-through and what we called a dress rehearsal, with little opportunity for corrective editing later. Difficulties were often compounded when performers found it next to impossible to communicate at the level needed by their intended 16-to-18-year-old viewing audience.

Very few schools used *Discovery*, even in Granadaland where Sidney had scattered his free TV sets, and he was not best pleased. Some of the arts programmes, where a relevant studio set could be designed and used, were maybe slightly more eye-catching. But these, too, attracted very few school users. And Sidney continued to rule out wholesale use of film (which would, of course, also have been more expensive). On one occasion, Peter Mullings, the enthusiastic director of many *Discovery* programmes, found himself, with a film can under his arm, sharing a lift with SLB. 'What's that? Film?' growled Sidney, 'Look, Peter, we're making *Television* programmes, not films!'

Not that the programmes didn't produce some delights. Lord Rothschild presented a *Discovery* lecture on human sperm, which featured a large mechanically-driven model of one of the little beasties in the studio – a premonition of *Monty Python*. On another occasion, a leading chemical technologist, asked to provide a short ad-lib to cover a film clip, went on and on, until someone suggested to the PA that she should throw away her stopwatch and use a calendar to time him.

SLB did not get on well with the first Head of Education Programmes whom he had appointed. This was Joe Weltman, who left to join the ITA (later the IBA) as education gauleiter and then became their Director of Programmes (whatever that meant). Gradually, our schools programmes changed in character – but it was a slow process. Series for younger pupils were produced, and the range of subjects was extended, although there was always a strong science strand. Sidney Bernstein took rather less personal interest as time passed, although he could still make some dramatic intrusions. We built a somewhat fraught relationship with the Authority, whose education staff had a lack of realism matched only by the political correctness (and unrealism) of some of the advisers on its educational advisory committee. Granada had its own schools advisory committee, a loyal group which included some sturdily practical practising teachers.

Soon, there were adult education programme series as well, but this was never a strong area. Immensely practical series (buying a house, using the NHS) were stymied by impractical transmission times when members of the target audience could not get near their television sets. Later, it became a matter of persuading the Authority to classify quite different series as 'adult education' in a somewhat cynical attempt to fulfil the required quota – although there were honourable exceptions.

By the time home video recorders became generally available, our schools output looked very different from the earlier years. The few studio series incorporated much film footage, bringing the outside world on to the school TV screen using our own filmed sequences and also the work of talented film makers from the world of cinema. *Messengers* and *Picture Box* (this latter lovingly cared for by John Coop over many years, and one of the most used and useful of junior school series) built up significant audiences even before schools acquired the means to record programmes for later use. Soon, Granada's programmes for schools were attracting some of the biggest schools audiences, as school tape recorders became essential equipment in classrooms and laboratories. Programme budgets got a bit larger. It was realised that series on 'hard' subjects such as the sciences, shot entirely on film and with voiceover commentaries, were not only what British teachers wanted; they also had a big sales potential overseas. Our film crews brought back footage from Europe, the USA and the Middle East for scientific and geographical programmes, some of which became standard material for the teaching of their subjects. Maybe programming lacked the innovative excitements of some earlier efforts, such as, for example, the live current affairs series *Afternoon Edition* which featured probably the first-ever television phone-in, or the *Discovery* programme when we linked up via the satellite Telstar with a computer in Boston, Massachusetts. But the programmes made in the 1970s and 1980s more than justified the time and money spent making them, giving Granada a high reputation among teachers throughout Britain, and indeed, throughout much of the world. It was an immensely rewarding activity for those of us who worked on them, too.

But life was still never very easy. The demands which schools broadcasting make on a television station can cause immense irritation. Programmes, and the printed material which accompanies them (later, computer software as well) simply have to be planned a year or so ahead and produced strictly on time. And the work cannot be done by just anybody who happens to be without a current assignment. At the same time, it can be disheartening to work hard to create products which one's colleagues never see. But yes, it was rewarding, and often great fun.

Sidney could still make a characteristic appearance. One afternoon I was summoned to his Manchester office. Sidney had got hold of one of the booklets accompanying a school series, and he didn't like it: 'Why are you wasting money on things like this? Look at the page size. Look at the margins. Far too wide. Waste. We have a man at Golden Square, Alan Pinnock, who could design a far better job than this. Why don't you use him?'

I told him that Alan had, in fact, designed this booklet, as he did all our similar publications. He appeared not to have heard me, and went on looking at the printed pages. Then: 'In that case, Jack, what's troubling you?'

There seemed to be no answer to that. We chatted a few minutes longer, Sidney now friendly and on his best behaviour. Then, typically, he walked me over to the door and saw me out. he thanked me for 'coming to see' him. 'I'm always here, you know.'

Quite.

Once, in the days when the Dove aircraft shuttled between Heathrow and Ringway, ferrying Granada people to and fro, I was offered a flight back to Manchester on the plane by Margaret Hewitson, who very efficiently arranged travel at the London end. It was a lunchtime flight, and she told me that I would be sharing it with Cecil Bernstein, with whom I had not had many contacts. He was most anxious, said Margaret, to apologise to me that he would only have lunch for one aboard, as he hadn't known he was to have company. I grabbed a snack at Golden Square, then joined CGB in the limousine which took us to the airport.

Once airborne (Cecil white-knuckled, for he hated flying) I awaited with some interest for him to start lunch. A Harrod's hamper? A little lobster salad and some cold pheasant? Washed down with ... ?

He opened his briefcase and took out a brown paper bag, from which he took out a sandwich. He examined its contents. 'Ugh! She knows I hate salmon! Do please have one of these with me.'

I ate a tinned salmon sandwich, and later half a banana which he also insisted I should accept. Here I was, high in the clouds in a private plane, sitting next to one of the owners of the company, munching tinned salmon. I'd never dreamt that television would be as glamorous as this.

A terrible mistake ...

Liz Sutherland

I joined Granada on 16 June 1958 for the perfectly adequate salary of £8 a week and started in the Contestants Department, working for the theatrical Eve Caneva on *Twenty One*. The first transmission was on 3 July 1958 and the Contestants Department was involved in finding suitable participants. Even then, the chance to appear on television drew thousands of applications. Eventually the balloon went up about cheating – the complaint was made by a contestant who was a waiter at the famous Bell Inn, Aston Clinton.

Other quiz programmes needed contestants – *Spot the Tune, Make Up Your Mind, Concentration, Criss Cross Quiz* and *Junior Criss Cross Quiz*. Quiz masters included Chris Howland, Jeremy Hawke and (a young) Bob Holness.

Chelsea at Eight and then *Nine* was the big Studio 10 production. Charles Laughton topped the bill one week; another week a very striking-looking woman was standing in the wings, almost wringing her hands with nerves – the great Maria Callas. A young American comedian had a hilarious routine as a drunk scoutmaster; he grew up to be Johnny Carson.

In January 1959 I passed a Board for Production Assistants and moved to Manchester to start as a trainee under the wing of Margaret Wood on *Shadow Squad*. It was a hard routine of rehearsals and live transmission and my reaction on first seeing her at work in a control room was, 'This is a terrible mistake, I'll NEVER be able to do this.'

Trainees often had to assist Senior PAs on Drama. One week I was assigned to Rosemary Clarke, working for Silvio Narizzano on *Shadow of a Pale Horse*. During dress rehearsal the pale horse had (of course) left its mark and Silvio called down for the manure to be removed. No one seemed keen to do this, so in a flash Silvio was on the floor with a shovel in his own fair hands, doing what all good directors have to do ... I was terribly impressed!

Then I was transferred to a another programme which was to prove the beginning of many things – *What the Papers Say* with director Mike Wooller, producer Tim Hewat, PA Jane Nicholl; and Jeremy Isaacs was involved, too.

Mike had appalling writing and it was a weekly challenge to translate his scribbled shots into a clean script. And then the shots had to be called. One memorable programme had 115 shots to be called in 12 minutes 24 seconds – and I do mean 24 seconds – or was it 27? Pre-fading grams at 11 minutes 54 seconds did no more than guarantee the final notes of the signature would be there *if* there was time to fade them up at the very end.

Two particular *WTPS* broadcasts linger. When I joined the programme, Jane suggested that for Week 1 I should just watch her; in Week 2, I would do the rehearsal and she would do transmission; and in Week 3 I would do it all. Week 1 – no problems. Week 2 – I set about the rehearsal and all went well. I was just making way for her at the control desk when she said, 'OK, you do transmission.' There wasn't time to do anything, but take a huge gulp – Mike grinned – I checked the time with transmission control and went for it. Fifteen minutes later I had finished my first live transmission.

Some weeks later Bernard Levin was the presenter and broke the *Broadcasting Act* throughout the programme. Capital punishment was still in existence and Levin opened the programme with the chilling phrase, 'It is not given to many of us to know the hour of our death, but in x hours and y minutes —— will be hanged by the neck until he is dead.' He kept coming back to this at two-minute intervals during the programme, noting the reducing time left to the prisoner each time. The lighting and set had been changed to a plain flat with just the shadow of bars cast behind Levin at the desk. From that night on, I have been against capital punishment.

Tim Hewat produced *Searchlight*, the forerunner of *World in Action* in the middle of 1959. Mike Wooller was again the director and Pauline Lawson the PA. Still a trainee, I went too. The programmes were shot on film and then introduced from Studio 10 by Kenneth Allsop. The subjects alternated between good news and bad news; a vivid 'bad' one was 'Dirty Food' in which a stall-holder in a London open-air market lifted his cat off the meat block and then dug spirals of ingrained dirt from the damp surface.

At the end of August I had made it – a real first year production assistant; and now it would be possible, one day, to earn £1000 a year! That ambition was soon realised as the ACTT Union battled successfully to have some of the 'licence to print money' shared with staff. And I was able to move back to London where I was assigned to *The Army Game* – produced by Peter Eton and directed by Max Morgan-Witts. A regular cast was Alfie Bass, Bill Fraser, Harry Fowler, Ted Lune and Mario Fabrizi. It was a grinding routine of office work on Monday, outside rehearsal Tuesday to Thursday, and studio rehearsal and live transmission on Friday. On Thursday evenings Max plotted his camera scripts with great care, moving little cardboard camera pedestals with string cables around the floor plan, all to be translated into a camera script with matching camera cards. *The Army Game* was extremely popular and regularly in the Top Ten ratings. There was never any difficulty in getting a live audience to fill the dress circle at Studio 10.

One Friday morning everyone arrived except one. Phone calls were made to his home, eventually raising a mumbled answer – he was clearly not feeling well. I was sent to bring him to the studio. He was in bed when I arrived and it was obvious that he had been on a monumental blinder the night before and was still extremely drunk. Eventually I got him to the studio where it was clear that he couldn't possibly do the show. After a quick conference between Max and the cast the part was shared out and the action re-plotted. It was a tense afternoon, but everyone did a terrific job. It may not have been the most elegant episode, but the audience probably didn't notice the joins.

During 1960 there was a sea-going version of *The Army Game* called *Mess Mates*, again produced by Peter Eton and starring Dick Emery, Archie Duncan, Fulton Mackay and Bobby Metcalfe. It was not particularly successful and only ran for one season.

Then there was the even less successful *Colonel Trumper's Private War*, perhaps a forerunner of *Dad's Army*, but without any of that classic's quality despite an interesting cast of Dennis Price, Moray Watson, Bill Gaunt and Warren Mitchell. The series was cancelled after only six transmissions.

Then I was assigned to the very successful *Spot the Tune* presented by Pete Murray and the delightful Marion Ryan. The director was Phil Casson who has the best laugh of anyone in the business. It was mostly a giggle, except that the final programme in the series ended with 'The Party's Over' which reduced Marion Ryan and quite a few of us to tears.

After a three-month strike by Equity in the autumn of 1961 it was back to Chelsea with Phil Casson again, for *Swing Along* with Marion Ryan and the King Brothers. A certain Des O'Connor was also part of the show – and he would keep changing lyrics of the songs, which was much against the rules of the PRS in those days. My happiest memory of that particular show was of Marion giving me a pair of tickets for one of Frank Sinatra's concerts. It was *the* event of the year and tickets were like gold dust.

In September 1962 I heard that Tim Hewat was setting up a new series and I volunteered to work on it. Tim made it very clear that I would spend all the time in the office typing scripts and transcripts and I could not, repeat not, expect to go out with the film crew. Two months later I was with him and a full crew in Hamburg! It was the start of *World in Action*.

But before that got really started there was the Cuba missile crisis. Having previously made the *Cuba Si* documentary, Tim was asked to make a special as the crisis developed. It was the first time I had worked through the night and as the news bulletins got worse and worse, it was really quite frightening to be in the dark and deserted offices wondering if the sun would ever rise again over Carnaby Street.

For *World in Action* Tim had recruited a remarkable group of talented people among them Mike Wooller, Bill Grundy, Alex Valentine, Stephen Peet, Louis Wolfers (who worked as a director cameraman and was assisted by Gavrik Losey, son of the famous Joe). The adviser/consultants were Michael Shanks of the *Financial Times* and David Floyd of the *Daily*

Telegraph; researchers included Clare Ash, Diane Farris and Dick Fontaine. And significantly, he chose to break the current affairs convention and chose two voices – Wilfrid Thomas and Derek Cooper – neither of whom would ever appear in vision.

The *WIA* office was on the fourth floor of the company's London office in Golden Square, complete with cutting rooms, film library, and viewing room as well as the long production office. It was well isolated from the rest of the company and set the style for the team and the programmes. Occasionally 'outsiders' would struggle up the stairs or across the walkway from the third floor. A long table covered in newspapers and scripts and telephones dominated the whole room. Tim Hewat sat at the end of the table and ruled the roost. Weekly post-mortem meetings were held after every transmission and everyone's opinion was invited, including that of Mrs Smith, our long-suffering tea lady, whose occasional 'Oh, yes, it was quite interesting' was high praise!

Peter Heinze headed the editing team including Gene Ellis, Terry Rawlings and Tony Osborne. They often worked through the night and more often than not, the cutting copy (with well-reinforced splices) was the transmission copy.

In those distant extravagant days, SLB and Denis Forman had agreed that Tim could make some pilot programmes that might or might not be transmitted. Alex went off to Italy and made a film contrasting the poverty of the south and the riches of the north. Another programme compared the standard of living between similar families in Northern England (Crosby), France (Lille), Germany and Italy. Bill Grundy and Tim planned an exposé of *Der Spiegel*, the sensational magazine produced by the controversial Axel Springer.

So we went to Hamburg and checked into the Atlantic Hotel. After three days and two nights' hard work, everyone had earned a night off; so next stop – the famous Reiperbahn. A difficult decision for me: whether to be ladylike and plead a headache, or go with them? To this day I am not completely convinced about what I saw; surely that stunning looking woman in that bar who was so pleasant to me can't have been a *man*?

World in Action went on the air for the first time on Monday 7 January 1963 with a programme about the arms race. Carefully cast look-alikes for Kennedy and Khruschev glared at each other across a large table map with model missiles stacked in America and the USSR, all shot in a meeting room at the back of Golden Square.

A film about the Congo, still under Belgian administration, was next and made by Alex Valentine. Programme 3 was a chilling film by Stephen Peet about East Germany, way beyond the Berlin Wall. Mike Wooller made a film about Rhodesia (sic), which was followed by the first 'profile' programme, on President de Gaulle who was busily opposing Britain's interested in the Common Market.

In early 1963, during one of the coldest winters any of us could remember, the next location for me was Newcastle for a film about Lord Hailsham who had been appointed Minister for the North-East, an area of massive unemployment. There were programmes about supermarkets and fashion, and then the first row with the IBA. The subject was defence and despite arguments at the highest level between Granada and the Authority, the programme was not transmitted. As the arguments got more and more heated Tim sent me out for a long walk, taking a file with me. Only later did I realise that the file contained the only version of the script so hand-on-heart, Granada could tell the IBA that there wasn't a script for them to see.

An outbreak of typhoid in Zermatt threatened to ruin the winter sports season of 1963 and so *WIA* flew there to find out how the rich were reacting. There wasn't time for any of us to get typhoid jabs before we left, so the only precautions we could take was to avoid all food and drink. In Geneva I bought wine and chocolate in large quantities and that was all we had to eat and drink until we got down from the mountains.

On the return journey, we had no more than 90 seconds to connect with the mainline express, so everyone, including Tim and Mike and David Samuelson (cameraman) and Arthur Bradburn (sound recordist), helped to shift 40 or 50 items of baggage and equipment across the platforms. We made it!

A couple of weeks later no particular subject been agreed at the Wednesday meeting so I took a long lunch. When I got back everyone had gone to Greece – to do a film about the heated and increasingly violent dispute between the Greek monarchy and government.

Towards the end of May, nothing of interest seemed to be happening and again the weekly meeting had not agreed a definite subject. During that afternoon our assistant cameraman wandered in and said that a cabinet minister had resigned. Tim pricked up his ears, sent out for the papers and the name of Profumo was in the headlines. Tim then disappeared for 36 hours, to work out what the competition might do. He returned saying that *WIA* would do a profile of Colonel Ivgeny Ivanov, the mystery Russian 'other man' in the Profumo/Keeler affair.

Someone located a picture – the only picture of this KGB agent – and I was sent out to get it from Churchill's Club off Bond Street. I had to pay well over a hundred pounds – in cash – which was a fortune in those days. But it was the only picture of Ivanov and, enlarged and made into a huge jigsaw – with a question mark in the centre – it was the start of the film. At the end of the programme, the eyes were slotted in. Cliché stuff now, but effective then.

The first series ended in June and everyone went on holiday. After a month in Spain and France, I got back to the office only to be sent off to Glasgow to research the Great Train Robbery. I arrived in Glasgow, not really knowing where to start, and settled for one of the banks that had suffered in the robbery. I was shown into the manager's office and found a typical Scottish bank manager – silver-haired, horn-rimmed glasses, navy suit, white shirt! Astonishingly, he did not have any problem in agreeing to let a crew come to the bank a few days later and film a lot of money. And when we turned up again, there were tens of thousands of pounds stacked on the counter!

The robbery was reconstructed on the Bluebell Line in Sussex. Designer Dan Snyder created a life-size cardboard cut-out of a diesel locomotive, secured it to the Bluebell engine, which duly steamed up and down the track in the middle of the night. And we filmed mailbags being thrown down the embankment by the bridge on the main line where the train had been stopped; and at the farm where the robbers had stayed to count their loot.

Before that programme was transmitted, *WIA* made a profile of Lord Denning, the Master of the Rolls who was conducting an enquiry into the Profumo Affair. Mandy Rice-Davies was to be a witness and she had agreed to be filmed. Early one morning Tim sent me to Dolphin Square to make sure she didn't change her mind. She didn't seem particularly surprised when she opened the door to me, wearing a very skimpy baby-doll night-dress, and retired to bed for a while, leaving me to look at the few books she had – mostly by Georgette Heyer. It was during her response to Lord Astor's statement that her allegations were completely untrue that she coined the immortal phrase, 'Well, he would, wouldn't he?'

The second series started in September 1963. New researchers had arrived: the late, lamented Arnold Bulka who teamed up with Brian (now Professor) Winston and Jenny Izard, now the very successful producer Jenny Barraclough. Mike Hodges, who later became a feature-film director – *Get Carter* and *Croupier* – also joined the team as a researcher-director.

In early 1964 a film about the Army was planned, *The Thin Red Line*. *WIA* hired a studio at Elstree and long-standing film union rules and regulations were totally ignored that Friday as we continued well past normal hours without complaint or overtime claim. Perhaps ten thousand toy soldiers set out across a map of the world painted on the studio floor had something to do with it.

1964 was Olympics year and for the first time the Games were to be held in Asia, in Tokyo. It was decided that ITV would cover the Games so a group was put together from several companies. Tim Hewat was to be the Granada producer working with Bill Ward of ATV. One evening in April, while having a drink in the Coffee Pot, Tim asked if I would like to be the PA – would I!

It was the experience of a lifetime. Towards the end of the Games the Pacific cable broke somewhere near Wake Island and there was no way of getting the regular evening broadcasts to London. Memorably, Bill Ward saved ITV's bacon by flying one commentator out to Hawaii for a night, where a line to London could be found. And it was in Tokyo that the first semi-portable Ampex VT machine was seen as a prototype. VT recording and editing had arrived a couple of years earlier, but Granada forbade editing (which was done with copper scissors) unless permission was given from Golden Square. How times have changed!

In Tim Hewat's absence in Tokyo, Alex Valentine became producer of the third series of *WIA*. However, Alex was taken ill some months later, and Derek Granger took over. During this time, a gruesome programme about Bronchitis was made. It opened with a shot of coffins being carried from house after house in a typical Coronation Street. Ken Ashton was the director and was mightily proud of the repulsive shot of early morning sun back-lighting sputum on the cobbles!

Meanwhile Tim Hewat was planning another project to replace *WIA*. It started as *The World Tonight*, but soon became *The World Tomorrow*. There were four bureaux around the world – London (with new researchers Brian Moser and Ingrid Floering), New York (John Macdonald and Jane Nicholl), Rome (Hugh Pitt and James Burke) and Tokyo (John Maher). One programme involved filming a pregnant ewe in Scotland, the fertilised eggs being transferred to a rabbit which was then flown to Tokyo where Johnny Maher had arranged a full police escort for the unsuspecting bunny from Haneda Airport to a sheep farm somewhere in Japan.

When the series ended, the bureaux closed down. Tim Hewat wrote to Max Morgan Witts, then editor of *Tomorrow's World* at the BBC, commending the talents of James Burke who duly became everyone's guide to the moon.

There were regular inserts from London into *Scene at 6.30*. A director and PA had to go to ITN in the middle of the day and send whatever story or interview up the line. One week I was assigned to this chore which was to be directed by a young man who was still basically a trainee. He was terribly enthusiastic and intense and at the end of the two-minute item, more or less collapsed on the control desk panting, 'How did I do?' I was kindly patronising and said he'd done quite well. He eventually grew up to be Mike Newell and has done extremely well!

As the amount of production based in London became less and less, the centre of the universe moved more and more to Manchester. Along with many other people I was offered the chance to go north, but my reasons for not doing so were accepted by Victor Peers and clutching some redundancy money (much to my surprise) I left Granada in September 1966.

Seeing stars

ANN SUUDI

Ann Suudi was Casting Director 1956–68.

Cecil Bernstein, the brother with the limp and the stutter, engaged me to be a casting director for Granada Television the week the station went on the air. But Sidney, his elder and better — knowing that the struggling company could not afford to do much drama — was never one to let talent lie idle. So he assigned me to produce cine-variety packages to go on before the feature films in his leading theatres, notably Granada Tooting in London's southwest and Granada East Ham in the east, to which the famous old music hall, The Metropolitan in Edgware Road, was added when it was bought in tandem with the Chelsea Palace in King's Road.

Fortunately I knew the top vaudeville acts because, from 1949 at the BBC, I had worked with Henry Caldwell on his hugely-popular series *Cafe Continental*. But knowledge of stage presentation and lighting I had none and the learning curve was steep. Added to that, when I returned hungry and tired to my flat, Sidney phoned nightly to check on the take, both first house and second. But when the financial-rescuing network deal was done and the company's safety secured, the Granada determination to be the best at everything asserted itself, fuelled by the fact that Sidney's deepest desires were in drama.

His passion for plays by America's best was soon evidenced by a tremendous production of Arthur Miller's landmark *Death of a Salesman*, directed by Silvio Narizzano. For the title role of Willie Loman we brought from New York Albert Decker, a great shambling actor of pathetic power.

This was soon followed by Miller's *The Crucible* about the persecution of the so-called witches of Salem, directed by Henry Kaplan. We gave one of the leads to a developing Scottish actor called Sean Connery – and he seemed to turn out all right.

Henry followed with another American classic, Thornton Wilder's *The*

Skin of our Teeth. Vivien Leigh had made the kittenish role of Sabina her own in Old Vic productions in London and abroad. This great star, who had won an Oscar in *Gone with the Wind* some twenty years earlier, had nothing to gain and lots to lose by appearing live on television (pre-videotape) but at 44 she accepted the challenge. We took her to tea at the Dorchester to discuss the rest of the cast and she was the most enchanting person I ever met.

In Granada's great love affair with the north we revived a series of Lancashire plays and I cast in the leads two promising youngsters: Maggie Smith and Robert Stephens. They too, turned out all right.

That northern affair flowered fully when Tony Warren fashioned *Coronation Street*. So keen was Harry Elton to produce a pilot that the script was sent to me at the Welbeck Street Nursing Home the day I had twin daughters — and labour and Lancashire accents made an odd mixture.

By scouring the repertory companies we discovered Pat Phoenix and Margot Bryant, and Lynne Carol, and Doris Speed who breathed such gusto into the drab streetscape, and Arthur Leslie who made his Rovers' Return the best-known pub in Britain. We won Violet Carson from behind the piano in Wilfred Pickles's marathon radio show *Have a Go*. We recruited just one established actor: Jack Howarth, who first trod the boards in 1908! He had played on the West End stage and appeared in several films. And he made the sprightly Albert Tatlock a national character.

We also did a series of plays by that great Yorkshireman, J. B. Priestley. His later nuclear-disarmament tract *Doomsday for Dyson* – commissioned by Granada and directed by Silvio Narizzano – showed just how fraught live productions could be. I cast an experienced West End actor, Howard Marion Crawford, as a marshal in the RAF. But when his big close-up speech came, he dried — and it took excruciating seconds of prompting to get him going.

Shocks in a quite different sense followed my casting of Richard Harris to play his first lead opposite Patrick McGoohan in an IRA thriller, *The Iron Harp*, directed by Cliff Owen. The problem was not that in every rehearsal of a fight scene they belted each other for real, it was that they carried the brawl into the Festival Café (a Granada carry-over from the Festival of Britain) where Richard caused an awed hush by shouting at Patrick: 'I'll knock your FUCKING head off.' (In those days the F-word was not much used in public).

The Chelsea Palace became the best studio conversion in Britain and the home of our variety extravaganza *Chelsea at Nine*. I was obliged to negotiate, often abroad, for many of the greatest: Maria Callas (the memory of her performance still makes the back of my neck tingle), Yehudi Menuhin, Liberace, Jerome Robbins' New York Ballet and the Maurice Béjart Ballet from France. Billie Holiday, frail and close to death, sang her very last songs in *Chelsea*, but silly Cecil (Bernstein) had 'Love for Sale' edited out before transmission – and lost for ever.

A long association with the promoter Harold Davidson enabled me to negotiate musical specials for Granada Chelsea by Duke Ellington and his orchestra, Ella Fitzgerald, the Louis Armstrong All Stars and a series called *One Man's Music* in which Cleo Laine, backed by husband John Dankworth and his band, sang the songs of thirteen different composers.

But perhaps the greatest thrill of all was back in the growing Granada TV Centre in Manchester when Silvio Narizzano's first videotaped production of Tolstoy's *War and Peace* filled three of the four studios. In a cast of more than a hundred, we chose as the leads Daniel Massey, Kenneth Griffith and Nicol Williamson.

There was magic in the place that night, and this was recognised soon afterwards when the National Academy of Television Arts and Sciences in New York gave the show an Emmy, the first awarded to a British commercial television production. Sidney and everyone else deserved it.

Ann married Tim Hewat, a Granada producer, in 1959 and they have lived in Australia since 1970.

Industrial action

CAROLE TOWNSEND

I joined Granada as a temporary secretary in 1974 and became part of the staff in 1975. In 1976 I got very involved in my trade union. Granada was producing *Reports Action*. There was a major dispute about using Community Service Volunteers (CSV). The NATTKE shop (as it was then called) decided that the use of CSVs was unacceptable and that, if Granada insisted on using them instead of Granada staff, we would 'black' the show. There were endless meetings with the management.

The shop argument was that the use of CSVs was impeding NATTKE clerical staff getting better and more interesting jobs. Granada's argument was that NATTKE secretaries/clerical staff were dimbos and wouldn't be able to do the work of a CSV. A shop meeting was called – I reported back on the meeting we'd had with management and, of course, I dropped in nicely what had been said. Feelings were running very high that day with shouts from the floor of 'Black the show!' We did.

Then the big one in 1979. A strike which involved all the ITV companies.

The first time I met Andrew Quinn, the managing director of the company was the last day of work before the strike. Malcolm Foster and Lynn Lloyd of ACTT together with John Yates of ETU were sent for by Andrew. I got a phone call asking me to join them as Andrew wanted to know who the NATTKE shop steward was. I joined them on the sixth floor – not quite shaking in my shoes but not feeling too brave. I thought, what do I do when I get up there, I can't shake hands with him, it's not that sort of meeting. I got in, sat down and a more pleasant man I couldn't wish to meet. All he did was explain what this strike would mean to our members. He said other things as well but I just don't remember what they were.

I believe the strike lasted sixteen weeks and during that time I've never worked so hard. The joint shop stewards committee met each week to discuss tactics. One of the jobs I was given along with John Yates was to organise picket duty all over the country. I remember calling Elizabeth Price who had only been at Granada for about a month before the strike. I told her she was down on the roster for picket duty. She told me she thought she had a temporary job starting that week. I said I was sorry but everyone has to do their bit in this strike and if you feel that your temporary job is more important than this strike – let it be on your conscience. Needless to say she arrived for picket duty. What a prig I was.

After we got back to work there was a job vacancy on *This is Your Right*, a programme I really wanted to work on. I applied for the job and got an interview with the programme producer, Marjorie Giles, who gave me an awful time. However, after a bit of wrangling, I forced her to give me the job!

I can honestly say that the time on *TIYR* was the happiest in my working career. My producer was in training for the swimming Olympics. She was so dedicated that she never missed a day and won a cup from her team on retirement. The staff were in training too – with their elbows – at the bar in the Old School. After Marjorie retired, Pat Baker took over. I think we were pretty awful to her – she couldn't take Marjorie's place (no one could) but I think she was too serious for us.

SHORT ENDS

Brian Armstrong, Phil Birnbaum, Diana Bramwell, Brian Cosgrove,
Bill Gilmour, Lois Richardson, Roy Stonehouse

—pages 266–9

Did Sidney Bernstein really compare maps of rainfall and population in order to decide to apply for the northern franchise? He never denied it and it became the first of the Granada legends. The programme makers themselves provided many others. The following is a selection:

Granada began in fine linguistic style. It said goodnight at closedown in three languages: Welsh, Manx and English. Its most famous programme, *Coronation Street*, has been dubbed into Thai. However, in the matter of tongues, not all was plain sailing ... In 1968 *World in Action* was in Czechoslovakia during the Russian invasion. Its crew of three pulled up for lunch in some lost little town. They were presented with a menu in handwritten Czech. From this fathomless obscurity the producer thought he recognised the Czech for 'omelette' grandly entitled 'a Monaco'. He ordered three, to be accompanied by 'patates frites'. The meal duly arrived.

Monaco omelettes proved to be 6-inch wide jam tarts with ersatz cream extruded over the top. These were served on a bed of chips. After a pause, the cameraman said, 'I'm ever so glad you didn't know the Czech for gravy.' (BA)

Granada frequently ran foul of authority. Exasperated by a run of exposés in the 1960s, the ITA summoned the Granada board, headed by Sidney Bernstein, to debate the renewal of the franchise. The meeting began acerbically. ITA: 'The file of complaints against Granada is fatter than those of all the other contractors put together!' SLB: 'We consider that as a compliment'. (BA)

A researcher who moved from the BBC to Granada was struck by one difference in technique. Faulty equipment at the Beeb was painstakingly ticketed – 'line hold inoperative', 'reverse scan failure', 'black levels substandard' and such technical minutiae. Arriving at Granada, he spotted three studio monitors parked outside the Maintenance Department. They all bore the single, felt-tipped word ... DUFF. (BA)

'Due impartiality' and 'balance' were regulatory checks in the early days which Granada, in its desire to shine light into dark corners, found irksome. *Searchlight*, the company's first current affairs programme, ran into trouble with its edition attacking dirty food. The ITA claimed that it showed bias to which Sidney Bernstein replied, 'What do you suggest I do? Restore the balance by making a programme attacking clean food?' (BA)

Lord Hailsham – who had compared commercial television to smallpox, bubonic plague and the Black Death – said at a meeting with Granada in

1958 that the company was politically biased against the Tory party. 'Why is it that every time your producers have politicians on programmes,' he asked, 'they invariably show the most unattractive and implausible Conservatives?' Victor Peers, a board member, answered with total truth. 'But, Lord Hailsham, we only put on the speakers who are sent to us by Central Office.' (BA)

Sir Jeremy Isaacs who later wrestled with the multi-million pound re-vamp of the Royal Opera House in Covent Garden, learned financial stringency when he produced *What the Papers Say* for Granada in 1957. After one obviously lavish edition, he received a crisp memo from Accounts: 'On Thurday, records show that in the making of the programme you sanctioned an expenditure of 19 shillings and 6 pence (just over 97p) on sandwiches, coffee and hospitality. This is more than the Welsh programme spends in a week.' (BA)

Sidney Bernstein may always have been immaculately dressed in a dark blue suit, but it is not actionable to say that most of his early staff were strangers to sartorial refinement – save one. A very small and strikingly dapper researcher joined the news staff. Day after day, he presented himself in a three-piece suit, starched white collar and serious tie. Moreover, he had a taste for very precise hats. Passing this tiny vision one day in the car park, Peter Eckersley, in the distressingly spacious dungarees then in vogue – stopped in admiration. 'My God,' he breathed, 'if there were two of you, I'd wear you as cufflinks.' (BA)

One thing the Granada management totally lacked was the ability to deal openly with their staff. How many people have turned up on a Monday to find someone else at their desk when they didn't even know their job was up for grabs? When I was Head of Music, Denis Forman suggested I should go over to Yorkshire TV to see how they ran the music department there. Eventually I made an appointment and drove over to Leeds but, when I got there, I had the feeling that I wasn't expected. But the Head of Music put on a great show of helpfulness, gave me an excellent lunch and plenty to drink. What he knew and I didn't was that his assistant had already moved to Manchester to take over my job. Denis was surprised that I was so angry when he gave me the heave-ho a week later. (DB)

Working on *Clouds of Glory*, Ken Russell's films about Coleridge and the Wordsworths involved daily explosions by the mercurial Mr Russell. While I was enjoying a quiet smoke at the back of Dove Cottage one day the first assistant came to say that Ken wanted to see me. I walked round to the front quoting Dorothy W's immortal line, 'What the fuck is it now?' to find Ken pointing at a witch's broom placed artistically by the designer outside the front door. 'How many times must I tell you not to park in shot?' he said. (DB)

I remember an evening in the Graphics Department, working late on my first animated film. The room was dark but for a pool of light where I was working. The door opened and in walked Sidney Bernstein. He asked what I was doing. I told him and he left without commenting. I was very nervous but I needn't have been. The next day I got a phone call offering any help I might need.

Life is not a straight road. Occasionally something happens the significance of which you don't realise at the time. It offers you a side road. A turn to the right or the left. That night in the Graphics Department, Sidney opened a side door for me for which I will always be grateful. It lead to me being given the facilities by Granada to complete my first film, which led to my first series and all the other things that came after. With fellow designer Mark Hall, I formed the successful Cosgrove Hall Animation Company which lists five BAFTAs, two International Emmies and the Prix Jeunesse among its many awards. (BC)

The day Neil Armstrong landed on the Moon I was floor managing for Les Chatfield on *The Dustbinmen* in Studio 6. I was, of course, dependent on the radio talk-back between the studio floor and the control gallery and reception was often appalling. Next day I sent a memo to the Head of Squawks and Squelches with copies to all sorts of other important people. 'At home last night I could hear Neil Armstrong more clearly from the surface of the Moon than, earlier in the day, I could hear Les Chatfield from the gallery of Studio 6.' The result was that John Fitzgerald Kennedy got us a new talk-back system. (BG)

Make Up Your Mind was a half-hour programme in which the contestants had to value objects correctly in order to win 'valuable' prizes. For one episode we managed, with great difficulty, to borrow a full-grown tiger for valuation. This wasn't one of your docile, drugged, toothless circus tigers but one of your honest-to-God, vicious 'show me a man and I'll eat him' animals. With great difficulty the huge beast was dragged into the studio snarling and growling at the floor manager whose main concern was that his insurance policy had been renewed. After some persuasion – in the shape of a raw leg of lamb – the animal settled down to life as a television personality.

During the transmission of the programme and the tiger's brief moment
of stardom a group of Manchester University students broke into the studio
as part of a Rag Week stunt. Amid hysterical screaming, laughter and mayhem on the studio floor, the tiger rose to his full majestic height and con-
fronted the intruders. After that, Granada was not the target of student
pranks for a very long time. (PB)

Whilst filming the deathbed scene of Lord Marchmain for *Brideshead
Revisited*, Lord Olivier and I were staying at the Worsley Arms, Hovingham.
It was impossible to be served breakfast before the 7 a.m. make-up call so
we ate after the full make-up and hair transformation was effected. We were
ushered into the restaurant and given a corner table *à deux* from where we
could observe the other guests while waiting for our breakfast to be served.
During the meal I realised that 'Sir' was becoming increasingly attentive to
me, patting my hand and flashing the notorious eyelashes in a most
flirtatious manner. Eventually, unable to stop myself, 'What are you playing
at?' I asked. Came the gentle and low reply, 'Well, my dear, all these people
are wondering why a young thing like you is having breakfast with one as
decrepit looking as me, so I thought I'd give them something to think
about.' (LR)

In 1972 I was asked to design *Country Matters*, a series based on short stories
by A. E. Coppard and H. E. Bates to be shot on film. One particular story
was set in the south of England and called for the creation of a working
farm in the 1930s, which was difficult as we rarely went more than 30 miles
from the studio for drama productions. The stockbroker-belt of Knutsford
in Cheshire was selected because it had unspoilt views of the countryside
and looked very much like Kent. But we had to create the farm by building
two oast houses with scaffold poles and façades, we laid out and planted a
large vegetable plot and paddock, modern additions to the original buildings
were disguised, and the livestock brought in. When *Country Matters* was
transmitted I picked up a newspaper to find that the television critic had
been much impressed. 'The designer should send his fee to God, he had very
little to do with this production.' I suppose I should have been flattered! (RS)

Timeline

A selective list of programmes from the first generation. Except in some special cases, a series is listed only under the year in which it first appeared with producer/director credits for the first episode only.

1954

Television Act provides for ITV franchises to be regulated under the IBA. Granada makes successful application for the Northern region – Lancashire and Yorkshire, five days a week

1956

GTV starts broadcasting on 3 May – Meet the People and A Tribute to the BBC
Look Back in Anger by John Osborne dir. Tony Richardson
What the Papers Say prod. Denis Forman dir. Guy Nottingham
Spot the Tune dir. Philip Jones
Zoo Time dir. William Gaskill

1957

The Army Game prod. Peter Eton dir. Milo Lewis
Chelsea at Nine prod. Denis Forman
Criss Cross Quiz prod. John Hamp dir. David Main
Death of a Salesman by Arthur Miller dir. Silvio Narizzano

1958

The Verdict is Yours prod. Harry Elton dir. Herbert Wise
Doomsday for Dyson by J. B. Priestley dir. Silvio Narizzano

1959

Searchlight prod. Tim Hewat/Jeremy Isaacs dir. Mike Wooller
No Fixed Abode by Clive Exton dir. James Ormerod

1960

All Our Yesterdays prod. Tim Hewat dir. Eric Harrison
Cinderella (Prokofiev) prod. Douglas Terry dir. Mark Stuart
Bootsie and Snudge prod. Peter Eton dir. Milo Lewis
Coronation Street by Tony Warren prod. Stuart Latham dir. Derek Bennett
Appointment with... (Malcolm Muggeridge interviews) prod. Pat Lagone dir.
   Max Morgan-Witts

1961

The Younger Generation prod. Peter Wildeblood
45 Cranley Drive prod. Tim Hewat dir. Mike Wooller

1962

University Challenge prod. Barrie Heads dir. Peter Plummer
The Odd Man by Edward Boyd prod. Jack Williams dir. Gordon Flemyng

1963

War and Peace prod. Derek Granger dir. Silvio Narizzano
World in Action prod. Tim Hewat dir. Phil Casson

1964

Granada in the North prod. David Plowright dir. Bob Hird
Cinema prod. Mike Wooller dir. Phil Casson
Seven Up prod. Tim Hewat dir. Paul Almond
Yeah! Yeah! Yeah! (New York meets the Beatles) prod. Granger/Eckersley/Fontaine
The Other Man by Giles Cooper dir. Gordon Flemyng
Wedding on Saturday (Prix Italia) prod./dir. Norman Swallow
The Villains prod. H. V. Kershaw dir. Richard Everitt (including first all location tape play)

1965

This England prod. Denis Mitchell/Norman Swallow
The Music of Lennon and McCartney prod. John Hamp dir. Phil Casson
Deckie Learner prod./dir. Michael Grigsby
The Man in Room 17 by John Kruse prod. Richard Everitt dir. David Cunliffe

1966

D. H. Lawrence Plays prod. Margaret Morris
The World Tomorrow prod. David Plowright
The State of the Nation prod. Brian Lapping dir. Roger Graef

1967

Ten Days that Shook the World prod. Grigori Alexandrov/Norman Swallow dir.
     Michael Darlow

Granada franchise changed to provide programmes for the North West seven days a week

1968

The Caesars by Philip Mackie prod. Philip Mackie dir. Derek Bennett

Rogues' Gallery by Peter Wildeblood prod. Peter Wildeblood
Nearest and Dearest prod. Peter Eckersley dir. June Howson
Cities at War prod. Mike Wooller dir. Michael Darlow
Nice Time prod. Mike Murphy dir. Stacy Waddey

1969

Big Breadwinner Hog by Robin Chapman prod. Robin Chapman dir. Mike Newell
Stones in the Park prod. Jo Durden-Smith dir. Leslie Woodhead
This is Your Right prod. Peter Heinze/Marjorie Giles dir. David Warwick
The System prod. John Finch (including first all film play)
The Dustbinmen prod. Jack Rosenthal/Richard Everitt dir. Les Chatfield
Stables Theatre prod. Gordon McDougall

1970

Barenboim on Beethoven prod. Douglas Terry dir. Christopher Nupen
Disappearing World prod. Brian Moser
A Family at War by John Finch prod. Richard Doubleday dir. June Howson
The Lovers by Jack Rosenthal prod. Jack Rosenthal dir. Michael Apted
The Man Who Wouldn't Keep Quiet prod./dir. Leslie Woodhead

1971

The Mosedale Horseshoe by Arthur Hopcraft prod. Peter Eckersley dir. Michael Apted
The Comedians prod. John Hamp dir. Walter Butler/David Warwick
Open Night prod. Peter Heinze/Derek Granger dir. Eric Harrison
Paper Roses by Dennis Potter prod. Kenith Trodd dir. Barry Davis
Roll on Four O'Clock by Colin Welland prod. Kenith Trodd dir. Roy Battersby
Seven plus Seven p/d Michael Apted

1972

Country Matters prod. Derek Granger dir. David Giles
Crown Court prod. Michael Dunlop dir. Peter Plummer
Another Sunday and Sweet FA by Jack Rosenthal prod. Peter Eckersley dir. Michael Apted
Whose Life Is It Anyway? by Brian Clark prod. Peter Eckersley dir. Richard Everitt

1973

Sam by John Finch prod. Michael Cox

1974

Childhood prod. James Brabazon
The Nearly Man by Arthur Hopcraft prod. Jonathan Powell
The Wheeltappers and Shunters Social Club prod. John Hamp dir. David Warwick

1975

Village Hall prod. Michael Dunlop dir. June Howson

1976

Ready When You are, Mr McGill by Jack Rosenthal prod. Michael Dunlop dir.
    Mike Newell
Three Days in Szczecin prod./dir. Leslie Woodhead
Decision prod. Roger Graef dir. Peter Mullings
The Krypton Factor prod. Jeremy Fox/Geoff Moore

1977

Hard Times prod. Peter Eckersley dir. John Irvin
The Christians prod. Mike Murphy
Philby, Burgess and MacLean prod. Jeremy Wallington dir. Gordon Flemyng
The Life and Death of Steve Biko (WIA) prod. Stephen Clarke/Mike Ryan
This Year, Next Year by John Finch prod. Howard Baker

1978

Clouds of Glory prod. Norman Swallow dir. Ken Russell
21 prod. Michael Apted dir. Margaret Bottomley
Best Play of the Year prod. Laurence Olivier
The Hunt for Dr Mengele (WIA) prod. Mike Beckham

1979

Gossip from the Forest by Thomas Keneally prod. Michael Dunlop dir. Brian Gibson
Talent by Victoria Wood prod. Peter Eckersley dir. Baz Taylor

1980

Camera prod. Maxine Baker
Staying On by Paul Scott prod. Irene Shubik dir. Silvio Narizzano
The Spoils of War by John Finch prod. Richard Everitt/James Brabazon
The Steel Papers (WIA) prod. John Blake/Stephen Segaller

1981

Brideshead Revisited by Evelyn Waugh prod. Derek Granger dir. Charles Sturridge
The Good Soldier by Ford Madox Ford prod. Peter Eckersley dir. Kevin Billington
A Lot of Happiness prod. Norman Swallow dir. Jack Gold

1982

First Royal Visit to Coronation Street. Launch of Channel 4.

1983

Brass by John Stevenson and Julian Roach prod. Bill Podmore dir. Gareth Jones
All for Love prod. Roy Roberts dir. Robert Knights
King Lear prod. Laurence Olivier dir. Michael Elliott
The Granada 500 prod. Jeremy Wallington dir. Eric Harrison

1984

The Adventures of Sherlock Holmes prod. Michael Cox dir. PaulAnnett
The Jewel in the Crown prod. Christopher Morahan dir. Christopher Morahan/Jim O'Brien

1985

Television prod. L. Woodhead/B. Blake/M. Beckham/D. Boulton/D. Liddiment
Bulman prod. Richard Everitt/Steve Hawes
The Practice prod. Sita Williams dir. Sarah Harding

1986

Lost Empires by J. B. Priestley prod. June Howson dir. Alan Grint
First Among Equals by Jeffrey Archer prod. Mervyn Watson dir. John Gorrie

1987

The Heat of the Day by Elizabeth Bowen prod. June Wyndham Davies dir. Christopher
    Morahan
Sword of Islam prod./dir. David Darlow
It Was Twenty Years Ago Today prod. Simon Albury dir. John Shepperd

1988

Game Set and Match by Len Deighton prod. Brian Armstrong dir. Ken Grieve
Small World by David Lodge prod. Steve Hawes dir. Robert Chetwyn

1989

A Tale of Two Cities by Charles Dickens prod. Roy Roberts dir. Philippe Monnier
After the War by Frederic Raphael prod. Michael Cox dir. John Madden

1990

Who Bombed Birmingham? prod. Mike Beckham
Why Lockerbie? prod. Leslie Woodhead

Broadcasting Act provides for de-regulation and sale of franchises to highest bidder.

Biographical notes

JIM ALLEN joined Granada (which he called The Wireworks) in the 1960s to write 12 episodes of *Coronation Street*. Wrote for the BBC: *The Lump* 1967, *The Rank and File* 1971, *Days of Hope* 1976. Other works include *The Spongers* 1978, *United Kingdom* 1981 and *The Gathering Seed* 1983. Died 1999.

MICHAEL APTED. After work as a documentary maker and drama director at Granada, moved into feature films in the UK and USA. His directing credits include *Coal Miner's Daughter*, *Gorky Park*, *Gorillas in the Mist*, *The World is not Enough*, and *Enigma*. Alongside these he has continued to maintain the social document which began with *7 UP*. In 1999 he received the International Documentary Association Career Achievement Award.

BRIAN ARMSTRONG joined Granada in 1958 as a transmission controller. Became a researcher in 1962. Producer/director/performer 1964, later Head of Comedy. Executive Producer 1984–93. Credits include: *All Our Yesterdays, Cinema, Coronation Street, Cuckoo Waltz, Devenish, Game Set and Match, Leave it to Charlie, A Raging Calm, The Sinners, What the Papers Say, Wood and Walters, World in Action, Yanks Go Home.*

STAN BARSTOW. Television work includes *A Raging Calm* from his novel of the same name. A play, *Joby*, also from his novel. A documentary, *This England*. He adapted *South Riding* for the small screen.

LORD BIRT. Left Granada to make factual programmes at London Weekend where he and David Elstein formulated the 'bias against understanding' criticism of many current affairs programmes. He became Head of Features and Current Affairs at LWT, and later Programme Controller. He moved to the BBC in 1987 and became Director-General in 1992.

LESLEY BEAMES joined Granada in 1975 as a librarian and archivist. Became a drama researcher in 1979. Major credits: *The Jewel in the Crown, Brideshead Revisited, Spoils of War, King Lear, Coronation Street, Crown Court, Sherlock Holmes*. Left Granada in 1989 and freelanced at Border Television, before moving South for two years at GMTV and briefly at the BBC. Currently a JP.

DEREK BENNETT. Drama producer/director with Granada for twelve years. First director of *Coronation Street*. Directed plays by Shaw, Priestley, Peter Terson, Fay Weldon and many series, including *Maupassant, The Odd Man, The Caesars*. Left Granada in 1969 to freelance at Thames, and Yorkshire Television. Produced the *Experimental Drama* series.

BRIAN BLAKE joined Granada in 1966 as an information officer, and from 1967 to 1972 was a researcher and Associate Producer. From 1972 he worked as a Producer and Senior Producer on *World in Action*. Worked on many other Granada series including *What the Papers Say, Union World, History in Action, The Sporting Press* and *The History of Television*.

DAVID BOULTON joined Granada in 1966, edited *World in Action* in the mid-1970s, and founded the Granada Drama Documentary Unit with Leslie Woodhead in 1979. In the 1980s was successively Head of Granada Current Affairs and Local Programmes, and Commissioning Editor Arts and Features. He left Granada in 1991 and is currently a member of the Broadcasting Standards Commission.

JAMES BRABAZON. Granada producer 1970–81. Has worked as writer, actor, story editor, director and producer in film and television. Major credits are: *A Point in Time* 1972, *Childhood*, 1973–74; *Secret Orchards*, 1979; *Spoils of War*, 1979–81. Has also written acclaimed biographies of *Albert Schweitzer*, and *Dorothy L.Sayers*.

DIANA BRAMWELL joined Granada in 1959 as a production assistant. Became a researcher in 1964 on *What the Papers Say* and *All Our Yesterdays*, and then became Head of Music. Became an associate producer on arts programmes in 1972, and on various drama productions for the remainder of the 1970s.

ROBIN CHAPMAN. His work for the small screen, other than for Granada, includes the BAFTA-nominated *Blunt* and the comedy *Blore MP*. His feature films include *Triple Echo* and *Force Ten from Navarone*. He has also made several dramatisations for TV, has written seven novels, and has just completed a stage play. Was awarded the Edgar Allan Poe Award for the screen play *Skin*.

COLIN CLARK. Work other than for Granada includes Assistant Director *The Prince and the Showgirl*, 1956, Assistant to Laurence Olivier 1956–57, Producer documentaries, Channel 13, New York 1960–65. Producer and Director documentaries and drama series at ATV 1965–69. Retired to write books 1995. Died 2002.

BRIAN COSGROVE. Former Granada graphic designer and Programme Director. With Mark Hall he formed the Cosgrove Hall Animation Company, which lists six BAFTAs, two International Emmies and the Prix Jeunesse among its many awards. In 2000 the partners were presented with a special award by the Royal Television Society.

MICHAEL COX joined Granada in 1961 as a trainee floor manager. Became a programme director, producer and executive in the Drama department. Main credits: as a director: *Mr Rose, Rogues Gallery, The System*; as director and producer: *A Family at War*; as producer: *Sam, Holly, Victorian Scandals, After the War, The Adventures of Sherlock Holmes*. Published *A Study in Celluloid* (Jeremy Brett as Holmes) 1999.

RICHARD CREASEY. Since leaving Granada Richard has worked in an executive capacity in ITV for many years, including fourteen years as Central/ATV's longest-serving programme chief.

HARRY ELTON is a retired Canadian broadcaster who worked at Granada from 1957 to 1963, during which time he was responsible for the introduction of *Coronation Street*. He worked for the Canadian Broadcasting Corporation as performer, producer and manager for twenty years, and since retiring has taught oral English in China.

RICHARD EVERITT joined Granada in 1959 after serving as cameraman/floor manager at GTV9 at Melbourne, Australia. Floor manager at Granada until 1961. Producer/ director from 1963 to 1983. Programmes involved in included *D. H. Lawrence, Rogues' Gallery, Country Matters*. Producer *Man in Room 17, Corridor People, Coronation Street, Dustbinmen, XYY Man, Strangers* and *Spoils of War*. Executive drama producer from 1983 to 1989.

JOHN FINCH. Writer/Editor/Producer: *Coronation Street*. 1960–68 Writer/creator various series, including *A Family at War, Sam, This Year Next Year, Flesh and Blood, Spoils of*

War. Producer of *The System*. Many plays for the BBC, some adaptations and one novel, *Cuddon Return* 1979. Several awards. Granada left him in the 1980s.

ANNA FORD joined Granada in 1974 as a researcher on documentaries in the *World in Action* office. Became a presenter after Granada tested women for on-screen jobs in the same year. Then worked on schools programmes and daily for *Granada Reports*. Left to join the BBC's *Man Alive* in 1976.

SIR DENIS FORMAN joined Granada 1955. Appointed Managing Director 1965. Chairman from 1974 to 1987. In addition to involvement in most Granada programmes from 1956 to 1987, initiated *What the Papers Say, World in Action* (with Tim Hewat), *Disappearing World, The Christians, The Jewel in the Crown, Man and Music*. Personally involved particularly in *The Verdict is Yours, A Family at War, The Man in Room 17, It's Dark Outside*.

NORMAN FRISBY joined Granada in 1959 to run the Press Office in Manchester and represented the company in countries throughout the world. Publications include, *Television in the University 1964, What is a TV Centre, 1968–74*, and *The Granada Years 1981–87*. When he retired in 1988 he was the longest serving publicist in British Broadcasting.

MARJORIE GILES joined Granada on 1 May 1956 and retired in 1983. Was involved either as researcher or producer in every type of programme from documentary and drama to education and even sport.

BILL GILMOUR joined Granada in 1967. Floor manager and film production manager on *The Sinners* and *Country Matters, The Lovers* and *The Dustbinmen*. Began directing in 1972. *Happy Returns* by Brian Clarke and *Some Enchanted Evening* by C. P. Taylor. Episodes of *Sam, The Spoils of War*, and *This Year Next Year* written by John Finch. 186 episodes of *Coronation Street*. Produced and directed the first series of *The Cuckoo Waltz*. Left Granada in 1989.

JOHNNIE HAMP transferred to Granada Television from the theatre group in the early 1960s and was promoted to Head of Light Entertainment in the early 1970s. Left Granada in 1987 to set up an independent production company. Major TV credits include *The Comedians, The Wheeltappers and Shunters Social Club, The International Pop Proms, Cinema, The Music of Lennon and McCartney, It's Woody Allen, Royal Galas, BAFTA Awards, The Early Beatles*. Numerous awards.

ERIC HARRISON. The Royal Television Society and the New York Festival Awards, and the Emmy Award for the *Bounds of Freedom* series of *Hypotheticals*. Credits include: *World in Action, The Royal Variety Show, What the Papers Say, University Challenge*, and many in the fields of news and current affairs and sport. Still works extensively for many production companies.

STEVE HAWES joined Granada as a researcher in 1976. Later produced the first few series of *Celebration*, the regional arts programme. Produced the documentary trilogy *Ways of Loving*. In the mid-1980s moved to drama, producing *Bulman, Floodtide* and *Small World*. Was joint Head of Drama with Michael Cox from 1987 to 1989. Still writes occasional episodes of *The Bill* and has written for *Maigret*.

BARRIE HEADS joined Granada in 1956 as head of research in the outside broadcasting department. Was later news editor, head of outside broadcasts, and executive producer in charge of current affairs. As a producer worked on *All Our Yesterdays, What the Papers Say* and *University Challenge*. Executive producer on *World in Action* and *Scene at 6.30* and much of Granada's early political output. Spent his last 20 years as Managing Director of Granada Television International before retiring.

TIM HEWAT worked at Granada for ten years from 1957 to 1967. Originating producer series: *Searchlight, World in Action, All Our Yesterdays, The World Tomorrow, Here's Humph* and *One Man's Music*. Mini series and one-offs included: *Mighty and Mystical, Cuba Si, Sunday in September, Paris: The Cancer Within, White Jungle, Divided Union, 45 Cranley Drive* and *Seven Up*.

ARTHUR HOPCRAFT. Former *Guardian* journalist joined Granada in the 1960s as researcher/writer on *Scene at 6.30*. His first play, *The Mosedale Horseshoe*, was screened by Granada in 1971 and he continued to write many television dramas, including some adaptations, for both ITV and BBC. He received the BAFTA writer's award in 1985. Books include *Hunger*, 1968, *The Football Man* 1968, *Mid-Century Men* 1982.

CHRIS KELLY joined Granada from Anglia in 1965. Later produced drama, including the first two series of *Soldier Soldier*, all five series of *Kavanagh QC, Monsignor Renard* and the first series of *Without Motive*. Has produced four novels, two for children; *The War of Covent Garden* (1989), and *The Forest of the Night* (1991), Oxford University Press. Also two novels for adults, *Taking Leave* (1995) and *A Suit of Lights* (2000). Hodder & Stoughton.

GEOFFREY LANCASHIRE. Continuity scriptwriter for *Scene at 6.30, University Challenge*. 171 episodes *Coronation Street*, 36 episodes *United*, 4 episodes *Miracles Take Longer*. Adaptations of *Inheritance, Scenes from Provincial Life, Scenes from Married Life, Shabby Tiger, Rachel Rosing, Mrs Mouse are you Within?* Comedy: *Pardon the Expression, The Lovers, The Cuckoo Waltz, Foxy Lady, Goodnight Robert*.

H. K. LEWENHAK joined Granada in 1956. Directed the series *Under Fire, Youth Wants to Know* and *Zoo Time*. Left in 1959 to become Head of Features at Tyne Tees Television. From 1962 to 1964 was Head of Productions at Westward TV, and from 1964 to 1968 was a producer/director at ATV. He became closely involved in educational television and then from 1976 to 1986 he was Head of International Television Training at Visnews.

LORD MACDONALD joined *World in Action* as an investigative reporter in 1967. Subsequently became joint editor and executive producer. Variously Head of Current Affairs, Local Programmes and Features. Left in 1985 to join Scottish Television.

WALTER MARINER joined Granada 1958 as Senior Cost Clerk. Became Floor Manager 1961. Promoted to Senior Floor Manager, Unit and Production Manager, then Series Planner on *A Family at War*. After 'Family' worked closely with Peter Eckersley in Drama until Peter gave up the job. Drama Planning Manager 1980 Drama Planning and Advance Planning Manager. Retired at sixty on 9 January 1987.

ANDY MAYER joined Granada in 1966 as a production trainee and left in 1975 having worked on local programmes, *Coronation Street*, current affairs and light entertainment. Left to join LWT where he remained for 13 years.

GRAEME MCDONALD OBE joined Granada in 1960 as a trainee director. Main credits as a director: *The Bulldog Breed, The Victorians, Dangerous Corner*. Joined BBC TV in 1966 sas a drama producer. Produced *The Wednesday Play* and *Play for Today* before becoming Head of Series and Serials, Head of Drama Group and eventually Controller of BBC 2. Died 1997.

GORDON McDOUGALL. Production trainee autumn 1963. Researcher *World in Action* 1964, researcher *Scene at 6.30* 1964, director *Scene at 6.30* 1965. Executive producer *Stables Theatre Company*, artistic director 1968–1971. Producer *Crown Court* 1973.

CLAUDIE MILNE joined Granada as a researcher in 1969 on a light entertainment show called *Nice Time*. Within two years she was working on *World In Action*. After six years on the programme, she became the producer of *Granada Reports*. In 1979 she went freelance, returning to Granada in 1981 to produce and direct a *Disappearing World*. In 1982 she founded Twenty Twenty Television one of Britain's most prestigious independent production companies.

CHRISTOPHER MORAHAN entered television in 1955 at the BBC as an assistant floor manager. Started directing at ATV by doing eighty episodes of *Emergency Ward Ten* in two years. In following years divided his time between BBC and ITV, including a number of the original *Z Cars*. Head of plays at BBC 1972–76. Many plays for Granada prior to rejoining in 1981 to produce and co-direct *The Jewel in the Crown*. Credits are really too numerous to mention.

PETER MULLINGS MBE joined Granada in 1956 as a floor manager. Produced or directed over 4,000 programmes for the company, including among others *What the Papers Say, University Challenge, Discovery, Big Band Show, Criss Cross Quiz, Connections, Zoo Time.* He was awarded the MBE for services to charity in 1981 and left the company in 1987.

PADDY OWEN served as a signals officer in the wartime invasion of France and was in Paris on VE Day. Finding it difficult to settle in civvy street, and having a yen to be involved in some capacity in show business she joined Granada where, she said, she found working conditions and informality similar to her wartime experience in SHAEF. She worked as a transmission controller at Granada until her retirement.

PATRICIA OWTRAM worked as a freelance researcher/scriptwriter from 1956 to 1957, then joined the staff as a researcher on programmes including *Under Fire, Youth is Asking,* and *People and Places.* Producer of children's programmes *Junior Criss Cross Quiz* and *It's Wizard.* Many educational series, *University Challenge, Criss Cross Quiz* and *All Our Yesterdays.*

DENIS PARKIN joined Granada in 1957 and worked on the Welsh programme and others before designing the sets for *Coronation Street* from its inception until 1964. Thereafter he worked on many plays, series and comedies until his retirement.

JEREMY PAUL. Series include *Upstairs Downstairs, The Duchess of Duke Street, Danger UXB, By The Sword Divided, Tales of the Unexpected, Lovejoy, Hetty Wainthrop Investigates, Midsomer Murders.* Scripts for *Sherlock Holmes, Country Matters* and various other adaptations. Edgar Alan Poe Award from Mystery Writers of America.

ALAN PLATER. Granada credits: *Fred,* 1964: *Three to a Cell* (in *The Villains*) 1964: *The Stars Look Down* (from A. J. Cronin) 1975: *By Christian Judges Condemned,* 1977: *Cribb: Wobble to Death* (from Peter Lovesey) 1981: *The Clarion Van* 1983: *Shades of Darkness: Bewitched* (from Edith Wharton) 1983: *The Intercessor* (from May Sinclair) 1983: *The Adventures of Sherlock Holmes: The Solitary Cyclist* and *The Man with the Twisted Lip* (from Conan Doyle) 1984: *The Patience of Maigret* and *Maigret and the Burglar's Wife* (from George Simenon) 1992.

DAVID PLOWRIGHT CBE joined Granada in 1957 as Northern News Editor. Producer of current affairs programmes, including *World in Action*, before being appointed Programme Controller in 1968. Became Managing Director in 1975 and Chairman from 1987 to 1992.

PHILIP PURSER. Television critic of the *News Chronicle* during its last three years, and of the *Sunday Telegraph* for its first 26 years, *Done Viewing* (1992). Seven novels, two biographies and a volume of memoirs. Co-author of *Halliwell's Television Companion* (1982 and 1986). Three television plays, three radio plays and two screenplays produced. Married to novelist Ann Purser, they no longer watch TV.

LOIS RICHARDSON joined Granada in 1968 as a make-up artist. Credits include: *Nearest and Dearest, A Family at War, Country Matters, Seasons of the Year, Childhood, The Stars Look Down, Laurence Olivier Presents, Staying On* and *King Lear*. Nominated for a BAFTA award for her work on *King Lear* in 1983

DAVID ROBINSON joined Granada in 1974 as a press officer and left the company in 1990.

JACK ROSENTHAL CBE joined Granada in 1955 as a researcher and then as Promotion Writer. Became a freelance writer in 1961. Over 260 TV comedy and drama credits, including 129 episodes of *Coronation Street*, 40 original plays and films. Nineteen national and international awards, including BAFTA's writer's award and Hall of Fame. Appointed CBE for services to drama.

MARK SHIVAS joined Granada in 1964 as assistant to the Head of the Story Department. In 1966 became a researcher on Scene at 6.30, then producer of *Margins of the Mind* and *Cinema*. Left Granada in 1969 to join the BBC.

JACK SMITH. Magdalen College, Oxford. Joined Granada as Schools Programme Producer in January 1962. Then executive producer educational programmes. Series as producer/director include: *A Place to Live, Experiment, Facts for Life, Evolution*. Books: *Let's Look at Spiders, Facts for Life*. Many articles in educational and scientific journals.

JOHN STEVENSON. Since 1976 has written almost 400 scripts of *Coronation Street*. Also wrote some 50 per cent of the scripts for the Hylda Baker series, *Nearest and Dearest*. Devised and wrote *The Last of the Baskets, How's Your Father* and *Mother's Ruin*. With Julian Roche, devised and wrote *Brass* and *The Brothers McGregor*. Contributed to a number of other Granada series.

ROY STONEHOUSE joined Granada in 1958 as design assistant. Became Head of Design in 1975. Retired in 1991. Credits include: *Country Matters, Hard Times, King Lear, Prime Suspect, Touch of Frost*. Nominated many times and eventually won BAFTA awards for Best Production Design.

JOHN STRETCH joined Granada in 1968 in the reference library after working in Liverpool city libraries following graduation from Jesus College, Oxford. He worked in Granada Script Department from 1984 to 1992, when he became a freelance drama researcher.

LIZ SUTHERLAND joined Granada Television in 1958. In 1965 joined ABC-TV which, in 1968, merged with Associated-Rediffusion to become Thames Television. After a year on *This Week* went freelance before returning to Thames as Unit Manager on *The World at War*. In 1985 became senior manager in the Director of Programmes Department. Left Thames in 1989 to freelance.

ANN SUUDI. Casting director at Granada from 1956 to 1968.

ARTHUR TAYLOR joined in 1968 as a researcher. Over a period of more than twenty years produced documentary and music programmes, with some directing later. Left Granada in 1991. Publications include *Brass Bands*, 1979; *Labour and Love*, 1983; *Guinness Book of Traditional Pub Games*, 1991; *The Somme, A River Journey*, 1995.

KENITH TRODD. TV producer dedicated to drama on film, first with the BBC, later as an independent. Produced major work by Jim Allen, Stephen Poliakoff and Colin Welland. Formed Kestrel Films with Ken Loach and Tony Garnett. Closely associated with the work of Dennis Potter including *Pennies from Heaven*, *The Singing Detective* and all the writer's later films.

JIM WALKER. Poached by GTV in 1968 for *Octopus* then *Campaign* then the local nightly news which changed its name every year. *World in Action* Producer during a 'retrench-ment' year – 1984. Devised and produced *Scramble*. Produced *Telethon* 1988 with Martyn Day. 1989 Produced *New North* series. October 1989 left GTV.

CLAUDE WHATHAM joined Granada in 1956 after training at the Old Vic Theatre School and working as a stage designer. He was a staff director until 1968. Subsequently directed many plays both at Granada and later at the BBC. He also worked on many drama series including *The Younger Generation*, *De Maupassant Stories*, *D. H. Lawrence* series, *Shadow Squad* and *Airport*. Plays included the television production of *Cider With Rosie* and *A Voyage Round My Father*.

PETER WILDEBLOOD. Writer and Producer. Published *Against the Law*, *A Way of Life*, *The Main Chance* and *West End People*. Wrote book and lyrics for the musical *The Crooked Mile*. For Granada he wrote and produced *Rogues Gallery*, *Six Shades of Black* and contributed another musical, *The People's Jack*, to the Stables Theatre project. Died 1999.

HERBERT WISE. Born in Vienna 1924 and came to England in 1938. Joined Granada in 1956 and remained with the company for four years before becoming a freelance. Worked on series such as *The Verdict is Yours* and *I Claudius*. Directed numerous plays both in the UK and abroad.

VICTORIA WOOD OBE. *Talent* and sequel *Nearly a Happy Ending*; *Happy Since I met you*; *Good Fun* and the pilot for *Wood and Walters*, all of which were produced by Peter Eckersley. Awarded OBE in 1997.

LESLIE WOODHEAD OBE joined Granada as a graduate trainee in 1961 and stayed for 28 years including a decade as producer and series producer with *World in Action*. From the 1970s he pioneered the development of dramatised documentaries, and made ten films for Granada's *Disappearing World* series. He helped to establish the Granada Centre for Visual Anthropology at Manchester University.

Index

Note: page numbers in *italics* refer to illustrations. Page numbers in **bold** refer to memoirs written by that person.